IMAGES
of America

JOHNSON CITY

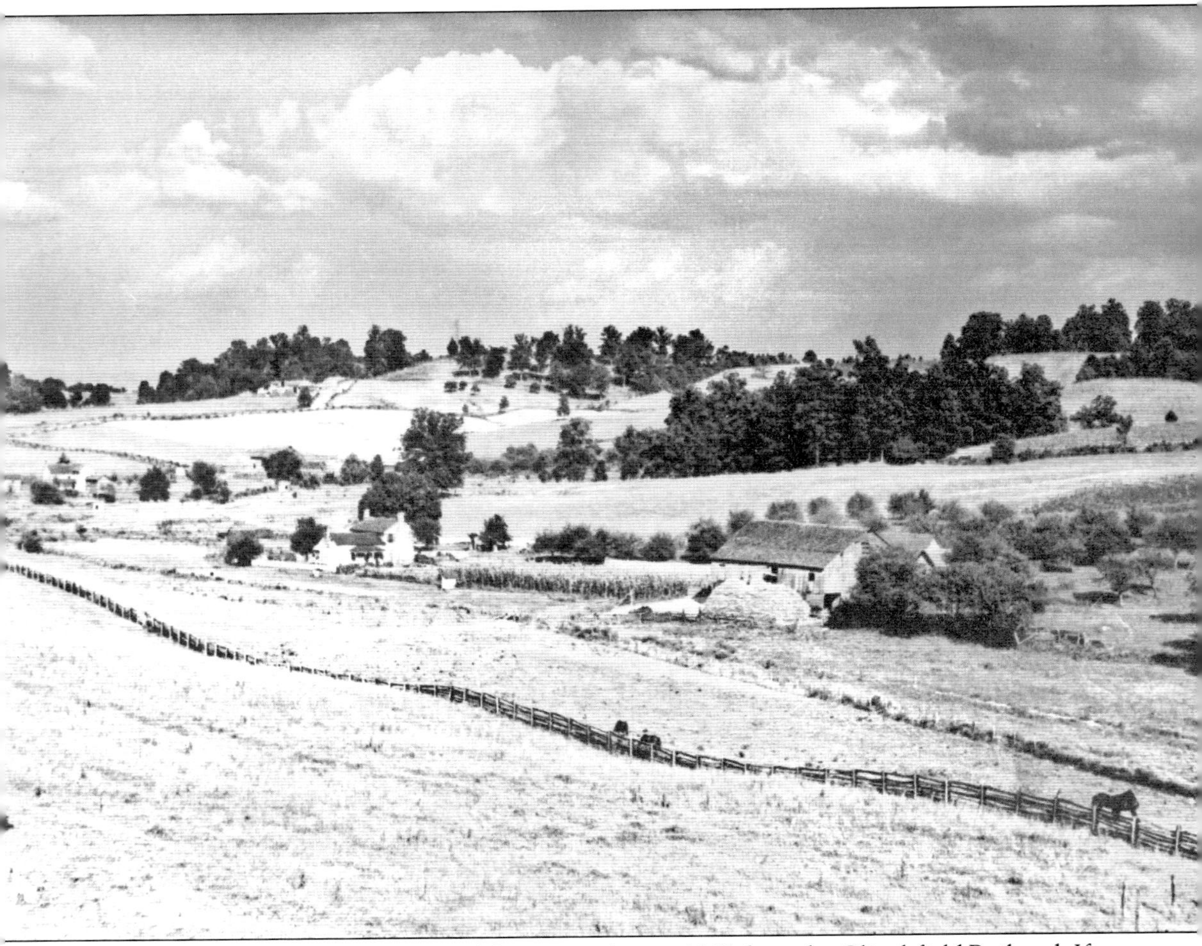

This scenic view of the D.A. Bond farm was taken in 1909 from the Clinchfield Railroad. If you took a picture from the same location today, you would see Fuddruckers just beyond the house in the middle, Lowe's on the left, and State of Franklin Road would run across the top part of the picture. (Courtesy of George and Margaret Holly.)

On the Cover: In the early 1930s, Pleny Brown stands at the counter of the Brown Milling Company general store, located at the intersection of what is now Brown's Mill Road and Roan Street. In true old country-store fashion, one could purchase candy, pop, dry goods, and other items by giving him a list, and he would fill the order. (Courtesy of Grace Brown Miller and June Miller Gouge.)

IMAGES
of America

JOHNSON CITY

Sonya A. Haskins

ARCADIA
PUBLISHING

ISBN 978-0-7385-1805-3

Published by Arcadia Publishing
Charleston, South Carolina

Printed in the United States of America

Library of Congress Catalog Card Number: 2005923390

For all general information contact Arcadia Publishing at:
Telephone 843-853-2070
Fax 843-853-0044
E-mail sales@arcadiapublishing.com
For customer service and orders:
Toll-Free 1-888-313-2665

Visit us on the Internet at www.arcadiapublishing.com

For my husband, Chris, who walked for me when I couldn't.

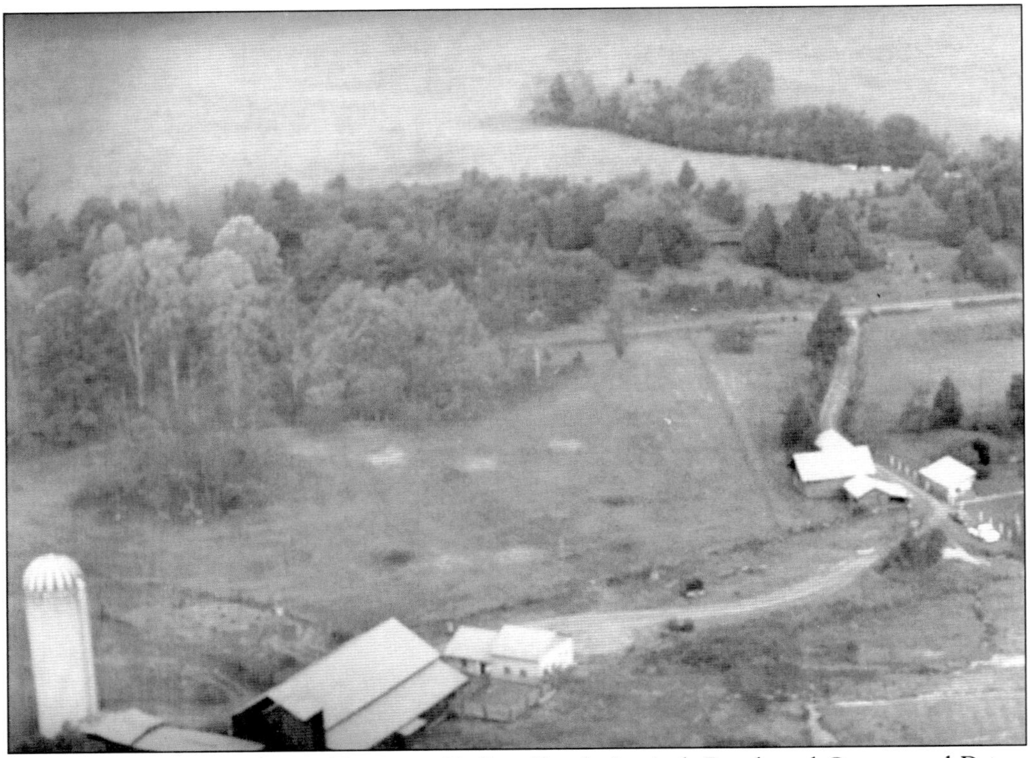

Willow Springs Dairy, located between Huffine Road, Antioch Road, and Greenwood Drive, was owned by Millard W. Wilson. According to Joe Wilson, a vast amount of land was originally obtained by Robert Young Sr. and his 13 sons from the Watauga Purchase in 1775. Johnson City purchased a portion of the land to create Willow Springs Park. (Photo by Joe L. Wilson, courtesy of William E. Wilson.)

Contents

Acknowledgments		6
Introduction		7
1.	Streets and Buildings	9
2.	Friends, Neighbors, and Families	23
3.	Railroads	49
4.	Religion	61
5.	Children	71
6.	Education	81
7.	Work	89
8.	Military	113
9.	Community	117
About the Author		128
Bibliography		128

Acknowledgments

I would especially like to thank Betty Jane Hylton, Sarah Walters, Margaret Holly, and Elaine Cantrell for the extensive work they've done to make certain our history isn't lost. Much appreciation is also extended to the other individuals whose names are listed with the photographs and postcards. Thank you for allowing me to share your stories.

Acknowledgment also goes to Adam Latham, acquisitions editor at Arcadia Publishing, for being helpful and encouraging throughout the conception and birth of this book.

I want to thank my friends—Heather Hull, Kim Jones, Steven and Liesl Huhn, Sandy Howard, Lori Keck, Marla Freeman, Susan Seaman, and the other moms in my homeschool group—for being encouraging and for believing in me.

Jimmy Neil Smith, Ned Irwin, Deborah Montanti, William Jones, and Carrie Jones have all helped in small yet meaningful ways. Lanette Depew, author of Images of America: *Elizabethton*, also provided guidance and encouragement.

Doug Thompson, of Doug Thompson's Picture Place, has been immensely helpful in the production of this book. I appreciate that he has allowed me to use several old photographs in his private collection, and I thank him for preserving contemporary lives with the beautiful pictures he produces.

David and Phyllis Parsley are the librarians of First Christian Church. Thank you for taking the time to meet with me on a Saturday and for doing such a marvelous job preserving the church history.

A special thanks goes to my husband, Chris, for holding down the fort while I worked on this book.

Finally, I would like to say thank you to my children—Sarah, Micah, Christopher, Daniel, and Hannah—for sacrificing a little bit of "mommy time" so that I could write.

INTRODUCTION

Though the area we now call Johnson City was initially known by several names, including Brush Creek, Haynesville, Johnson's Tank, and Johnson's Depot, ultimately Johnson City was the name chartered on December 1, 1869. The history of Johnson City itself would be incomplete without an introduction to the history of Upper East Tennessee.

Settlers began coming into this area in the late 1700s. The first permanent settlement was made in 1769 by Capt. William Bean on what is now called Boone's Creek. Around the same time, other settlers coming across the mountains from Virginia and North Carolina were building small settlements on Brush Creek.

The settlers called a meeting at the Watauga settlement, where the Sycamore Shoals park is now. At this meeting, they established the Watauga Association.

By 1784, local citizens were dissatisfied with their representation in the North Carolina government. Although Johnson City was still mostly farmland at that point, with a few scattered settlers, they were concerned about the lack of representation. There were frequent attacks by the Cherokees and other frontier tribes that had to be combated without the help of North Carolina militia, and local towns were building their own schools, roads, and courthouses. Thus, the Wataugans decided to secede from North Carolina, and they formed their own government, the state of Franklin, named for founding father Benjamin Franklin, but by 1789 it had collapsed. Rocky Mount, a few miles outside of Johnson City, was the United States Territorial Capital from 1790 to 1792. Then, in 1796, Tennessee was admitted as the 16th state of the union.

A stage line ran through the area by 1825, but true growth in the city began when the railroad line between Bristol and Knoxville was completed in Johnson City in 1858. With the coming of the railroad, Henry Johnson saw the potential of the area for growth. He had purchased a lot from Abraham Jobe and built a combination dwelling house and store, which was used as the railroad depot. The place was called Johnson's Tank for a while, because the steam engines obtained water there, and later was called to Johnson's Depot.

By the end of the 1800s, Johnson City was experiencing immense economic growth. The Johnson City Foundry and Machine Works was established in 1883. The *Enterprise*, the city's first newspaper, was published the same year. Tipton Jobe built Jobe's Opera House in 1884 and began offering a stylish form of entertainment.

While the railroad was an impetus for growth, it also threatened to ruin the city when the Charleston, Cincinnati, and Chicago Railroad collapsed in 1890. By 1893, several businesses failed, including the Carnegie Land Company, Carnegie Furnace Company, and the Embreeville Freehold Company.

The city was not destined for failure, however. Congressman Walter P. Brownlow initiated efforts that resulted in the development of the National Soldiers' Home in Johnson City in 1903. Then, in 1909, Johnson City was chosen as a site for one of the state's four normal schools to educate the state's public-school teachers. The school, which eventually developed into East Tennessee State University, opened in 1911, the same year that Johnson City became a stop on the state's highway route from Memphis to Bristol. In 1978, planning began to build a medical school at ETSU; the Johnson City Medical Center was completed in 1980. Interstate 26, between Interstate 81 and Asheville, North Carolina, opened in 2003, assuring our continued significance for travelers.

Since the development of Johnson City began, there have been a few names that stand out—Johnson, Jobe, Tipton, Taylor, Love, Crouch, and numerous others—but there also have been many people who have contributed to the history of the city in small yet meaningful ways. In this book, the reader will meet many of the more renowned citizens of Johnson City, as well as less well-known individuals. Hopefully, as local citizens or visitors to the area read the book and look at the images, a greater appreciation will be gained for driving on the State of Franklin Road, visiting the pond at the Veterans Administration, watching the trains on Legion Street, or just noticing others around us more carefully. There is much to be learned from the stories of history.

One

Streets and Buildings

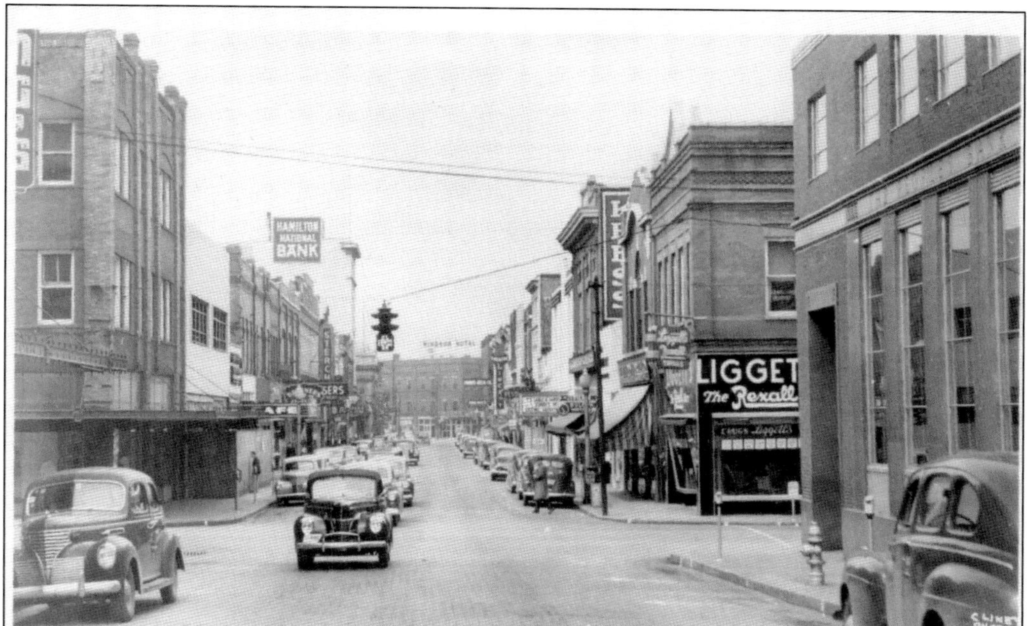

This postcard shows Windsor Hotel in the background, Hamilton National Bank on the left, and Liggett's drug store on the right. (Courtesy of Betty Jane Hylton.)

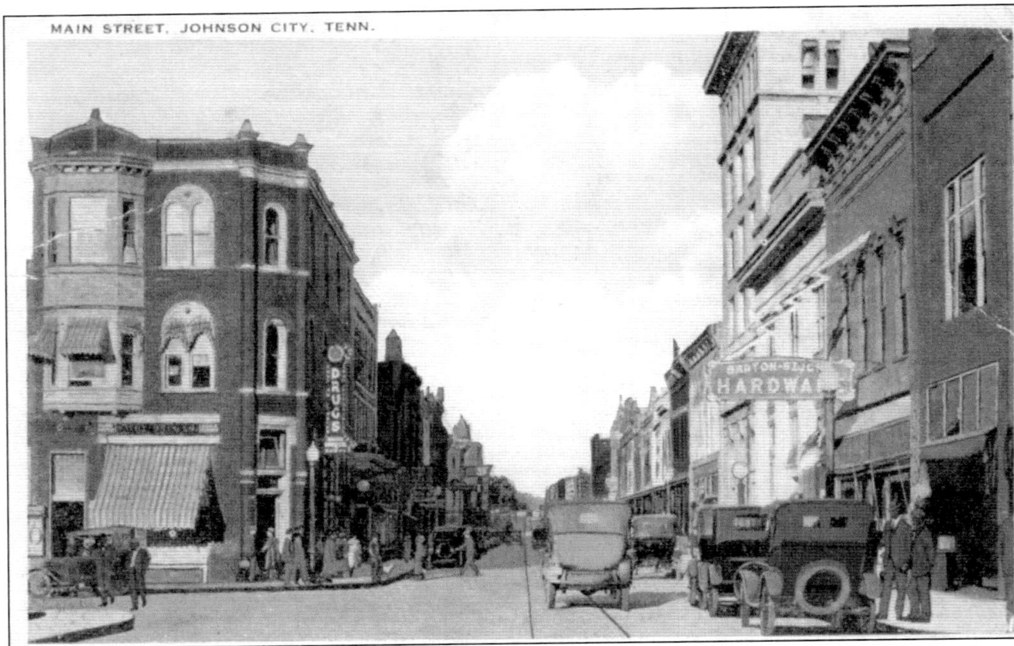

The back of this postcard is dated June 27, 1928, and has an interesting message: "Dear Paul, We arrived here last night about 7:40 p.m. Had a long ride on the train and while we were on the train a land slide fell ahead of the train and we had to [go] back about 5 miles. Stanley." (Courtesy of Betty Jane Hylton.)

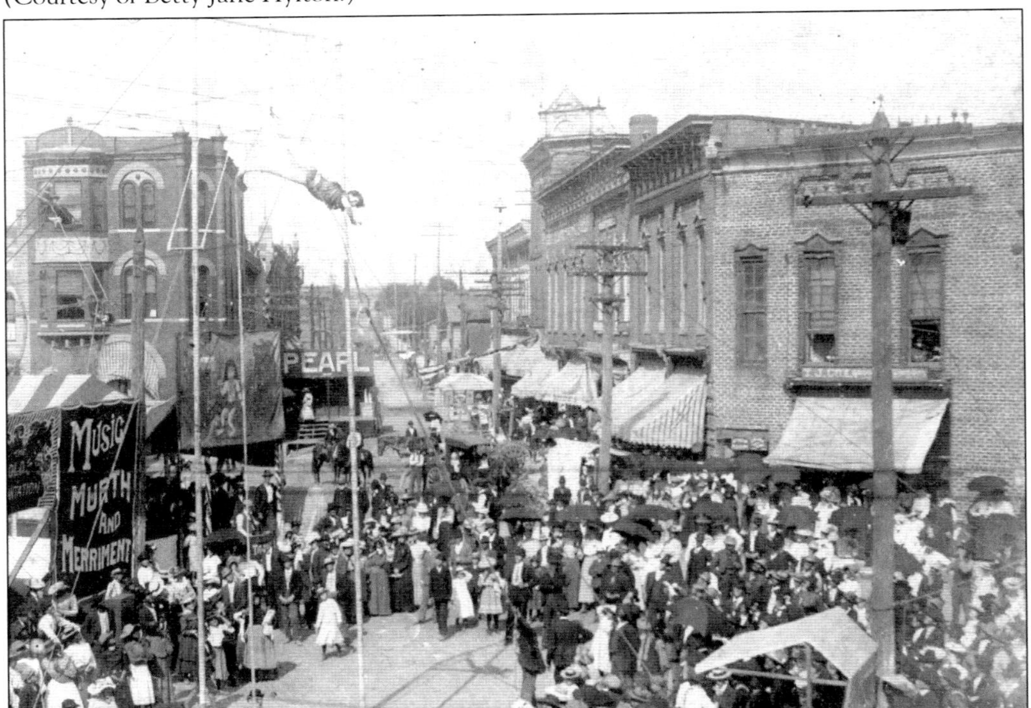

Here is a view of Main Street packed with people for the circus. A street performer can be seen high above the crowd. (Courtesy of Martha Stephenson.)

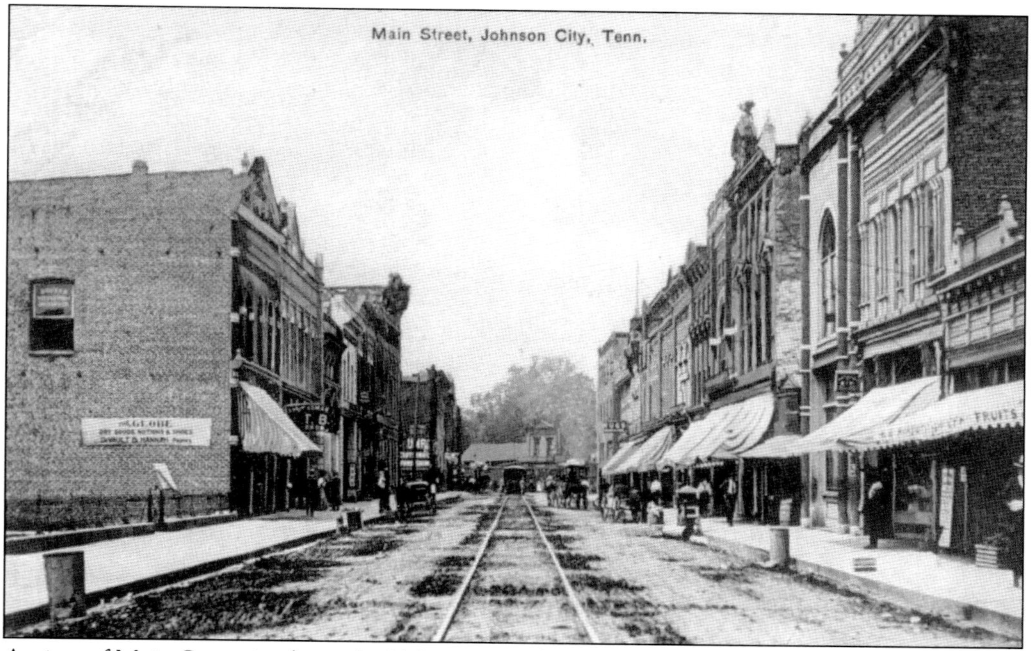

A view of Main Street in the early 20th century shows horses and buggies as well as a streetcar running down the middle of the street. An enlargement of the brick building on the left would reveal an advertisement for The Globe store, where proprietor DeVault B. Hannah sold "Dry Goods, Notions, & Shoes." (Courtesy of Betty Jane Hylton.)

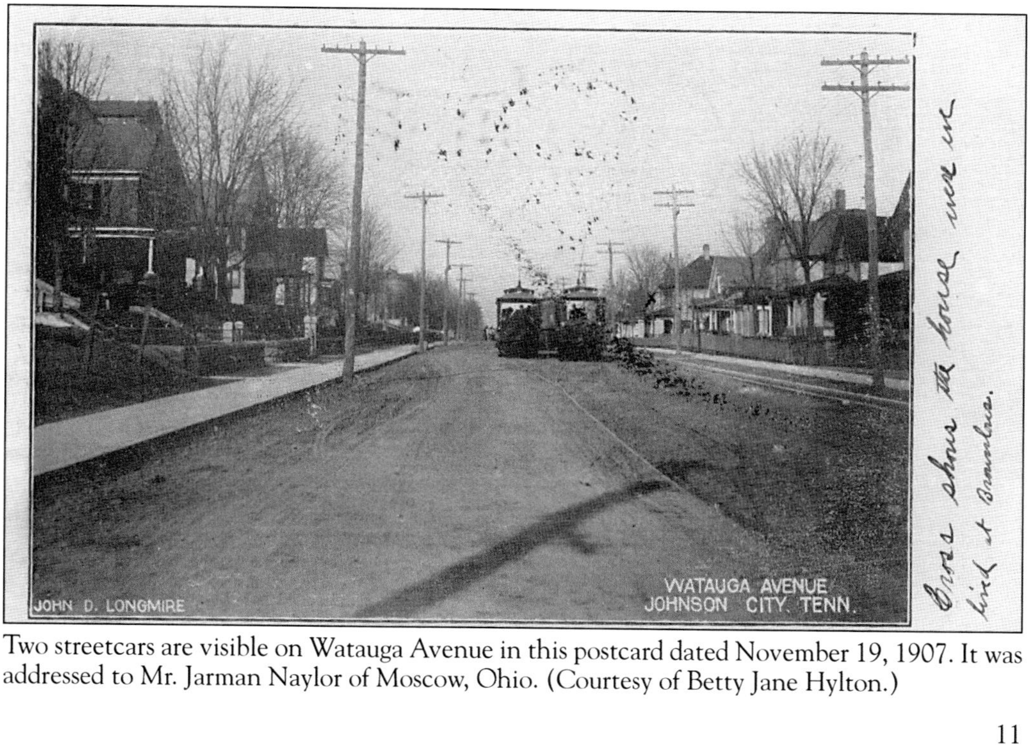

Two streetcars are visible on Watauga Avenue in this postcard dated November 19, 1907. It was addressed to Mr. Jarman Naylor of Moscow, Ohio. (Courtesy of Betty Jane Hylton.)

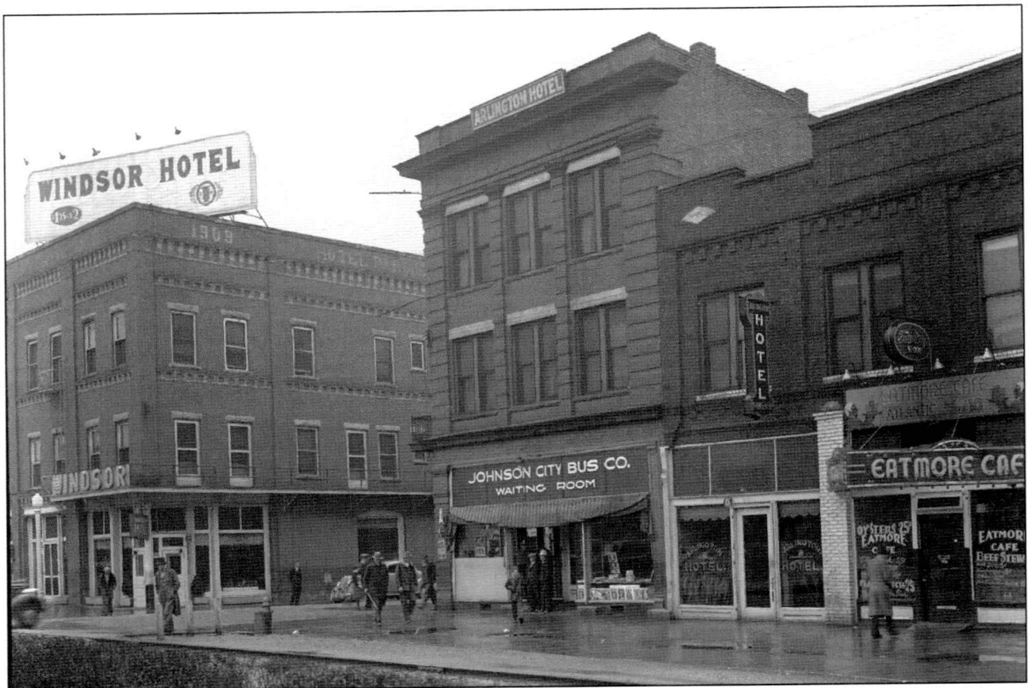

A view of downtown between Market Street and Main Street, taken March 4, 1939, shows the Windsor Hotel on the left, the Arlington Hotel in the middle, and the Eatmore Café on the right. Under the Arlington Hotel is the Johnson City Bus Company waiting room. (Courtesy of Doug Thompson.)

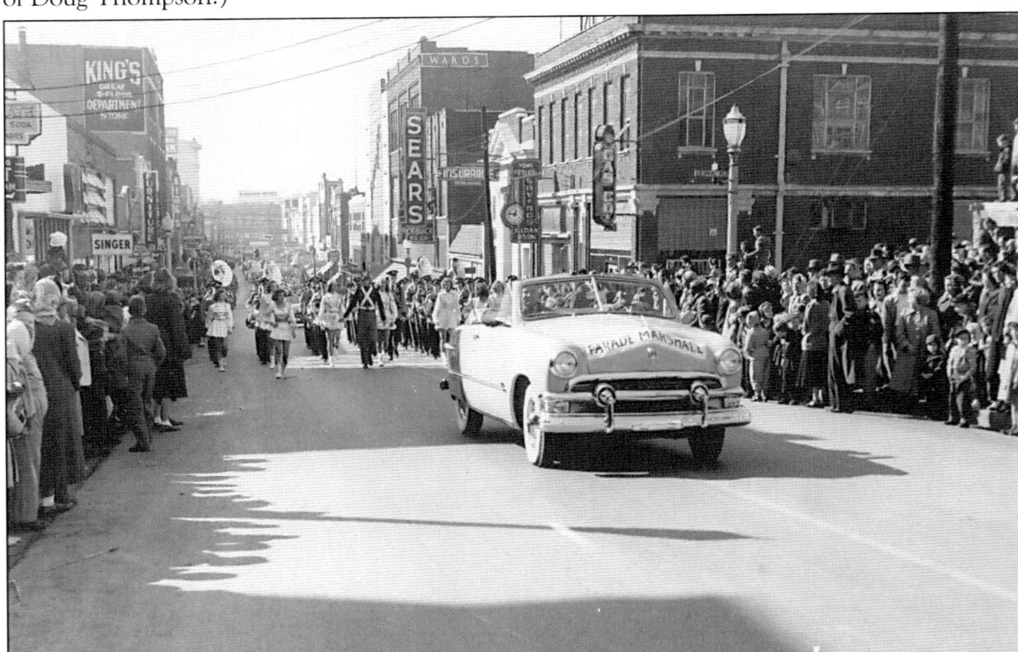

People line the streets for a Burley Bowl parade in downtown Johnson City in 1951. Local communities sponsored floats and queens for the parade. There was a football game afterward. (Courtesy of Doug Thompson.)

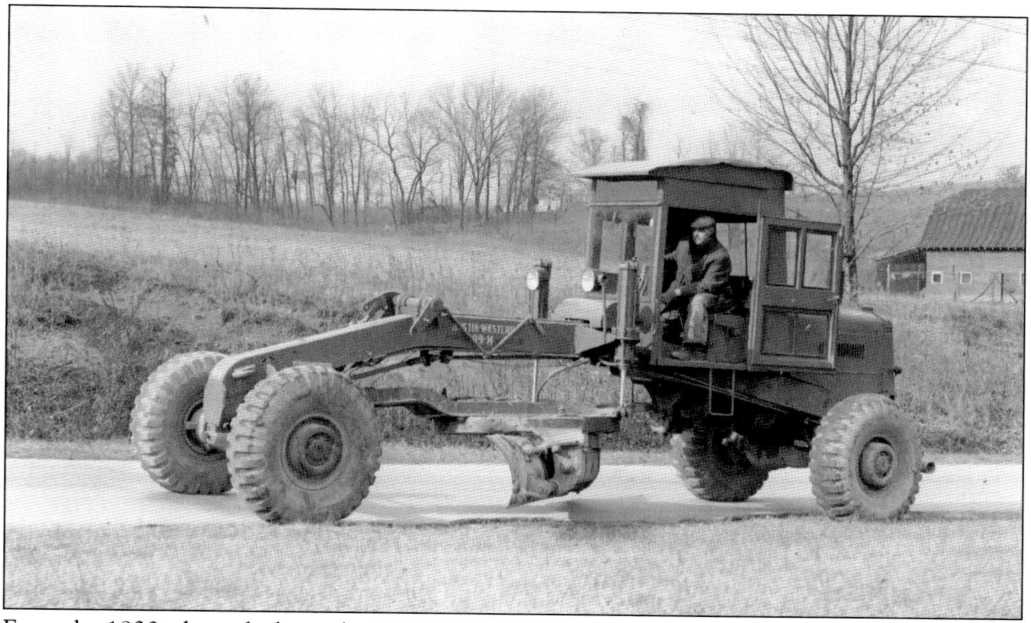

From the 1930s through the early 1960s, John A. Sherfey was employed by Washington County to maintain 200 miles of gravel roads. It was his responsibility, using the grader shown here, to keep the roads in good shape for travel. (Courtesy George and Margaret Holley.)

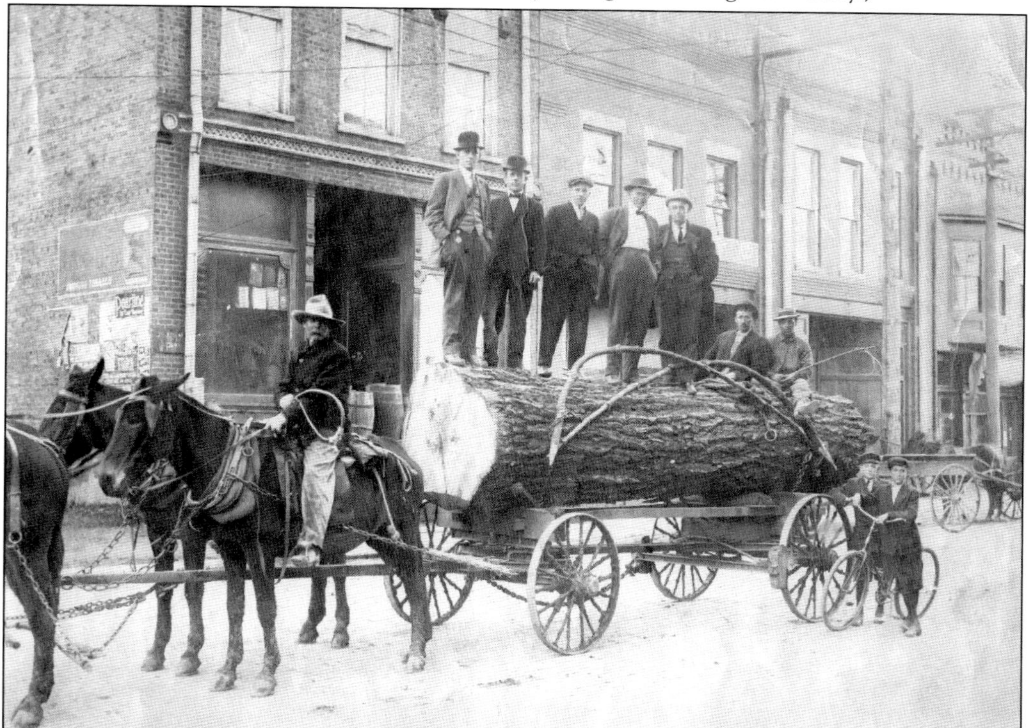

This photo was taken around the turn of the century of John Hopper (on the mule) and some unidentified men transporting a huge log through downtown Johnson City near the old arcade/bus station. John Hopper was born July 3, 1854, and was killed when hit by a train on July 17, 1928. (Courtesy of Don and Sarah Walters.)

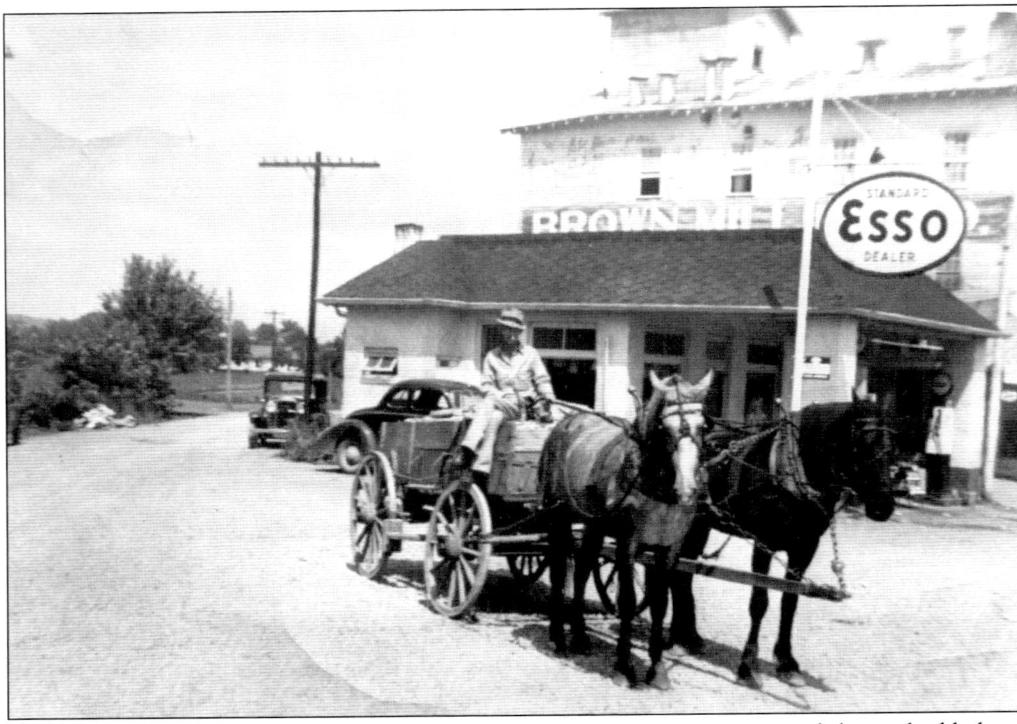

This wonderful photograph, taken in the early 1900s, contains two automobiles parked behind an unknown man on the traditional horse-and-buggy. The picture was taken outside the Brown Milling Company, probably where the man had gone to pick up some meal for his family or feed for his animals. (Courtesy of Grace Brown Miller and June Miller Gouge.)

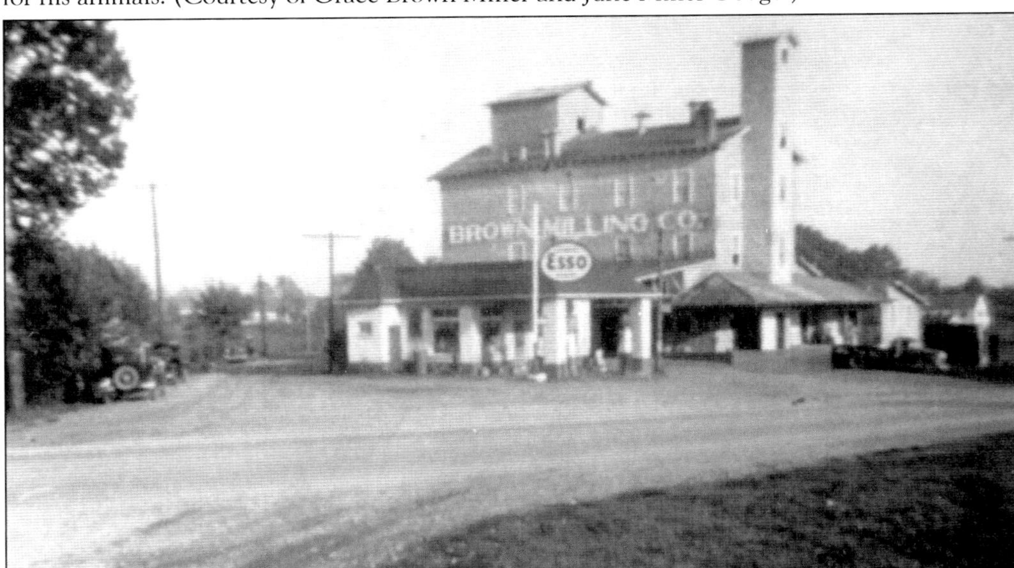

Most people probably wouldn't recognize this photo, taken in 1939, as the intersection of Brown's Mill Road and Roan Street. The road to the left is Brown's Mill, and the road going across the front of the photo is Roan Street. Today, Interstate 26 would be visible to the right. Brown's Mill Road was named after the Brown Milling Company. (Courtesy of Grace Brown Miller and June Miller Gouge.)

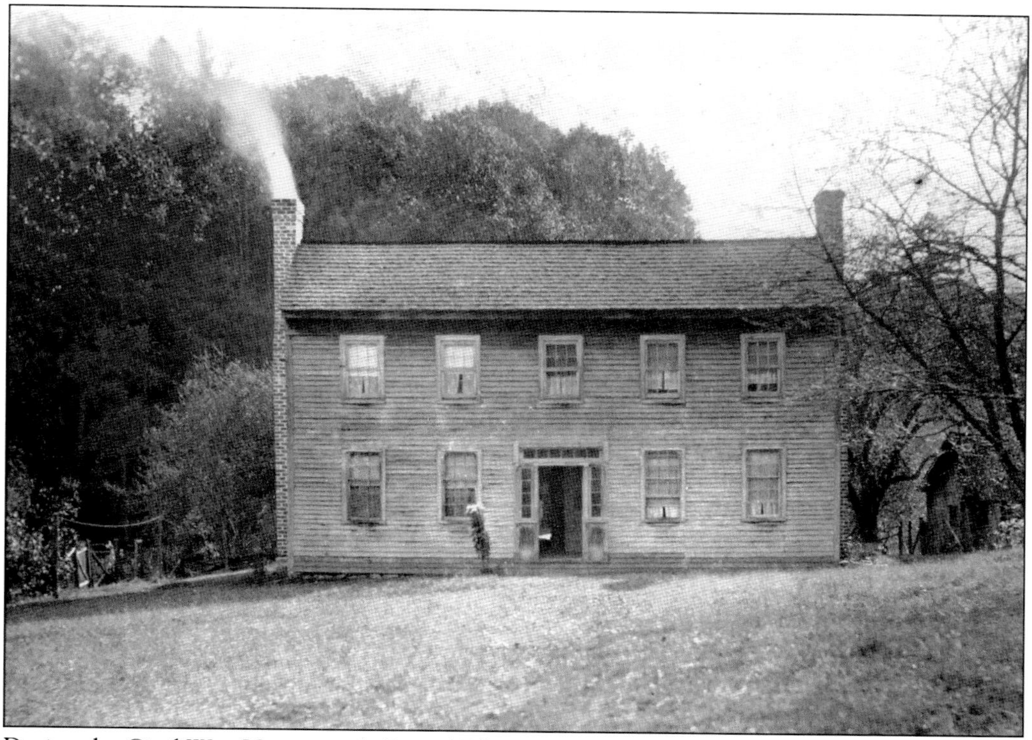

During the Civil War, Union guide Daniel Ellis took recruits from Johnson and Carter Counties through the Cumberland Gap to join the Union army. Ellis stopped for provisions at the home of Daniel and Susannah Wine Krouse. The family hid wheat between the studs. This photo of the Krouse house was taken c. 1918. (Courtesy of George and Margaret Holley.)

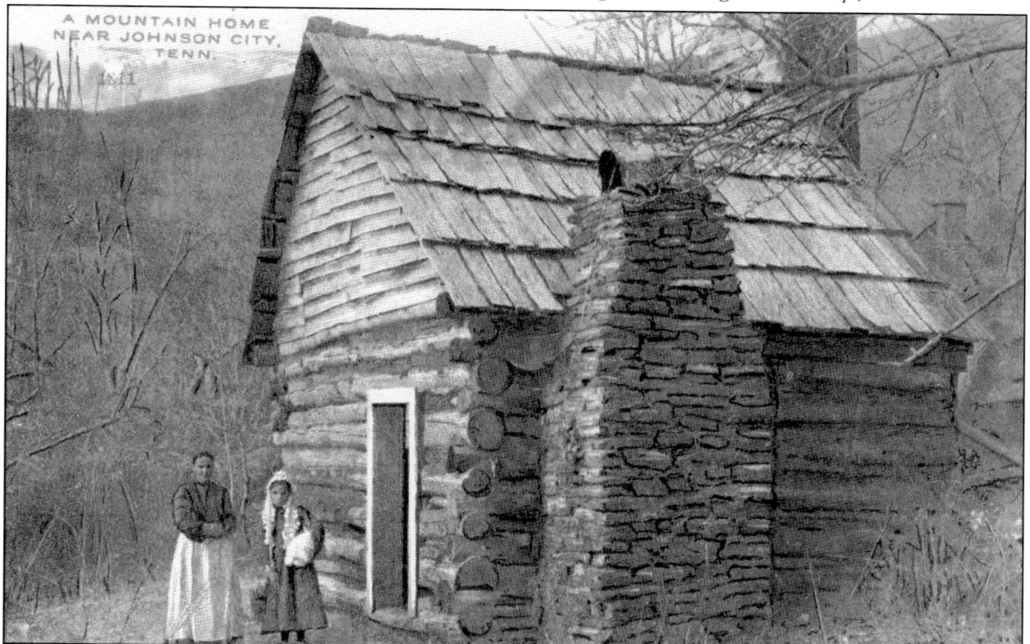

Postmarked in Johnson City, Tennessee, on June 5, 1913, this postcard of "a mountain home near Johnson City, Tenn[essee]" carried a 1¢ stamp. (Courtesy of Betty Jane Hylton.)

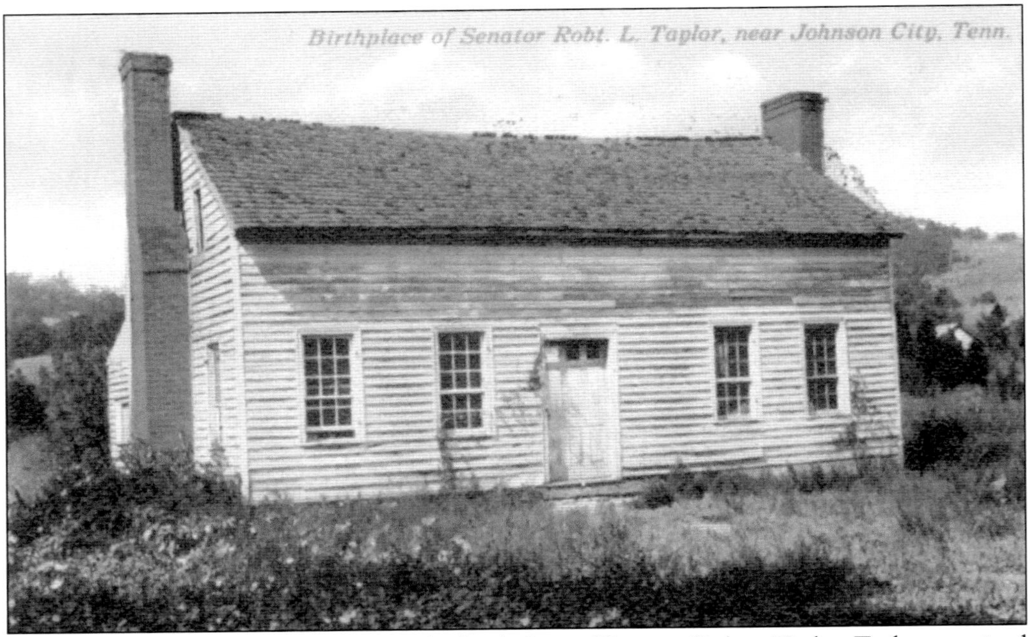

This small house in Happy Valley was the birthplace of Senator Robert Taylor. Taylor practiced law, participated in the newspaper business in Johnson City, and held numerous state offices, including three terms as governor of Tennessee. On the Democratic ticket, Robert won the first term as governor when he defeated his Republican brother, Alfred, in Tennessee's "War of the Roses" campaign of 1886. (Courtesy of Betty Jane Hylton.)

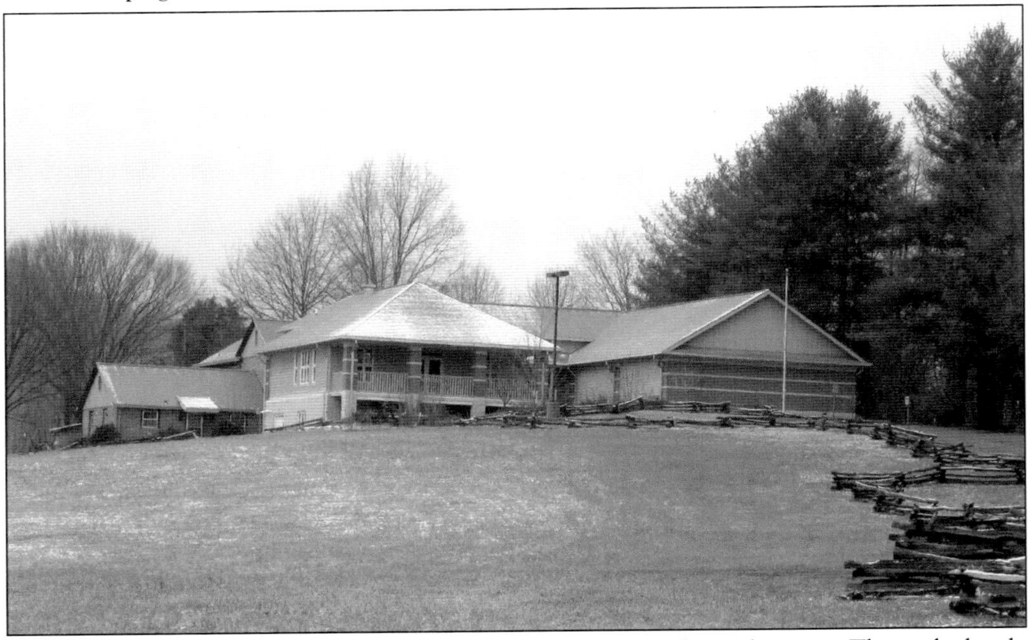

In 1788, Col. John Tipton established a pioneer homestead on this site. The only battle of the lost state of Franklin occurred near the farm in February 1788 between Colonel Tipton and Gov. John Sevier. The home was presented to Landon C. Haynes as a wedding present in the early 1800s and opened to the public as a historical site in 1971. (Photograph by Chris Haskins.)

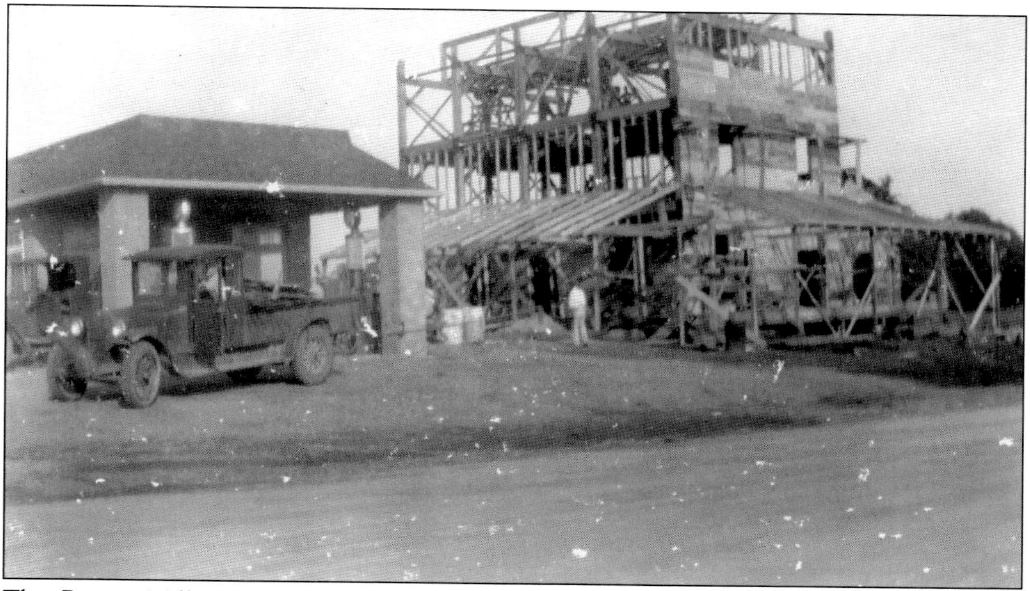

The Brown Milling Company, shown here in the first stages of construction, was built in the early 1920s by Joseph Brown. Brown had previously operated the Star Mill, shown on page 126, on Brush Creek with Leonard LaFollete. (Courtesy of Grace Brown Miller and June Miller Gouge.)

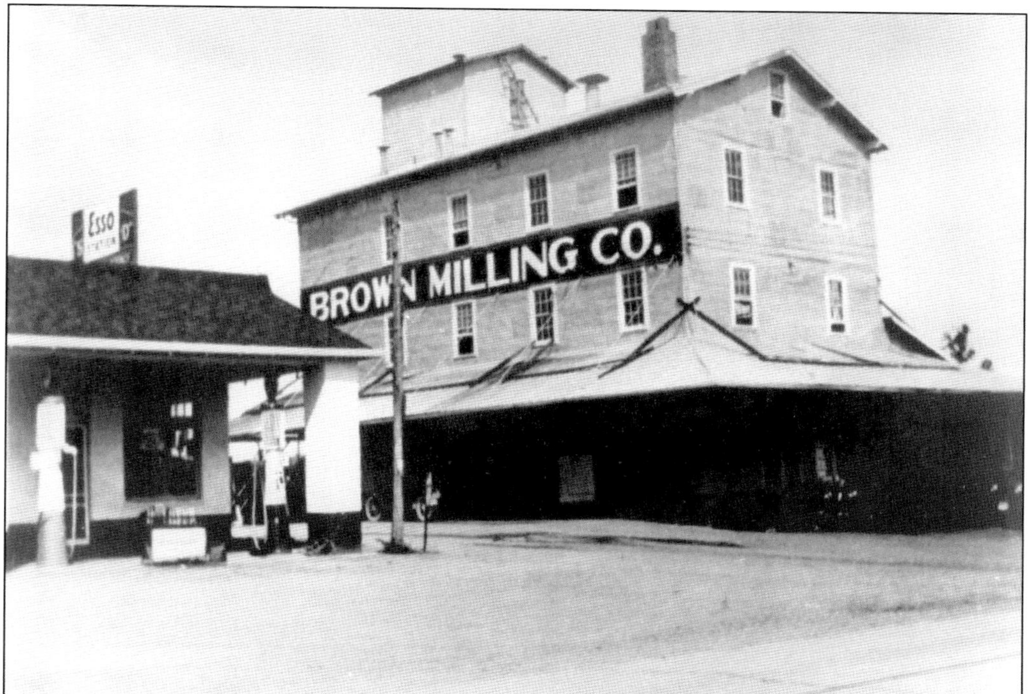

When Joseph Brown opened Brown Milling Company, he had an office, sold candy and pop, and had a gasoline station. Brown sold Esso oil in the gas station, seen here c. 1935. (Courtesy of Grace Brown Miller and June Miller Gouge.)

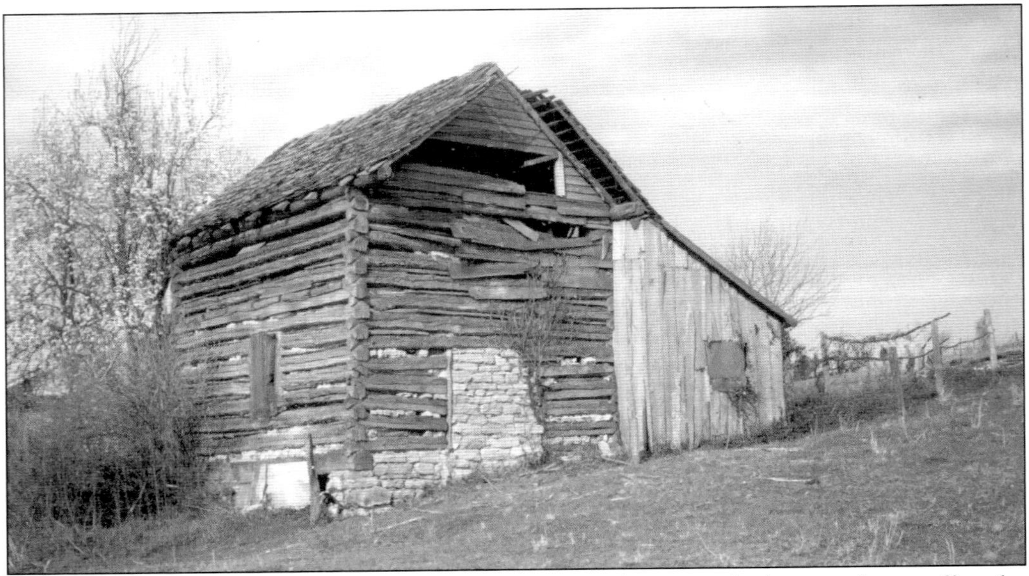

Jacob Krouse purchased this house from the Melvin family. Krouse built a new home off to the left (not shown here) in 1916. Jacob was a son of Daniel and Susannah Krouse and was married to Martha Pritchet. He died at age 94 in 1947 and is buried at the Snow Memorial Cemetery with his wife. (Photo was taken by Frank Tannewitz, courtesy of George and Margaret Holley.)

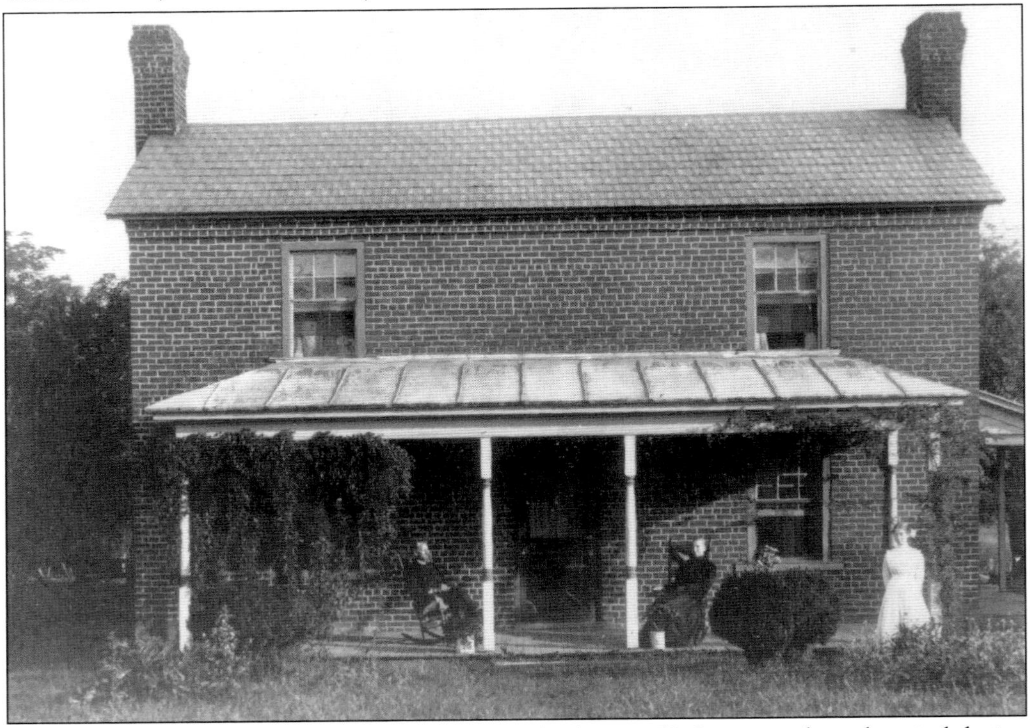

The Abraham and Magdalena Sherfey home was built in 1855. It was used as a hospital during the Civil War, and a battle occurred in a nearby cornfield. Magdalena was a midwife and raised herbs to use as medicine. This photo of James and Rebecca Sherfy Clark and their daughter, Edith, was taken in 1911. The home is on Woodlyn Road in Johnson City. (Courtesy of George and Margaret Holley.)

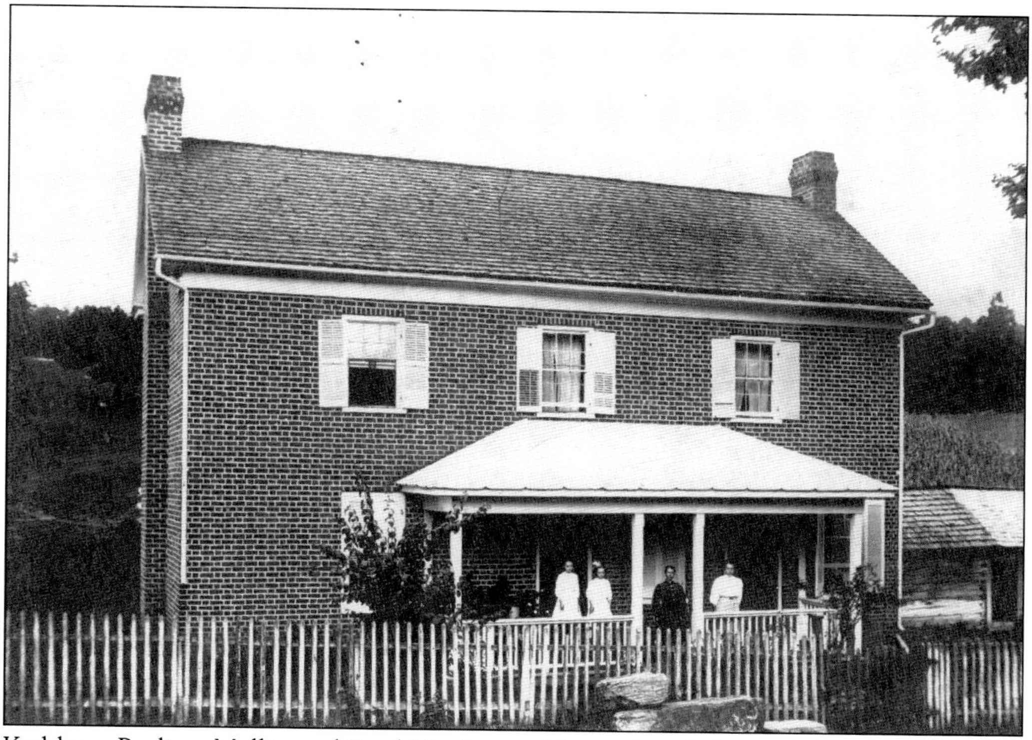

Kathleen, Pauline, Mollie, and Pearl Harrington (shown from left to right) pose on the front porch of their home on Claude Simmons Road. The home was originally built by Peter Miller in the early 1800s of handmade brick. (Courtesy of George and Margaret Holley.)

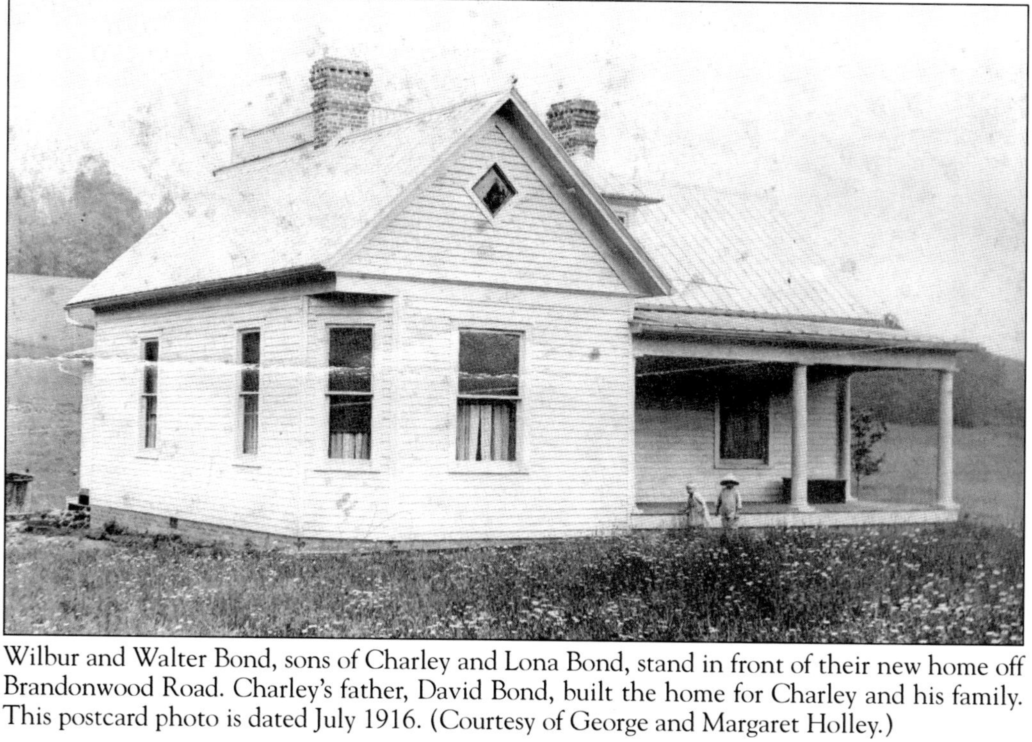

Wilbur and Walter Bond, sons of Charley and Lona Bond, stand in front of their new home off Brandonwood Road. Charley's father, David Bond, built the home for Charley and his family. This postcard photo is dated July 1916. (Courtesy of George and Margaret Holley.)

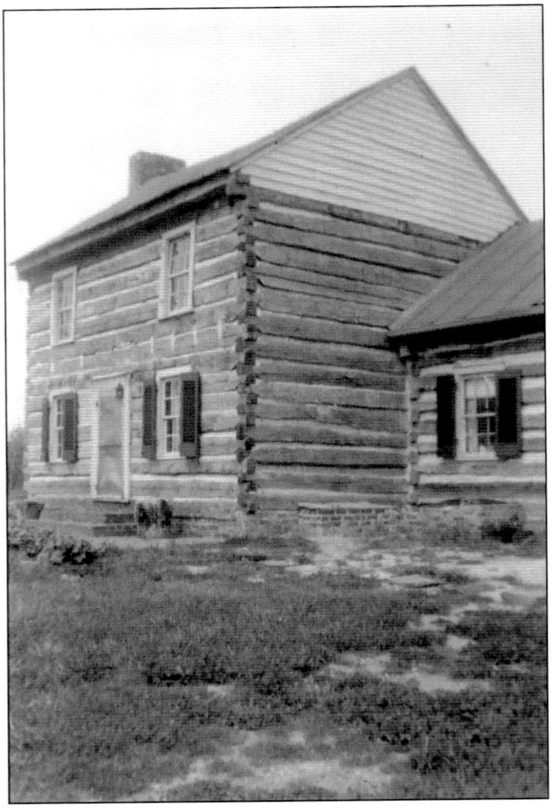

This log home was built in 1810 and was originally owned by the Hodge family in Boone's Creek. It was moved from the Boone Lake site to Crouch Road in 1952. Mary Dell Crouch had Paul E. Hashe rebuild the home to look exactly like the original except for the addition to the right side. Paul and Mary later got to know each other well and married in 1962. (Courtesy of Mary D. Hashe.)

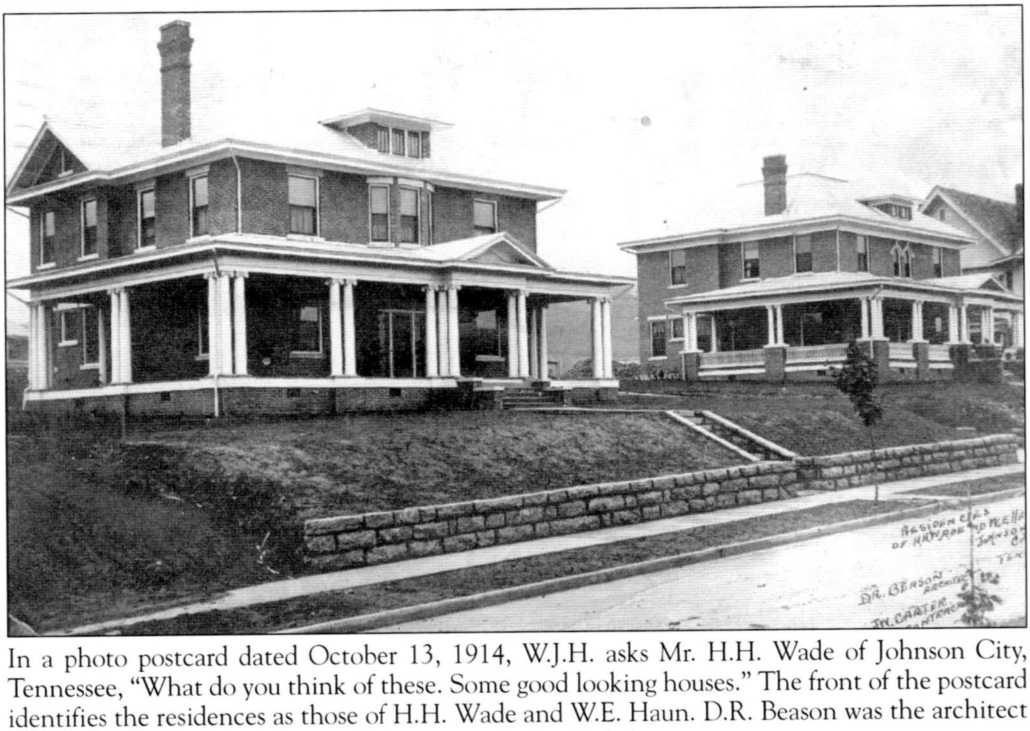

In a photo postcard dated October 13, 1914, W.J.H. asks Mr. H.H. Wade of Johnson City, Tennessee, "What do you think of these. Some good looking houses." The front of the postcard identifies the residences as those of H.H. Wade and W.E. Haun. D.R. Beason was the architect and J. Carter was the contractor. (Courtesy of Julia Wade.)

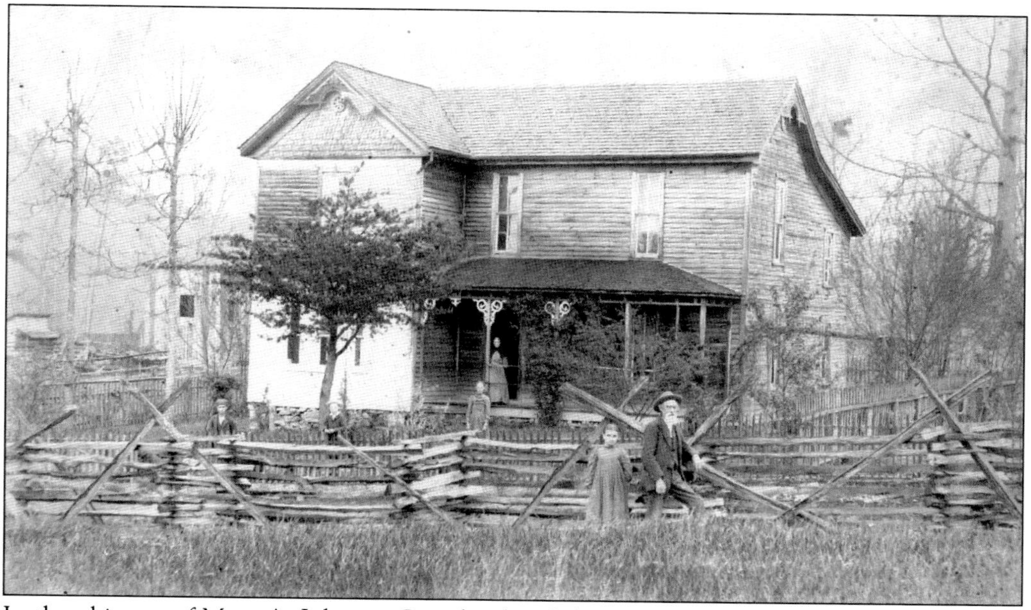

In the obituary of Mary A. Johnson Crumley, her father, Marshall Johnson, was proclaimed as "one of the bravest Confederate soldiers this section produced." Mary lived from September 14, 1875, to April 22, 1906, when she died from "the effect of carbolic acid poisoning." This is the Marshall Johnson home near Princeton Road c. 1885. Johnson is the man with the beard, and it is believed that the little girl beside him is Mary. (Courtesy of Don and Sarah Walters.)

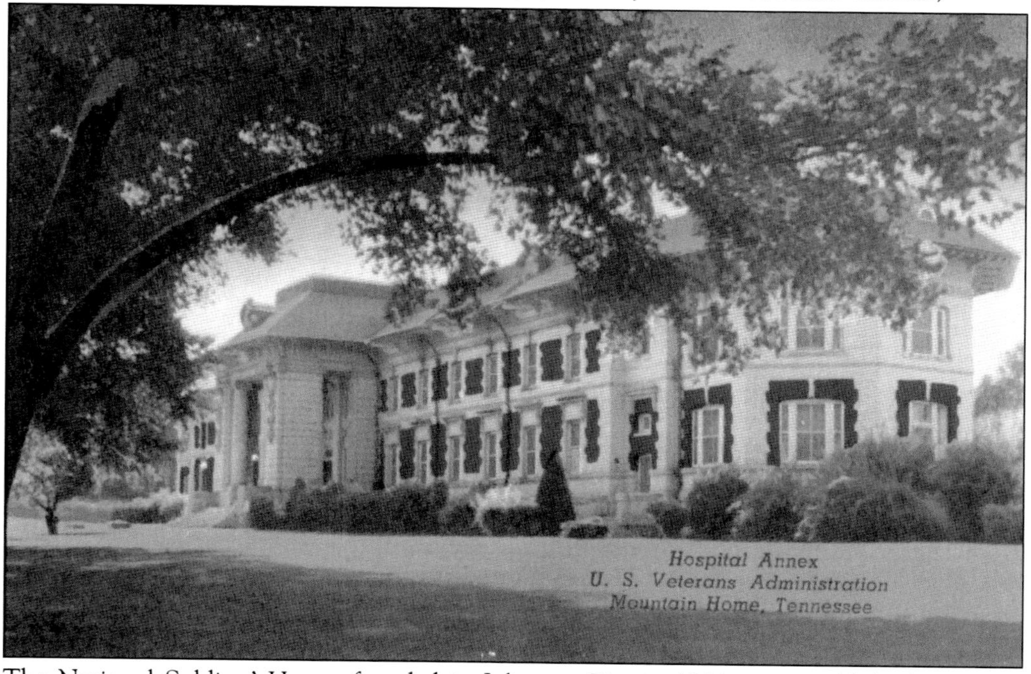

The National Soldiers' Home, founded in Johnson City in 1901, was established as a self-sufficient city. The home would provide services for soldiers, including veterans of the Spanish-American War, the Civil War, and the War of 1812. The National Soldiers' Home became known as the Veterans Administration Center at Mountain Home in 1930, and the name was later changed to the Veterans Affairs Medical Center. (Courtesy of Paul Stone.)

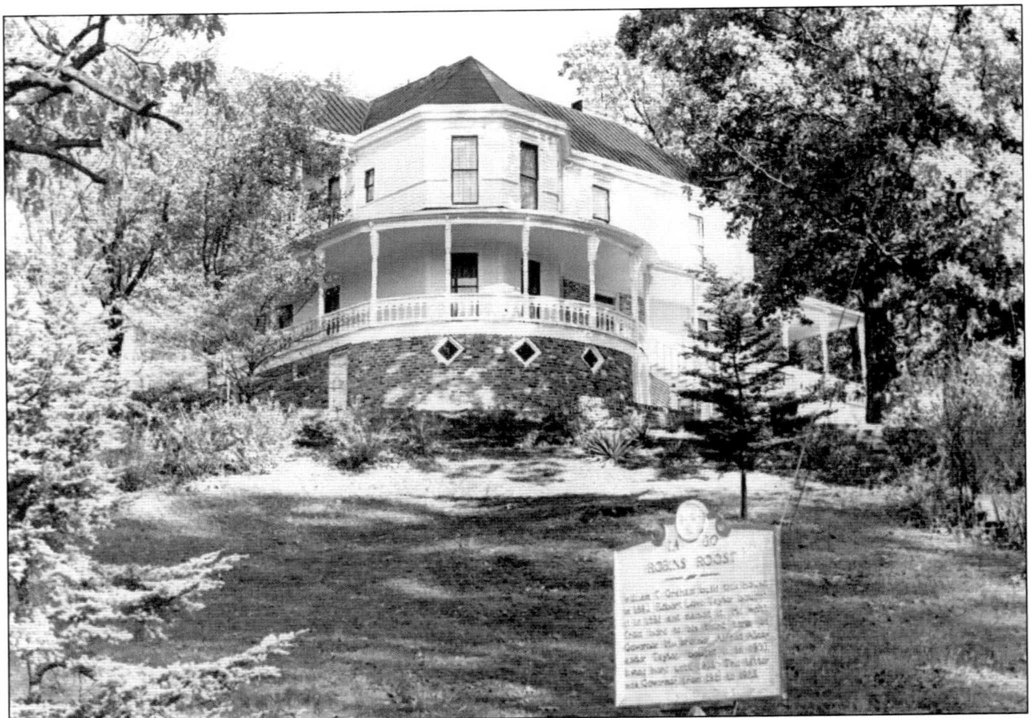

Robins Roost was built by William T. Graham in 1890. Gov. Robert Love Taylor lived in the house from 1892 to 1897, then his brother, Gov. Alfred A. Taylor, lived there from 1900 to 1903. Former mayor John G. Love says he used to dream of owning the home as a boy, so he and his wife purchased it in 1961. The top photo is an exterior view of the home, while the bottom photo is of the living room. (Courtesy of John G. and Etta Love.)

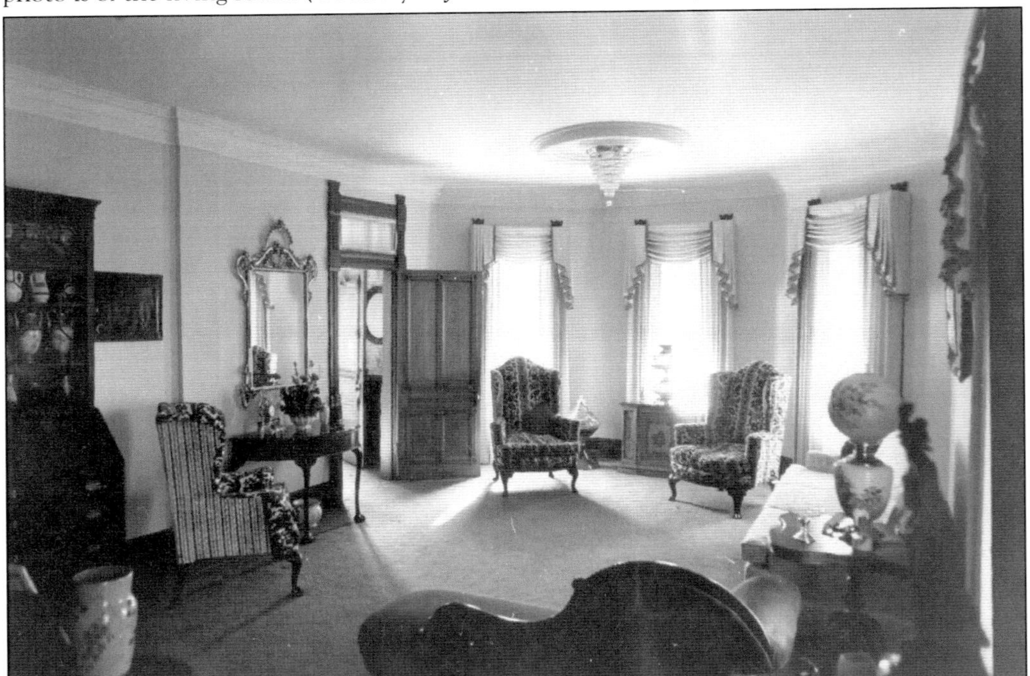

Two

Friends, Neighbors, and Families

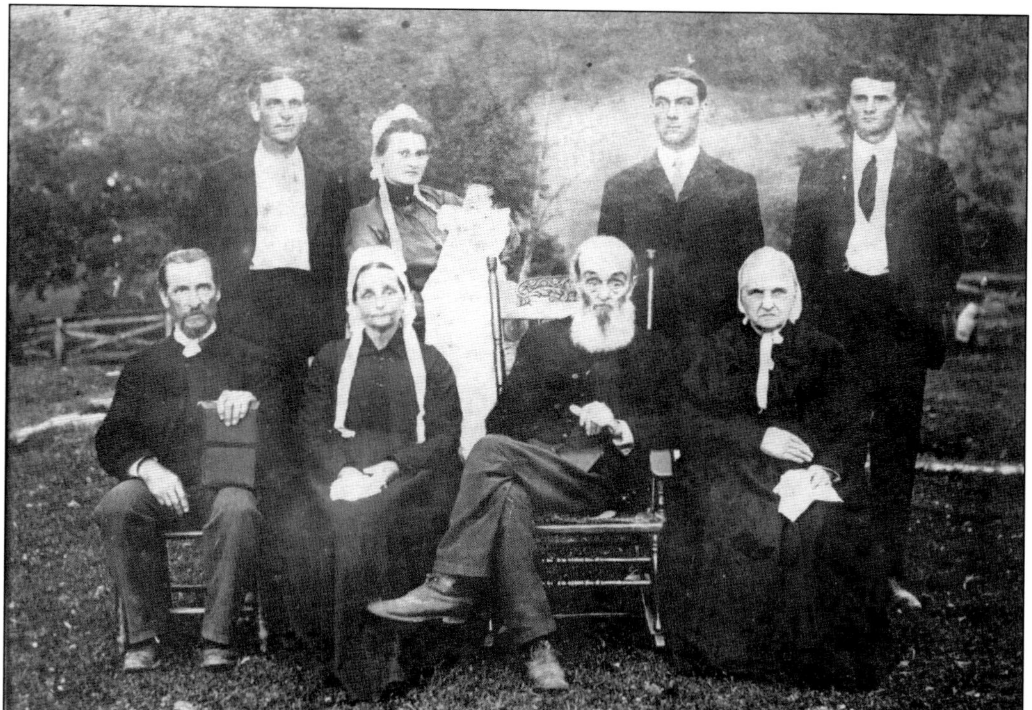

The birth of a new child was a popular reason to have photographs made in the early 1900s, just as it is today. This family photo celebrated four generations together. Pictured from left to right are (front row) John Garst, Rebecca Wine Garst, Joseph Wine, and Susana Wine Krouse; (back row) Joseph Garst, Lula Larimer Garst (holding a baby Garst), Samuel Garst, and Chris Larimer. (Courtesy of George and Margaret Holley.)

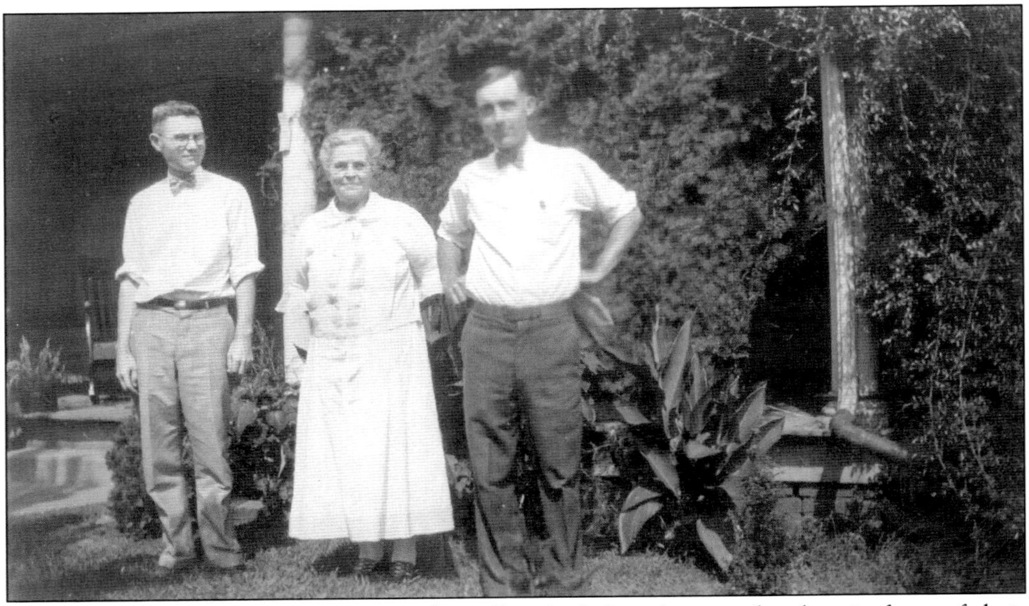

Grady Fine, Lucy Farley Fine, and William Fine had this photograph taken in front of their home on Lamont Street around 1910. (Courtesy of Barbara S. Hilton.)

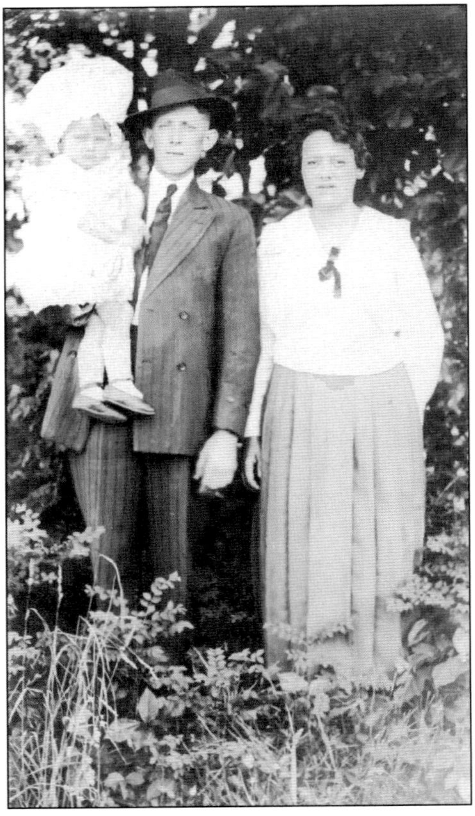

Moses and Nelle Miller pose with their daughter, Hazel, around 1922. Hazel was born August 16, 1918, and died on July 18, 1958. (Courtesy of Barbara S. Hilton.)

Solomon Slagel (September 16, 1855–October 24, 1939) and Mary Kate Henson (March 11, 1864–February 2, 1942) were married on January 18, 1884. The couple lived in the Sinking Creek area of Johnson City and had 13 children. (Courtesy of Betty Jane Hylton.)

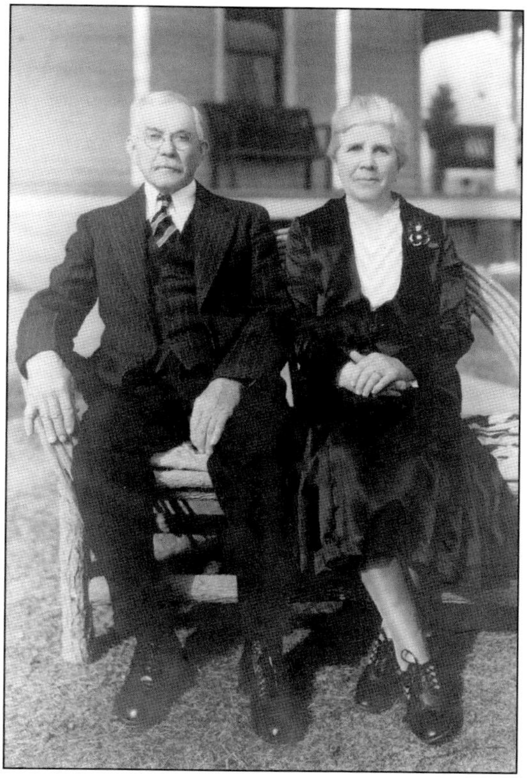

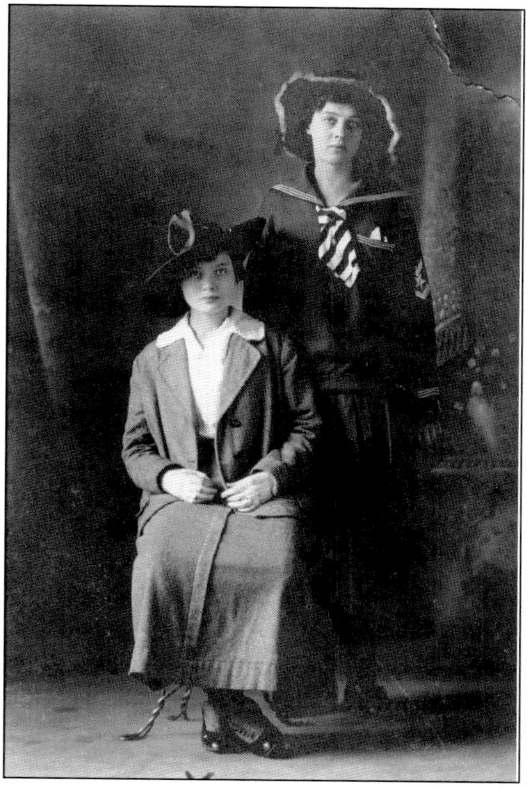

Dressed fashionably in early 20th-century clothing, Minnie (May 28, 1901–December 27, 1977) and Della (March 16, 1899–December 9, 1986) both chose serious expressions for their joint photo. (Courtesy of Bill and Mary Nelle Roberson.)

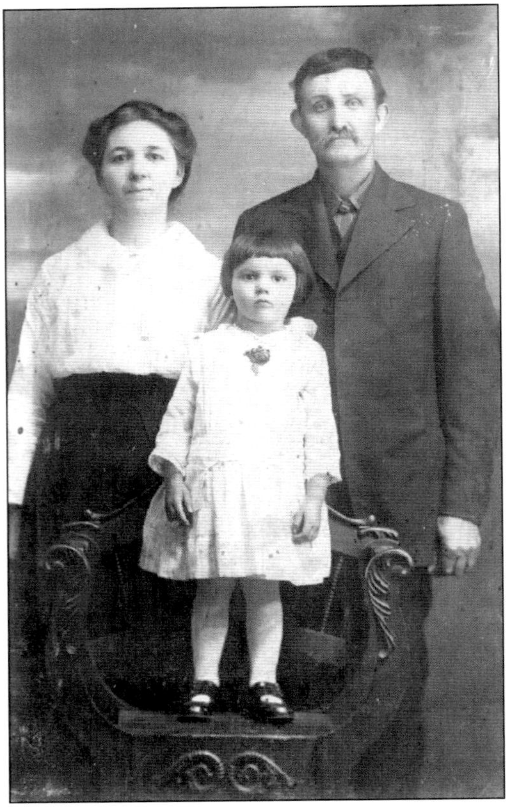

Axie Huffine Leach (February 1, 1871–March 28, 1937) and John Leach (September 26, 1869–March 19, 1937) had a beautiful picture taken with their daughter, Otta, around 1917. When Otta grew up, she married Sam Lecka, who died of a heart attack while driving his truck. (Courtesy of Elaine Cantrell.)

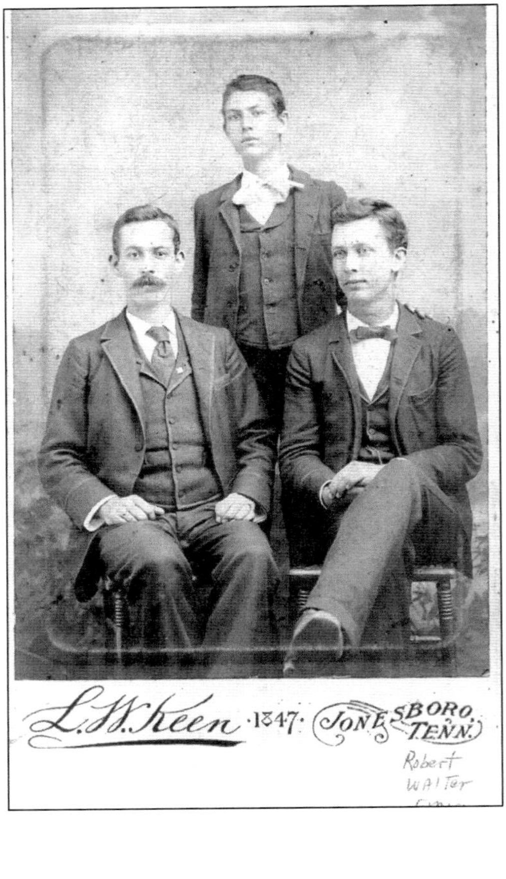

L.W. Keen took this photo of the Huffine brothers. Robert Milburn Huffine was 20 years old, Walter Sherman Huffine was 15, and Emory Taylor Huffine was 24 years of age when the photo was taken. (Courtesy of Elaine Cantrell.)

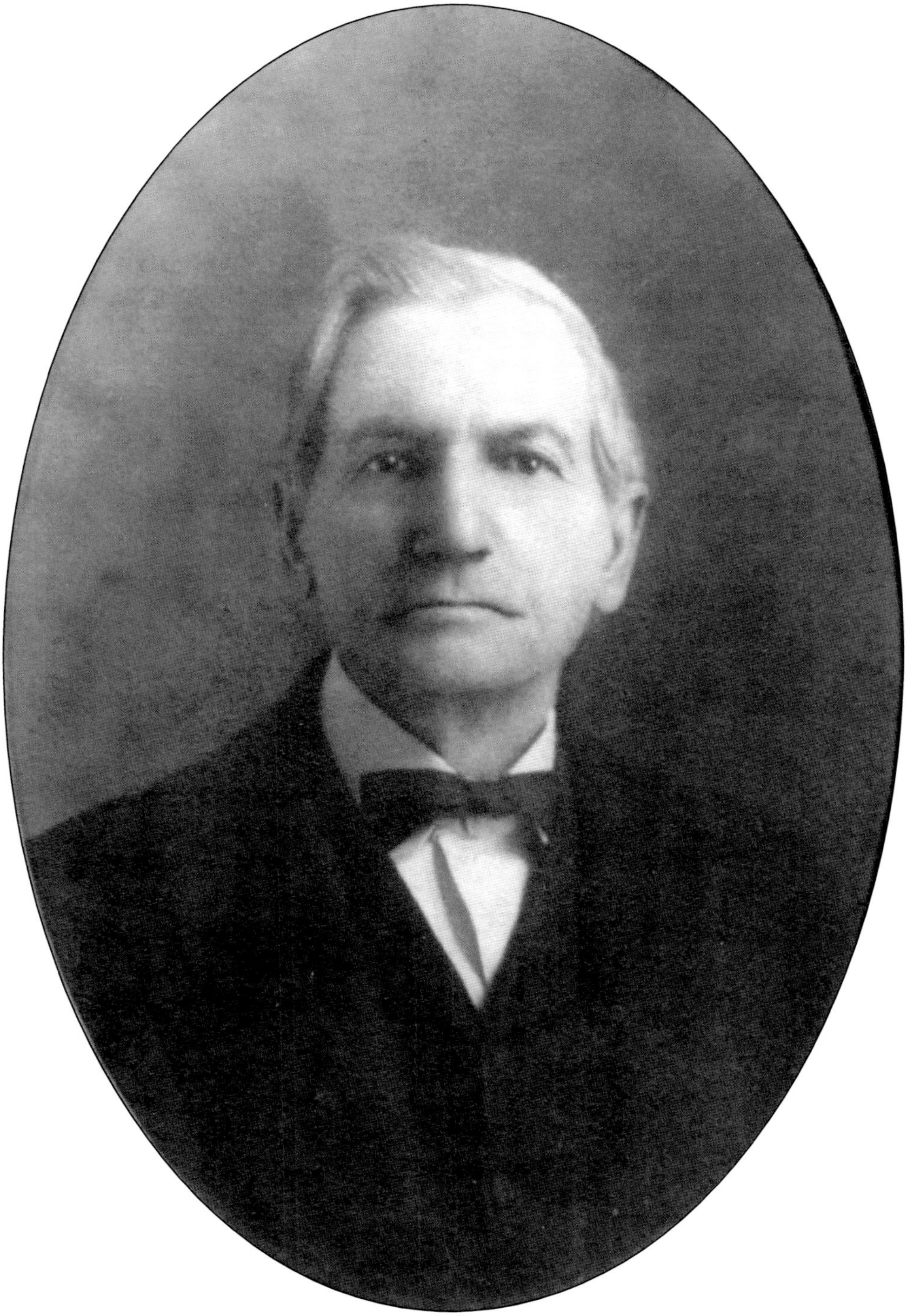

Dr. Abraham Jobe was a descendent of David Jobe, one of the area's first settlers, whose land grants covered what is now downtown Johnson City. Born in 1817, Jobe spoke three Native American languages and was a Union sympathizer. Abraham's primary interest was the practice of medicine, and he was at the bedside of ex-president Andrew Johnson when Johnson died. Jobe died in 1906. (Courtesy of Rocky Mount Historical Association.)

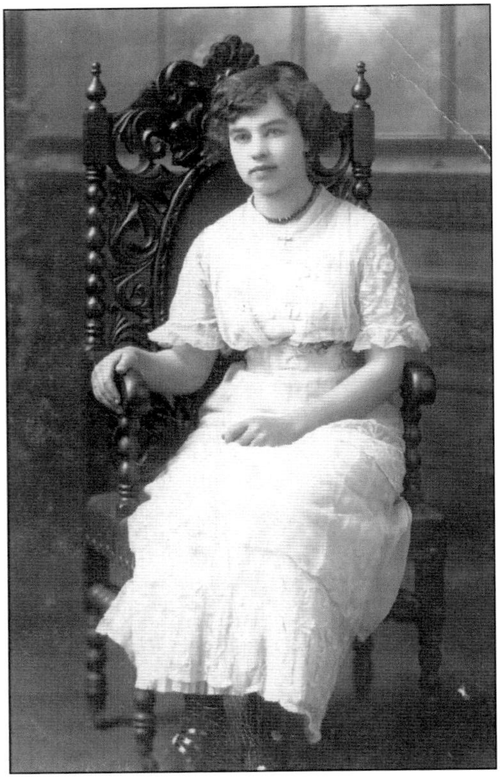

This well-preserved photo is a lovely example of early 20th-century photography. Goldie Huffine Scott lived from 1893 until 1980 and was around 20 years of age when this photo was taken. (Courtesy of Elaine Cantrell.)

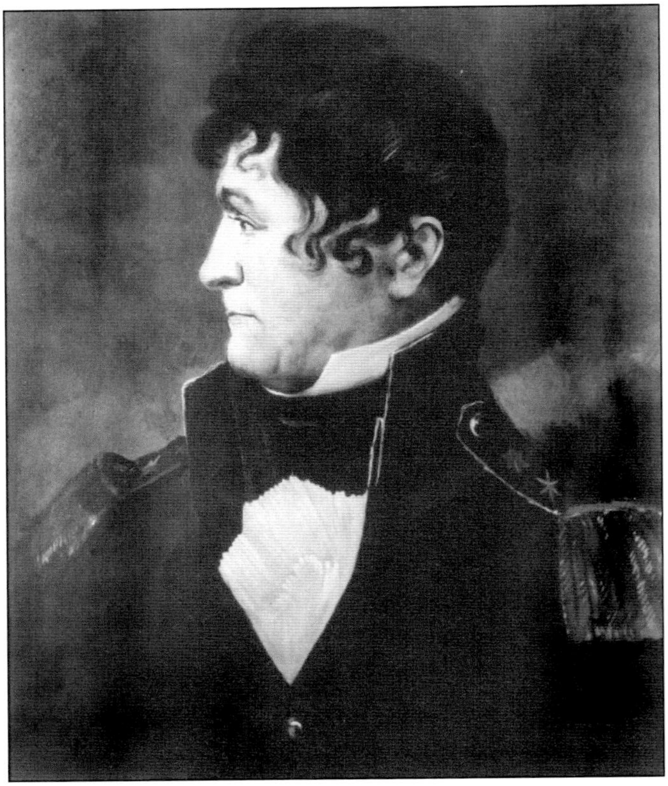

Brig. Gen. Nathaniel Taylor fought under Andrew Jackson. He was the great-great-grandfather of Senator Taylor. The brigadier general lived from 1771 to 1816. (Courtesy of the Rocky Mount Historical Association.)

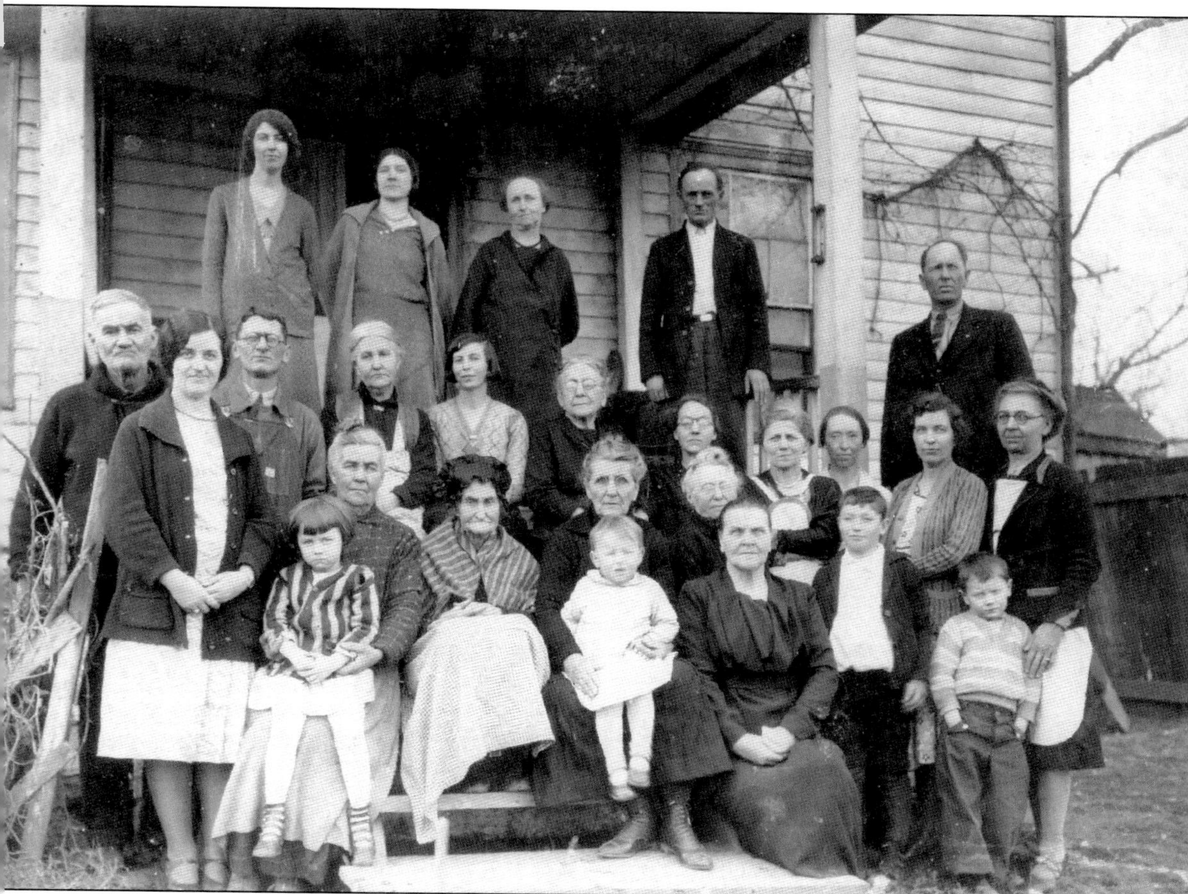

In the early 1900s, Vicie Leach allowed teachers to board in her home on Cherokee Road. Pictured here with "Aunt" Vicie Leach are, from left to right, the following: (front row) Ruby Estes, Emma Peoples (with Dorothy Crouch on her lap), Vicie Leach, Cordie Price (the child on her lap is unidentified), Mary Slagle, Mary Scott, Story Lad, and James Martin; (middle row) W.C. Keplinger, John Crouch, Mrs. Estes, Pauline Estes Crouch, Margie Huffine, Mamie Estes Martin, Florence Carr Carrier, Mrs. Story, Maude Estes Alphard, and Axie Huffine Leach; (back row) two unidentified ladies (possibly boarding teachers), Mrs. Keplinger, Mr. Keplinger, and Matt Martin. (Courtesy of Elaine Cantrell.)

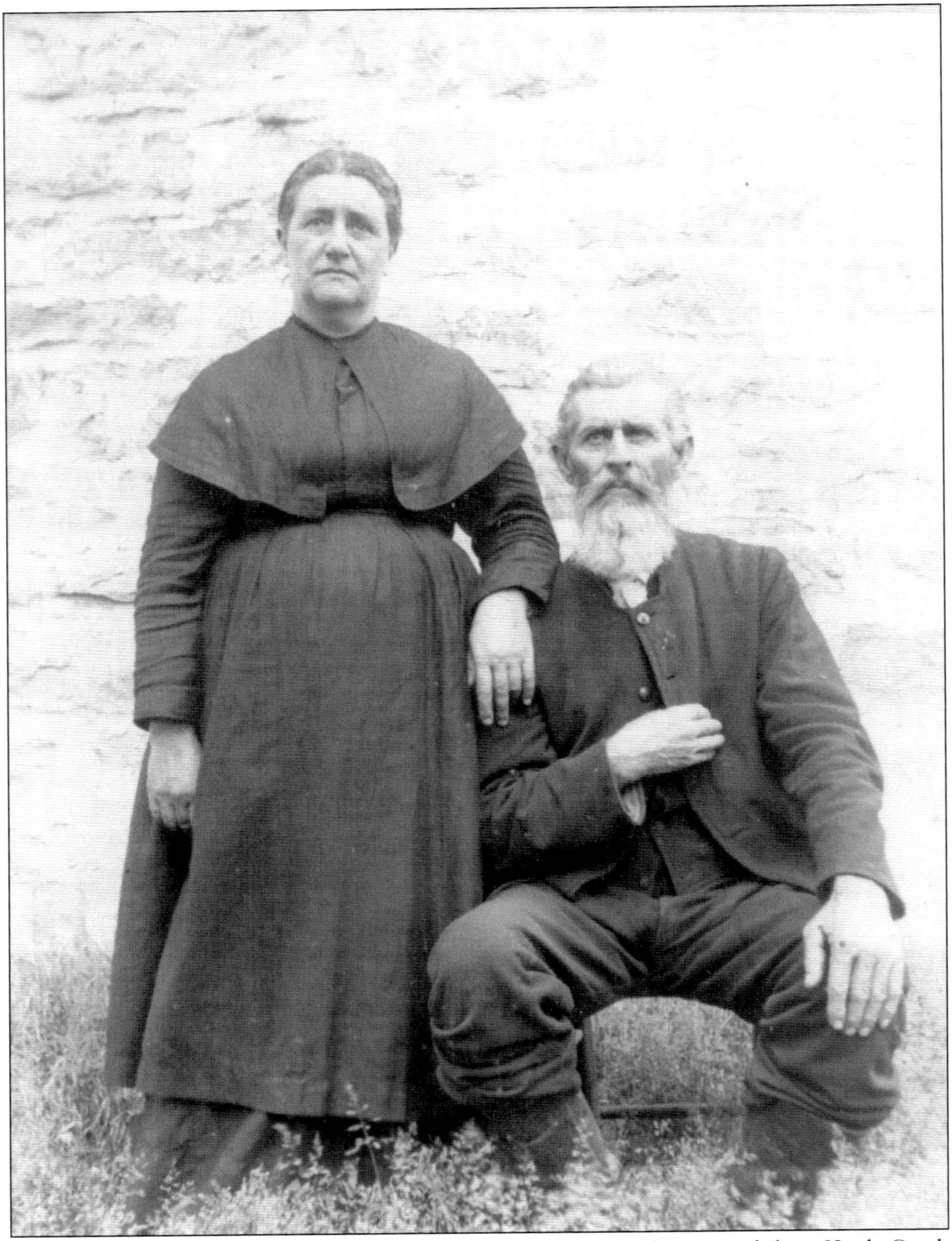

Isabell Krouse Sherfy and David Preston Sherfy pose by the chimney of their Knob Creek home in the early 1900s. Lt. David Sherfy served 4 years in the Union army and participated in 43 battles and skirmishes. George Holley, his granddaughter's husband, wrote a book about him entitled *David Preston Sherfy: Kinsman and Cavalryman*. (Courtesy of George and Margaret Holley.)

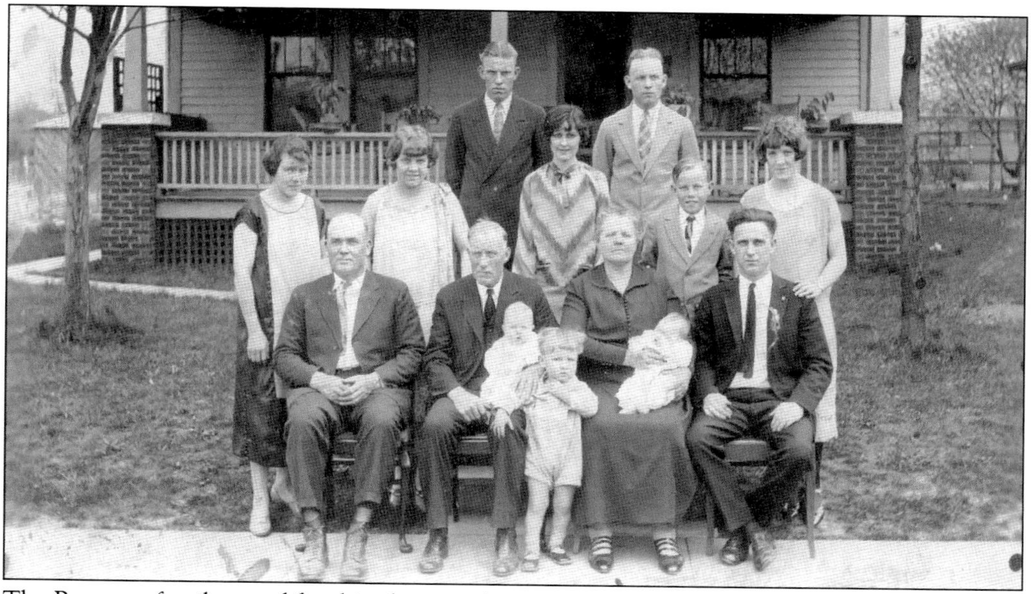

The Bowman family posed for this photo in August 1926. From left to right, the individuals are as follows: (front row) Ralph Eugene Scott Sr., Francis Patton Bowman holding baby Martin Francis Scott, child Ralph Eugene Scott Jr. (standing), Anna Smithson Bowman holding baby Louise Hankal, and William Hankal; (middle row) Selma Bowman Scott, Beatrice Love Bowman, unidentified, Walter Bowman, and Georgia Bowman Hankal; (back row) Bill and Lockie Bowman. (Courtesy of Elaine Cantrell.)

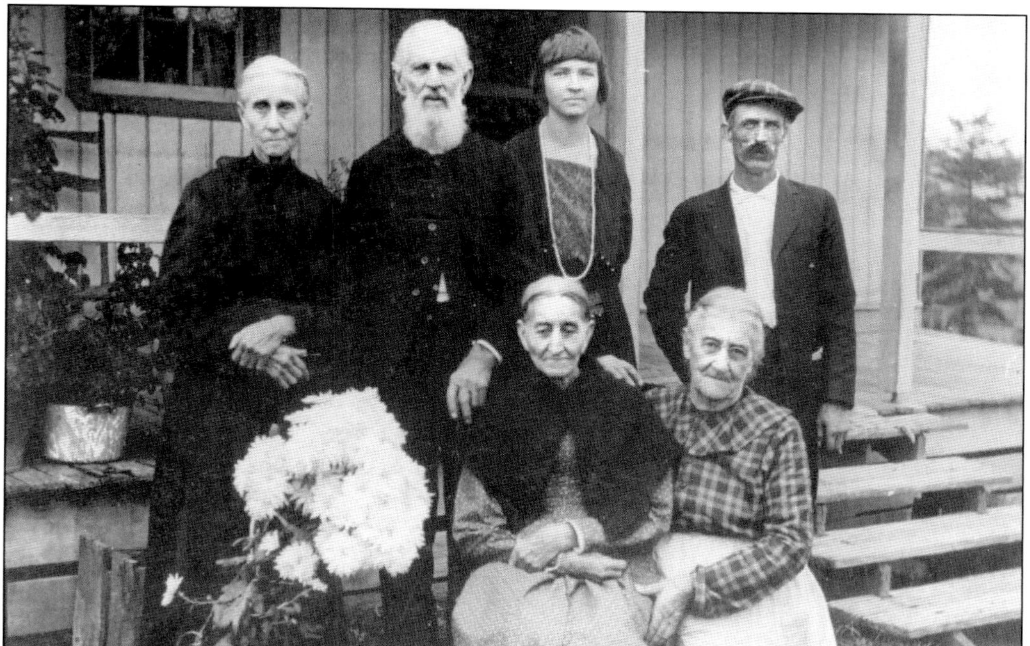

The Sherfey family had this picture taken on November 6, 1921. Pictured from left to right are (front row) Martha Sherfey Hodge and Isabell Krouse Sherfey; (back row) Sarah Sherfy Hodge, David P. Sherfey, Lelia Watson Sherfey, and Noah Hodge. (Courtesy of George and Margaret Holley.)

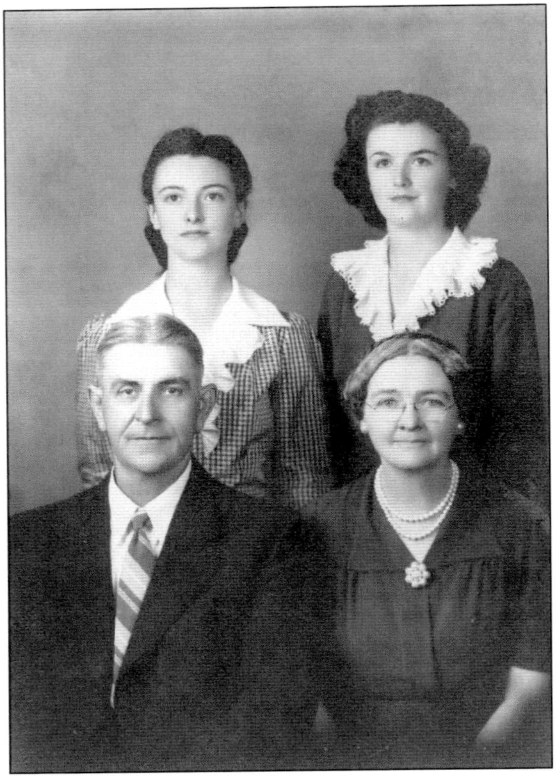

J.A. and Lelia Sherfey celebrated their 23rd wedding anniversary on June 11, 1944. To commemorate the occasion, they are pictured here with daughters (left to right) Helen, 21, and Margaret, 16. Margaret Sherfey grew up quite interested in history, particularly that of the Knob Creek area of Johnson City, and for numerous years has operated the Knob Creek Museum on Denny Mill Road. (Courtesy of George and Margaret Holley.)

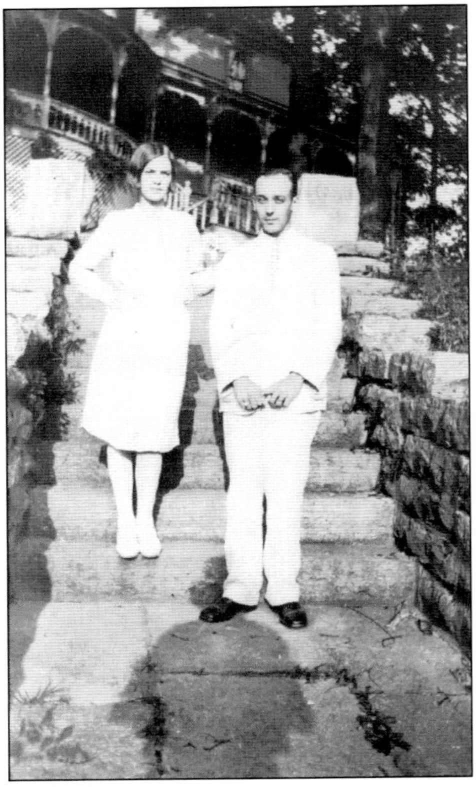

Robins Roost was a fashionable place to visit and have photos made in the early 1900s. This unidentified couple is standing on the steps leading up to the house. Robins Roost is shown on page 22. (Courtesy of John G. and Etta Love.)

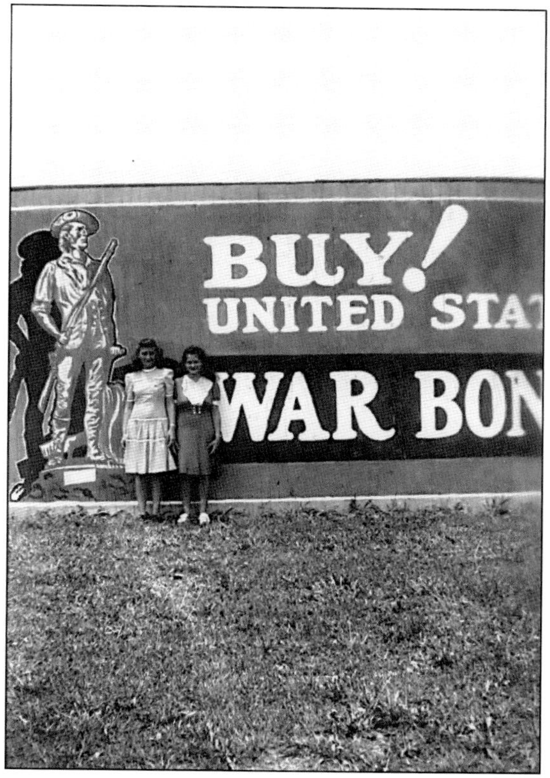

Hazel Miller Stout (left) and Dorothy Miller stand in front of an advertisement at a local stadium that Hazel's father-in-law Dewey took care of. The advertisement persuaded viewers to purchase war bonds. (Courtesy of Barbara S. Hilton.)

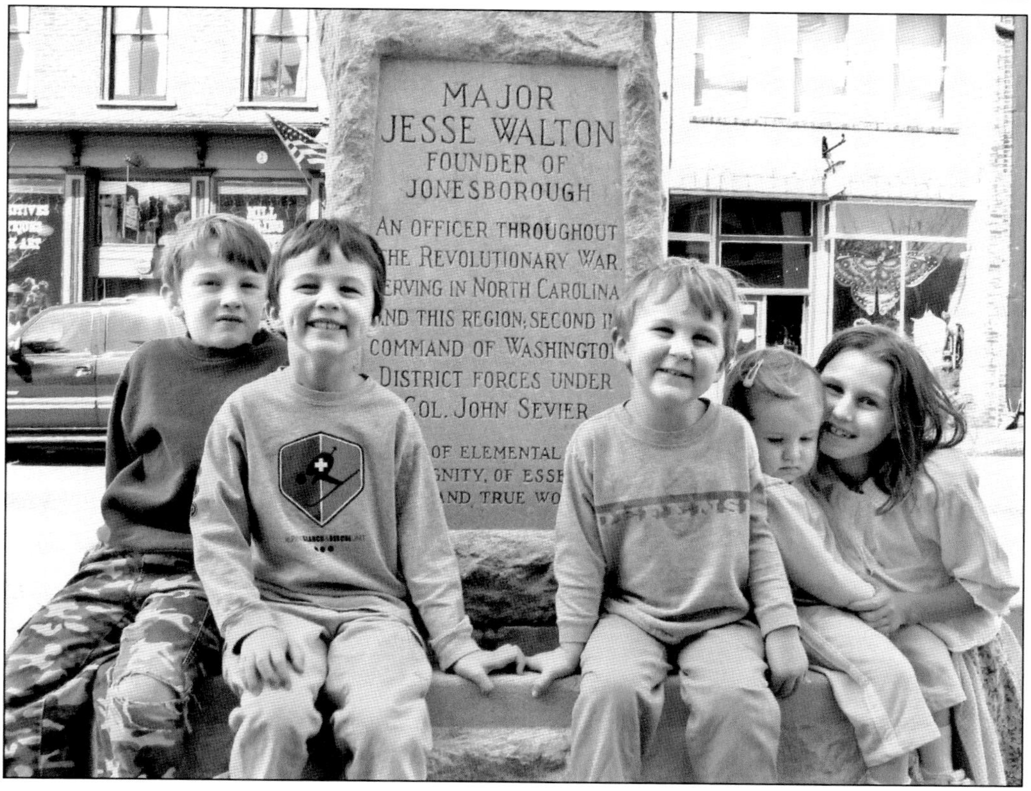

Pictured here, from left to right, are Micah, Christopher, Daniel, Hannah, and Sarah Haskins, enjoying an outing in front of the Washington County Courthouse in Jonesborough. The Haskins children are educated at home and visit sites in Johnson City, Jonesborough, and other Washington County towns to learn regional history. If you would like to learn more about Jonesborough, Tennessee's oldest incorporated town, which is about 10 miles from Johnson City, see Images of America: *Jonesborough*, by Sonya Haskins.

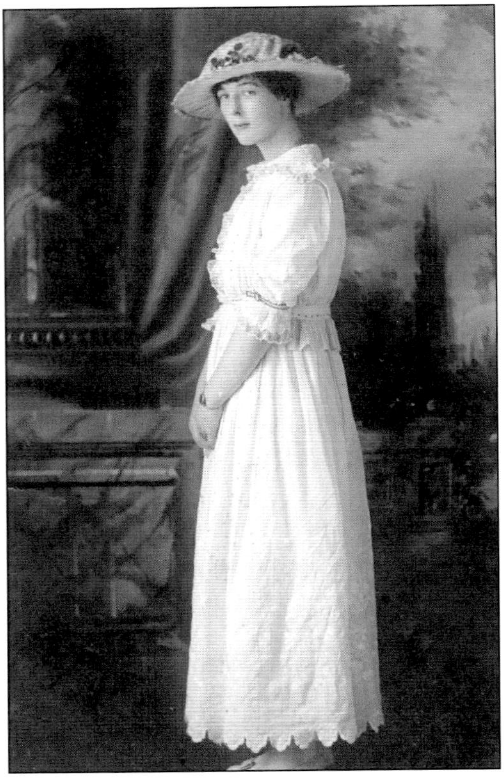

This is a beautiful photograph of Edith Buck Ward around 1930. Edith was a cousin of Lela Watson and Ina Dulaney. (Courtesy of George and Margaret Holley.)

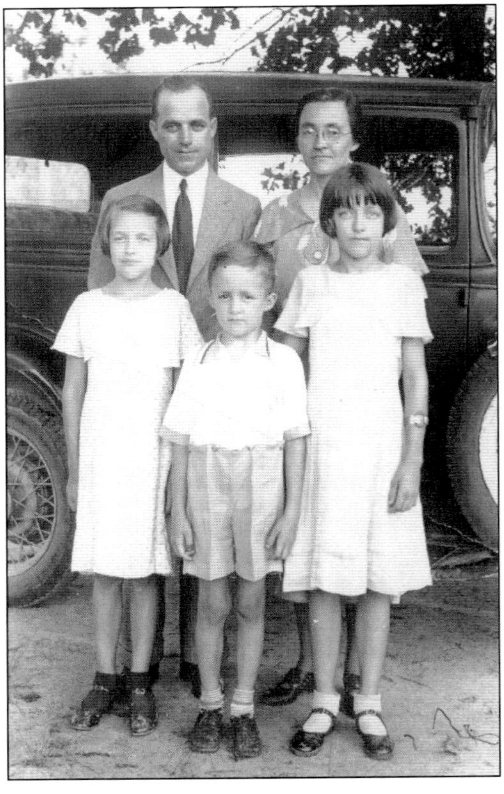

The back of this photo postcard wished recipients a "Merry Christmas" from Merlin C. and Pearl Shull and children Helen, 9, Merlin Jr., 7, and Anna Mae, 11. It was dated 1934. Merlin Shull was a pastor of the First Church of the Brethren on East Chilhowie Avenue. (Courtesy of George and Margaret Holley.)

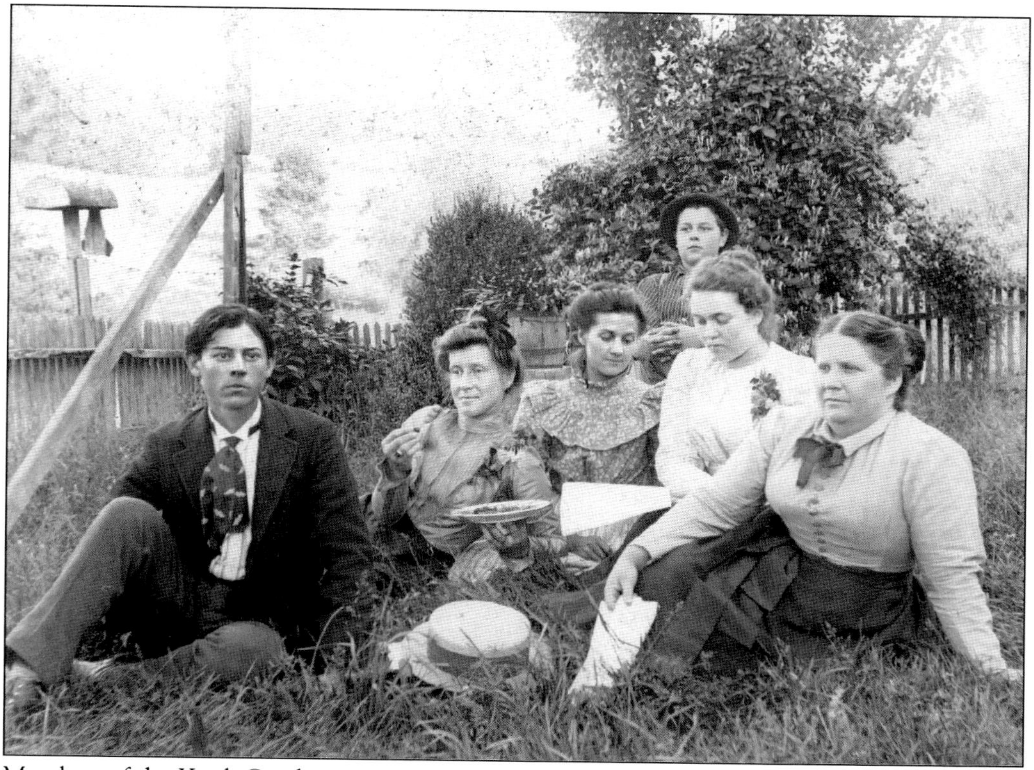

Members of the Knob Creek community enjoy a picnic in this photo from 1900. Pictured from left to right are Charley Hodge, Sarah Crumley, Gabie Goodman, Catherine Miller, Mary Reed, and (in the back) J.A. Sherfy. The last name "Sherfy" was sometimes spelled without the "e," but gradually it was added to the name on a regular basis in the 1900s. (Courtesy of George and Margaret Holley.)

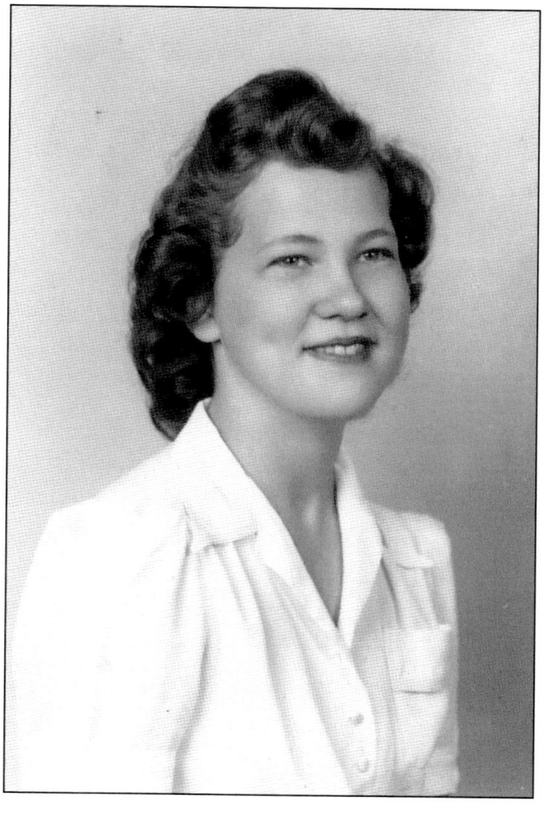

The use of photography was destined to become an important means to celebrate events like graduation. This was Elaine Scott's graduation photo from 1946. Elaine married James Cantrell in 1950. Today, though she battles cancer, Elaine is a marvelous family historian, organizing literally volumes of information, photos, and documents of families in Johnson City and the surrounding area.

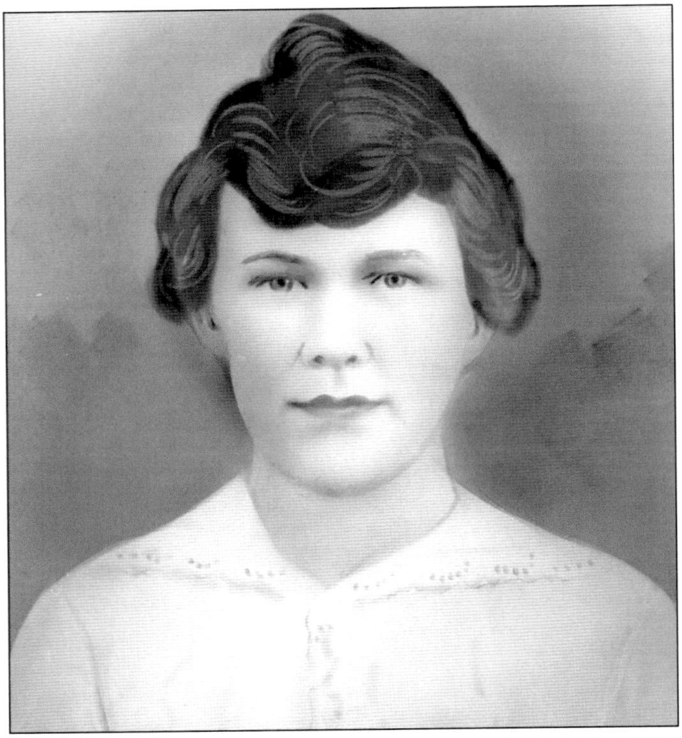

This gorgeous portrait of Ida Mae Scott was created shortly before her death. The daughter of Martin and Mary Scott, Ida Mae was only 18 when she succumbed to pneumonia on January 13, 1919. She is buried at the Speedwell cemetery on Cherokee Road. (Courtesy of Elaine Cantrell.)

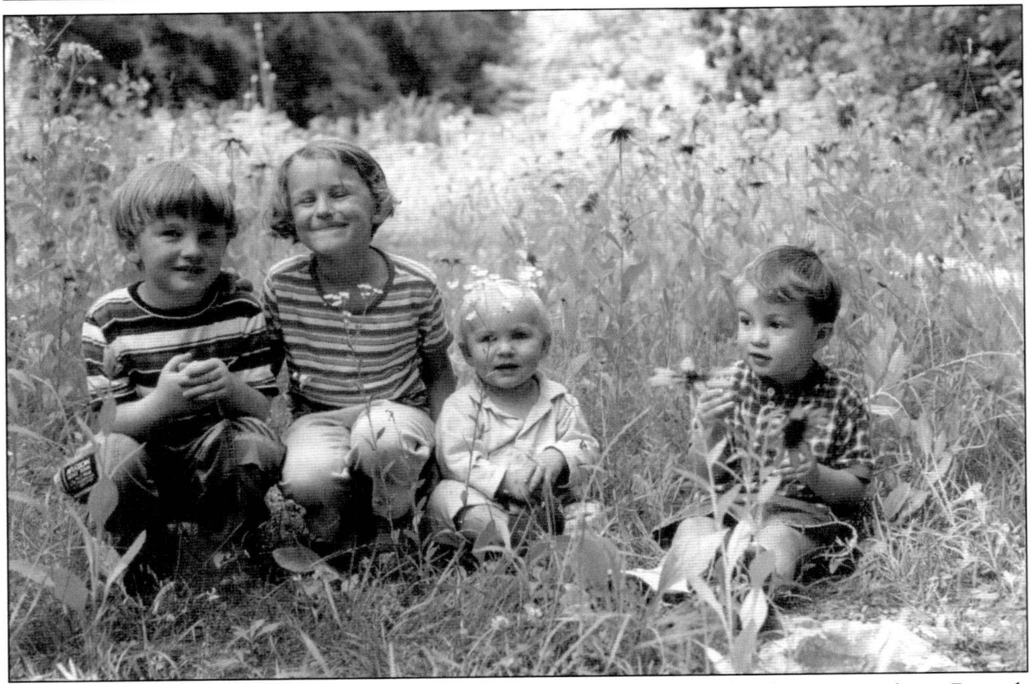

For visitors, the Tri-Cities area offers storytelling in Jonesborough, the racetrack in Bristol, and the opportunity to unwind in local parks. Doe River Gorge in Elizabethton is one area attraction that includes a mountain lake and a restored 19th-century railroad. Shown here on a gorge outing in 2002 are, from left to right, Micah, Sarah, Daniel, and Christopher Haskins. (Photograph by the author.)

Here is a marvelous example of the clothing and hairstyles that were typical in the early 1900s. The individuals in this Harrington family photograph, from left to right, are as follows: (front row) Susan, Richard, and Kathleen; (back row) Harry, Frank, Mollie, and Pearl. (Courtesy of George and Margaret Holley.)

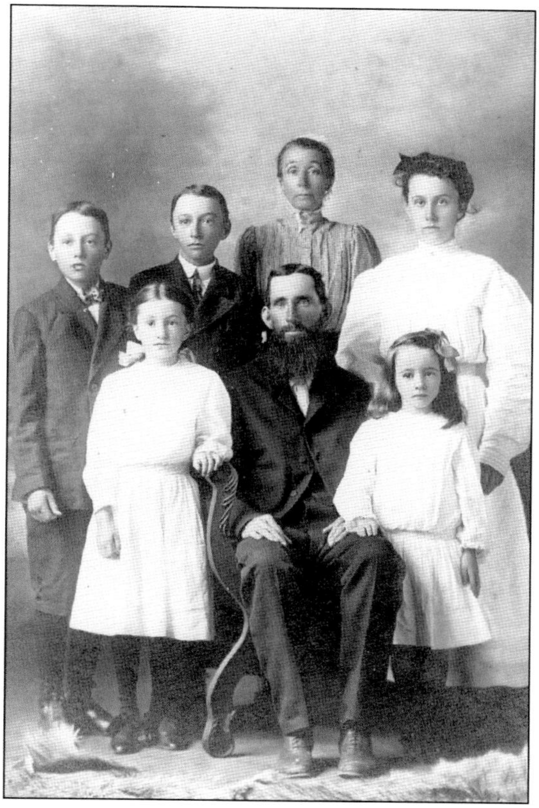

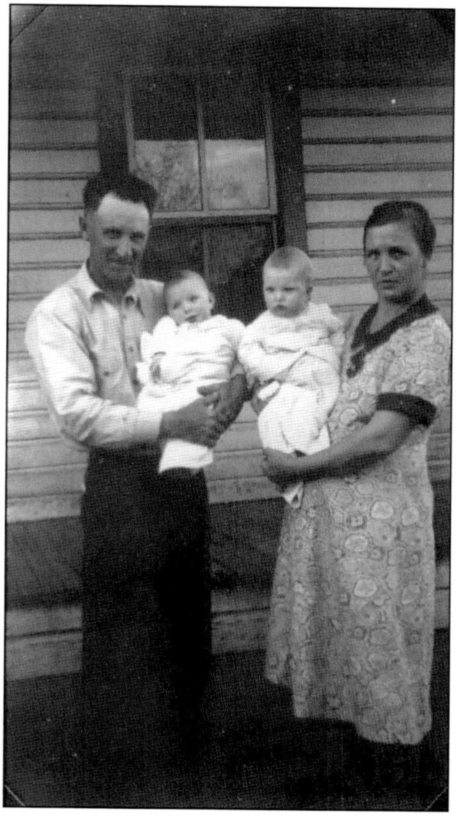

Hiram Jones, who worked as a supervisor for the Clinchfield Railroad, is pictured here with his wife, Carrie, and twin sons, John and Charles. The boys were born September 17, 1938. Hiram and Carrie lived in Erwin and had a total of 12 children. (Courtesy of Terry and Kim Jones.)

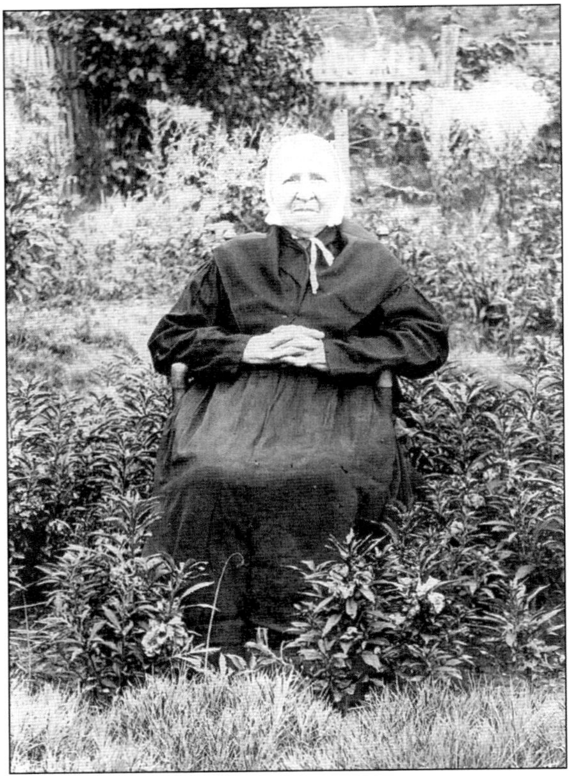

Here, Magdalena Garst, wife of Abraham Sherfy, is pictured in her flower bed at her home on Brush Creek in Johnson City during the summer of 1899. Magdalena was born August 7, 1816, and was buried in the Knob Creek Church cemetery when she died February 20, 1906. As a midwife during the Civil War, Magdalena nursed both Confederate and Union soldiers. (Courtesy of George and Margaret Holley.)

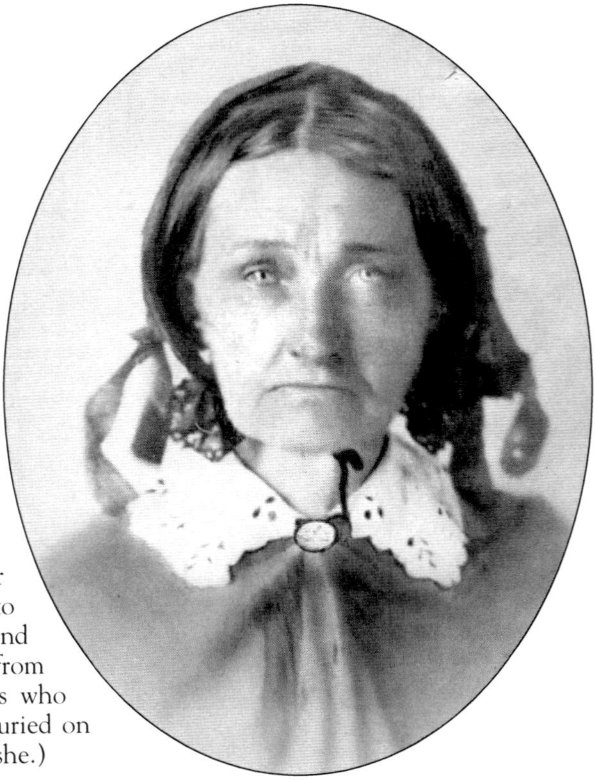

Nancy Epperson Crouch preferred a more traditional setting for her photograph. Nancy Epperson came to the Johnson City area from Kentucky and married Jonathan "Jackie" Crouch from Boone's Creek. She had four brothers who were Methodist preachers. Nancy is buried on Hyter's Farm. (Courtesy of Mary D. Hashe.)

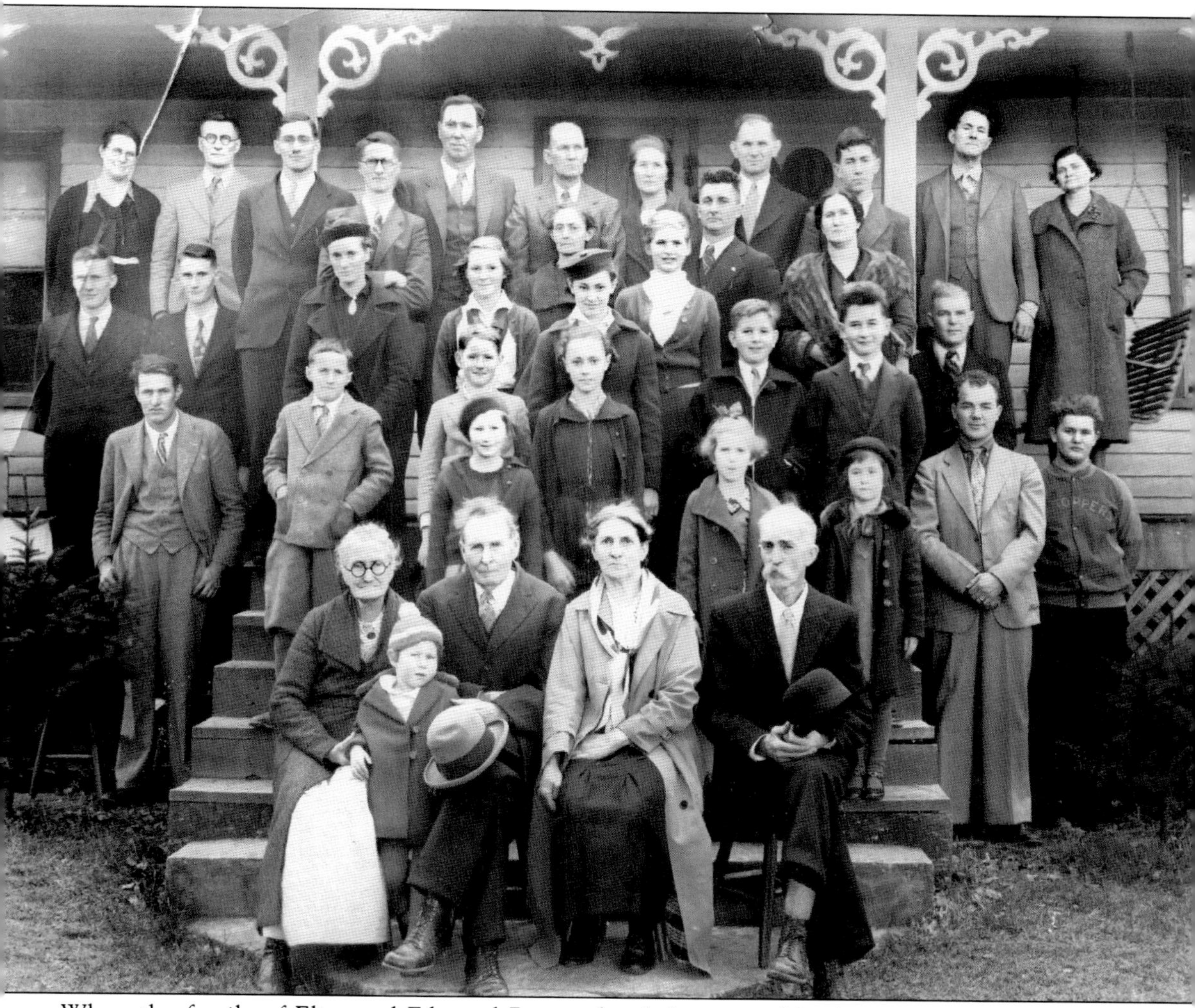

When the family of Eliza and Edmund Brown decided to assemble their 24 grandchildren for a family photograph, they managed to gather everyone at the family home. One of the grandchildren, Grace Brown, who would have been positioned on the right side of the photo just below the woman on the porch, is absent. As it was taking so long to coordinate the picture, Grace decided to go upstairs and read a book. (Courtesy of Grace Brown Miller and June Miller Gouge.)

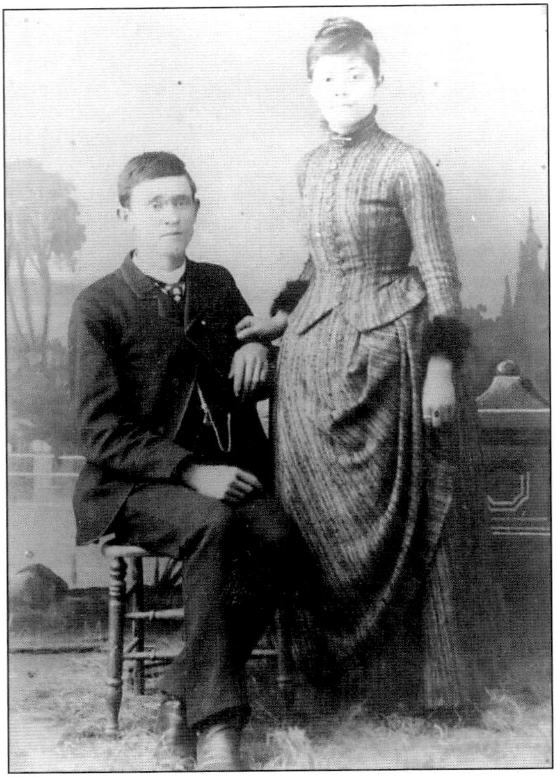

Bun and Crick Bowers Wolf, of Piney Flats, posed for this formal photo around 1920. (Courtesy of Mary D. Hashe.)

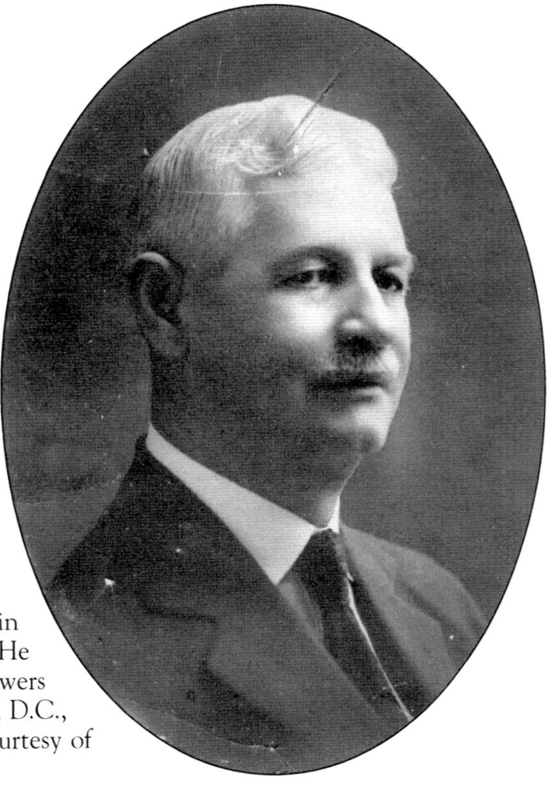

Henry Crouch was born in the late 1800s in his family's log cabin in Boone's Creek. He was the oldest son of Hyter and Sophia Bowers Crouch. Henry later moved to Washington, D.C., where he worked for the government. (Courtesy of Mary D. Hashe.)

Rev. Thomas Hyter Crouch started the First Baptist Church in Boone's Creek in 1881. Reverend Crouch lived from February 10, 1833, until June 11, 1894. (Courtesy of Mary D. Hashe.)

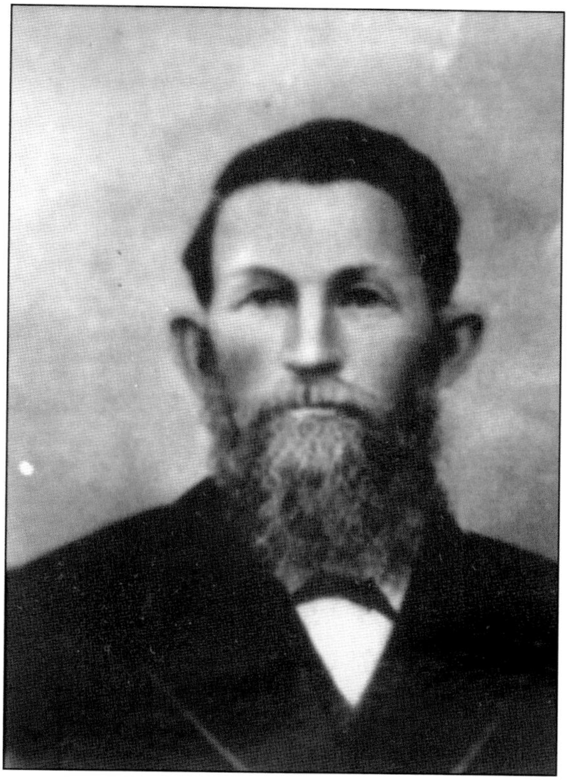

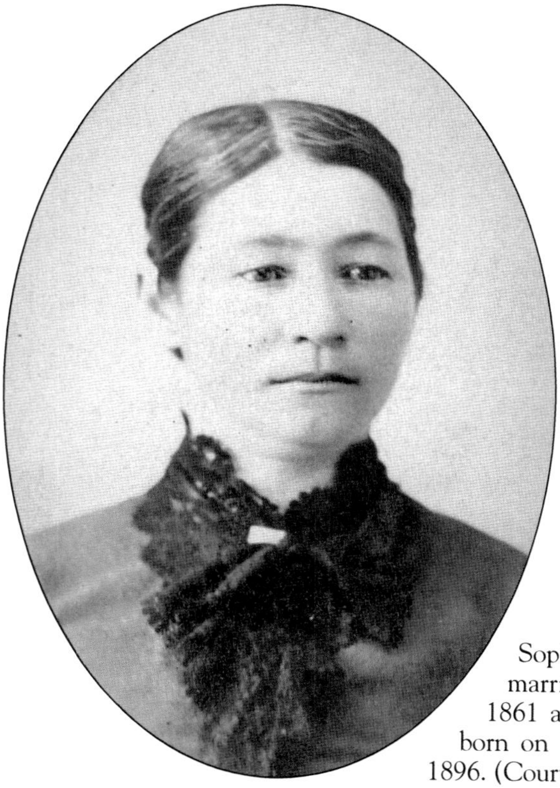

Sophia Bowers Crouch, from Piney Flats, married Rev. Thomas Hyter Crouch in March 1861 and moved to Boone's Creek. Sophia was born on December 1, 1837, and died January 20, 1896. (Courtesy of Mary D. Hashe.)

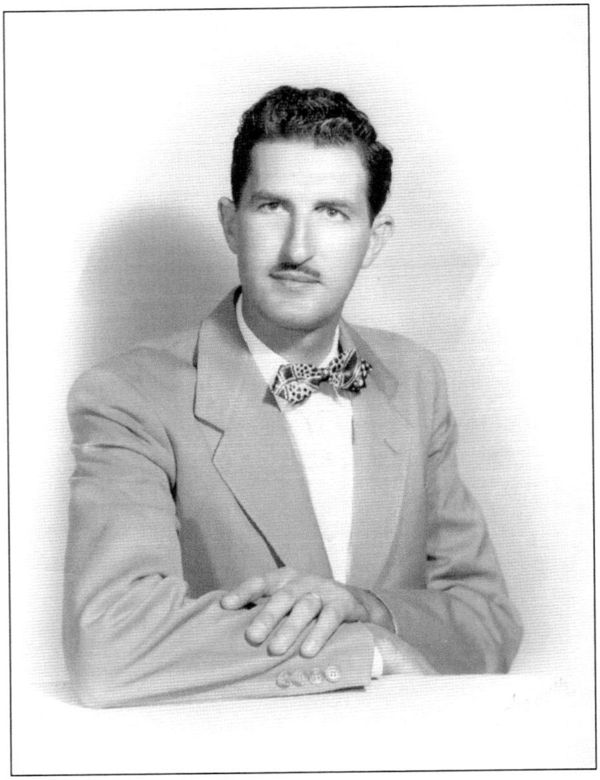

John G. Love Sr. is the son of Walter L. and Amelia Miller Love. John served as a commissioner and mayor in Johnson City in the late 1970s and early 1980s. Love helped organize the Johnson City Board of Realtors in the 1960s and served on the Tennessee Real Estate Commission. He is a former builder and developer and lives in Robins Roost. (Courtesy of John G. and Etta Love.)

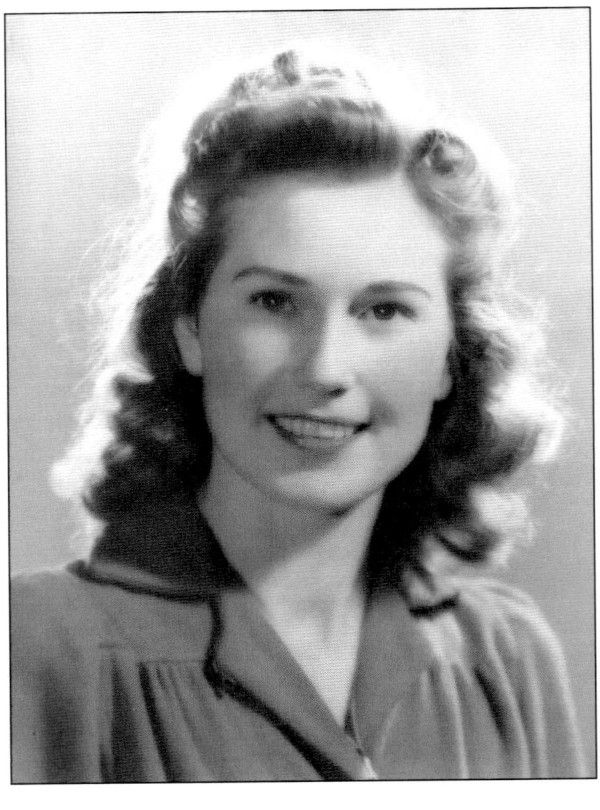

Etta Morgan graduated high school at age 16 and attended college in Ohio and Kentucky. After teaching school for a period, she came to Tennessee and worked as a social worker for the state. Etta married John G. Love in 1954. The daughter of L.C. and Betty Morgan, Etta is related to General John Hunt Morgan of Morgan's Raiders, a Confederate unit during the Civil War. (John G. and Etta Love.)

Around 1902, Bertie G. Miller traveled into the business district to purchase some red shoes for her toddler, AnnLea. While she was gone, the children's father placed his hunting rifle beside the fireplace. One of the preschool children accidentally discharged the rifle, killing AnnLea. Bertie never recovered from the loss and spoke of the tiny red shoes even unto death. (Courtesy of Grace Brown Miller and June Miller Gouge.)

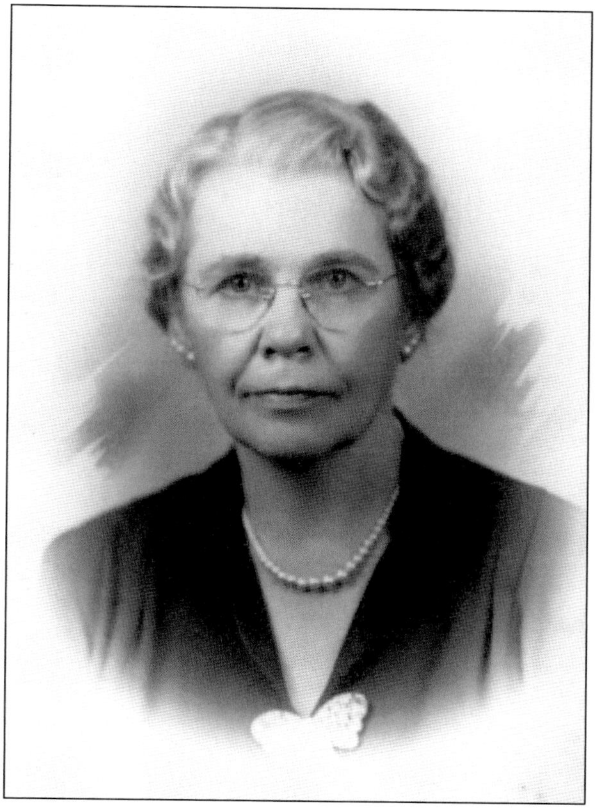

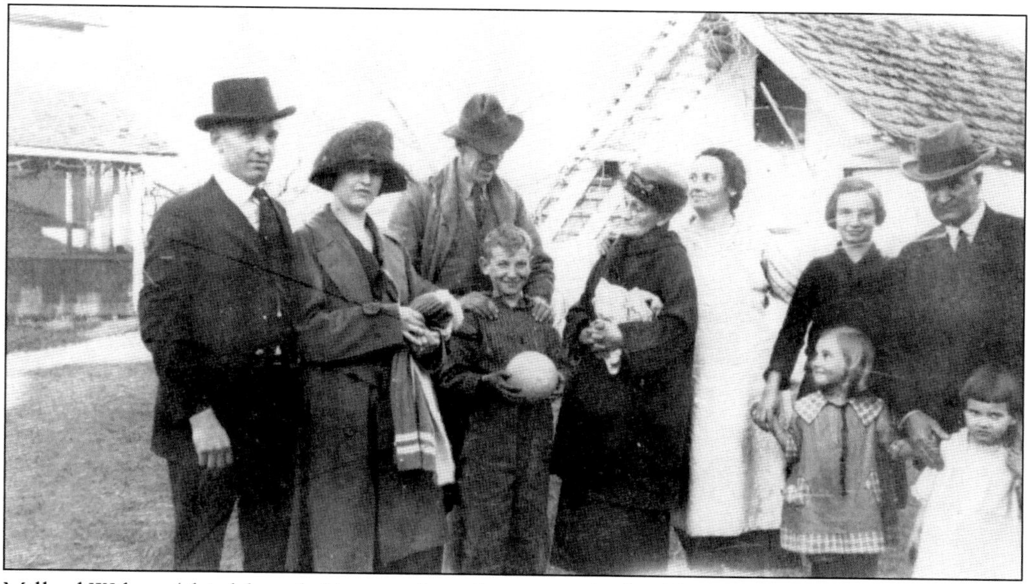

Millard Wilson (third from left) was a dairy farmer on the land between Huffine Road, Antioch Road, and Greenwood Drive. On page four, there is a photo of this dairy and information about the land. Pictured here, from left to right, are Byron Wilson, Cleo Wilson, Millard Wilson, Joe Wilson (holding the ball), Lilly Mae Wilson, Minnie Deakins Wilson, Mabel Wilson, Joyce Wilson, Joe Wilson, and Dorothy Wilson. (Courtesy of Robert and Darlene Wilson.)

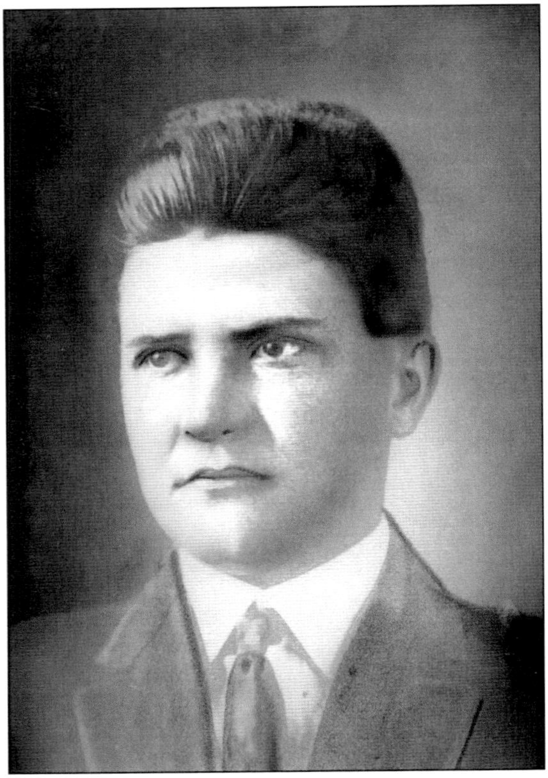

Clinton Mathias Wilhite was born in Bailey's Branch, North Carolina, on January 26, 1890, and after the Depression, he moved to Johnson City, where he lived at 101 Peachtree Street. This photograph was taken right before World War I, in which Wilhite served in the ambulance corps and was gassed three times. He died on May 13, 1965. (Courtesy of Robert and Darlene Wilson.)

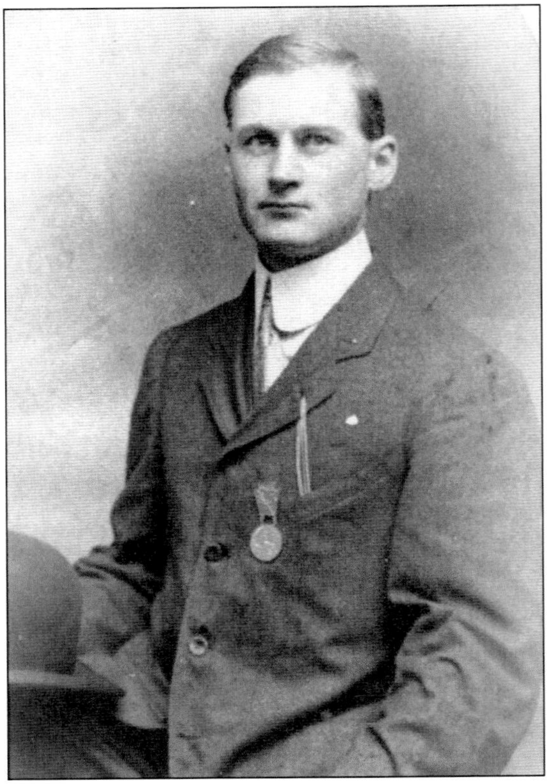

Ralph Waldo Crouch (January 4, 1881–1968) had this photo taken in 1903. Ralph married Nettie Bruce Bowers. (Courtesy of Mary D. Hashe.)

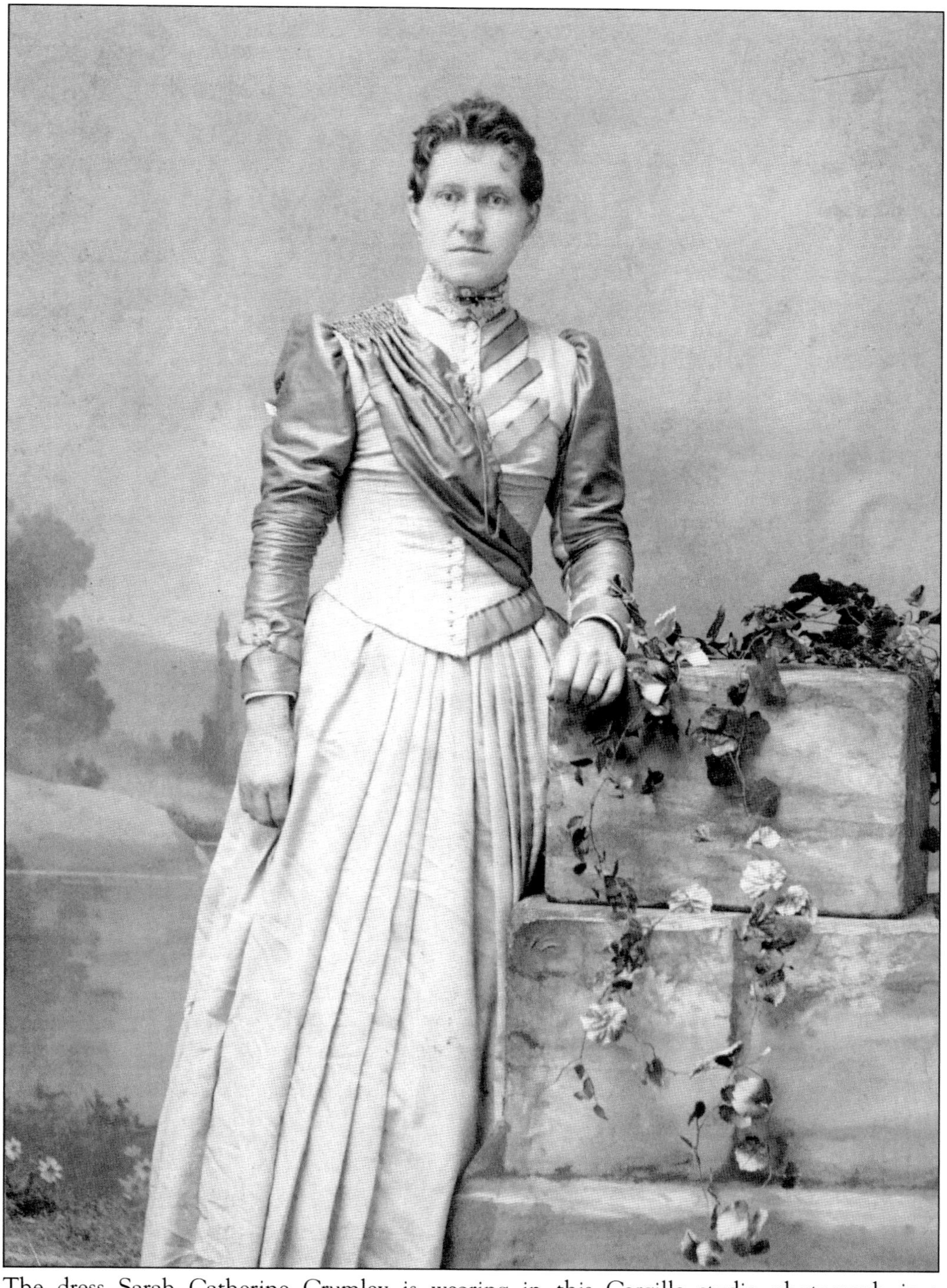

The dress Sarah Catherine Crumley is wearing in this Cargille studio photograph is a gorgeous example of turn-of-the-century clothing. As was customary in that time period, Sarah waited until all of her older brothers and sisters were married or deceased before she married her sweetheart. She was 51 years old when she married Samuel Krouse on January 25, 1917, at her home in the Knob Creek community. Sarah died on July 19, 1932. (Courtesy of Don and Sarah Walters.)

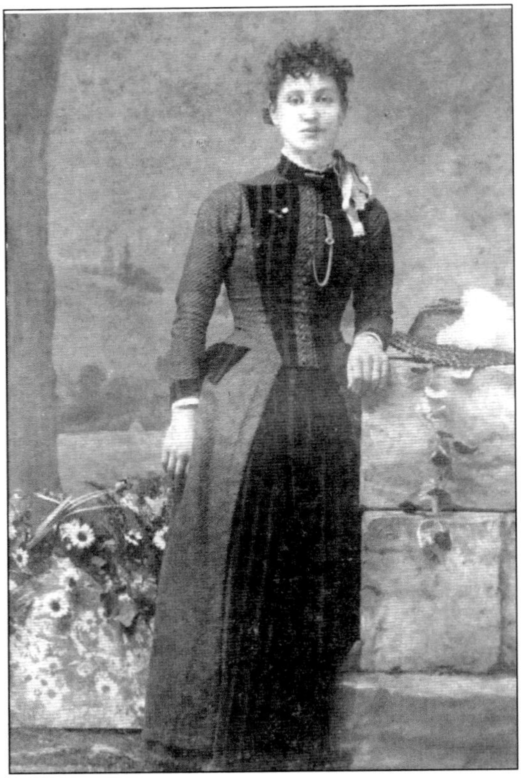

Martha Ann Crumley posed for this photo in the late 1800s. She lived from June 17, 1862, until July 24, 1903. (Courtesy of Don and Sarah Walters.)

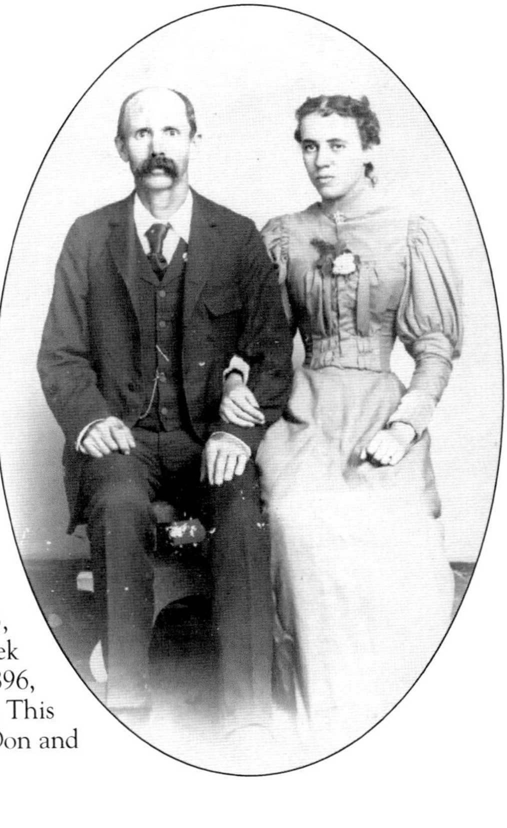

Thomas K. Crumley was born on October 25, 1856, at his parents' home in the Knob Creek community. He married Mary Alice around 1896, when she would have been about 21 years old. This is probably their wedding photo. (Courtesy of Don and Sarah Walters.)

This photo of John Hopper, a farmer in the Knob Creek community, was taken around 1885. He had eight children. (Courtesy of Don and Sarah Walters.)

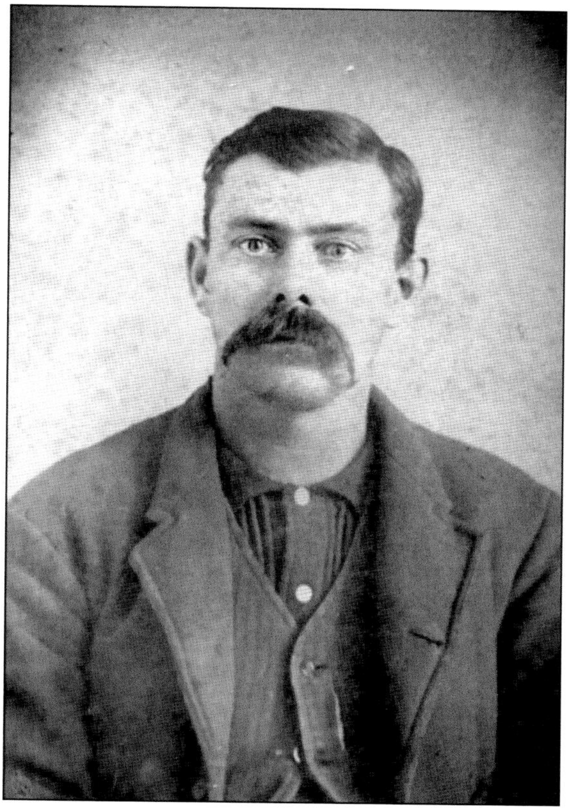

The Hopper family poses beside the back porch of the John Hopper home on Hopper Road in 1905. The individuals, from left to right, are as follows: Jennie Miller Hopper, John Hopper, Addie Hopper Church, an unidentified friend, Roy B. Hopper, Dusty Hoover, Carrie Hopper Hoover, Mae Hopper France, Mary Cain Hopper, John Hopper, Mattie Hopper Vines, Noah Vines, Edith Vines, and Roy Vines. (Courtesy of Don and Sarah Walters.)

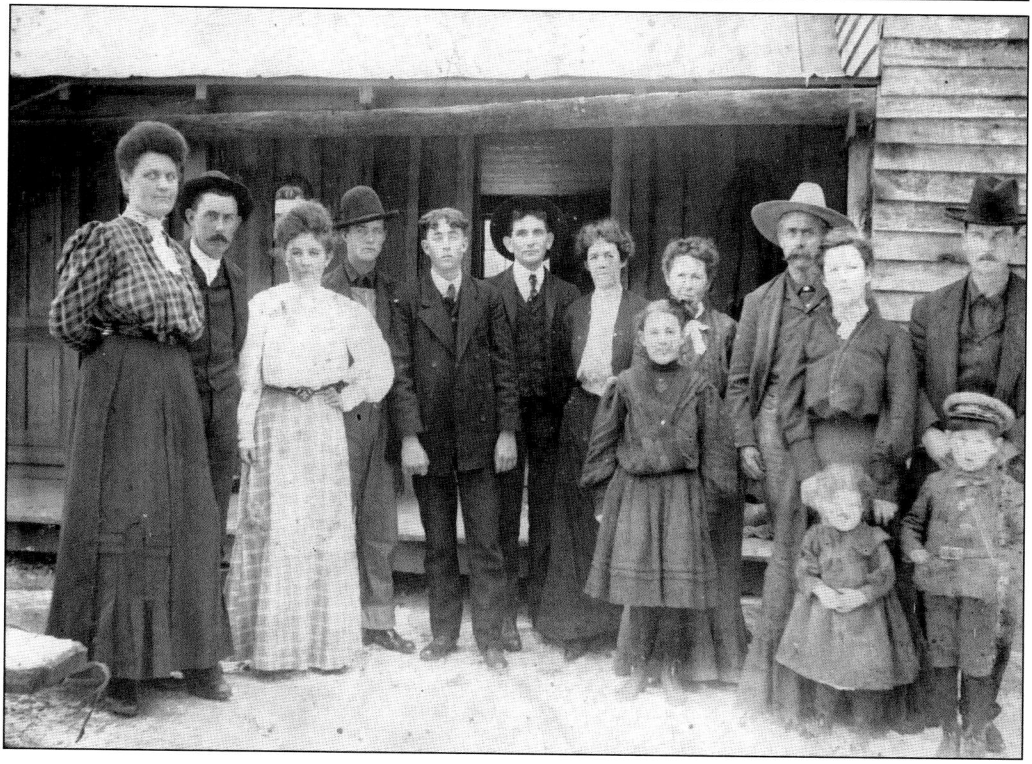

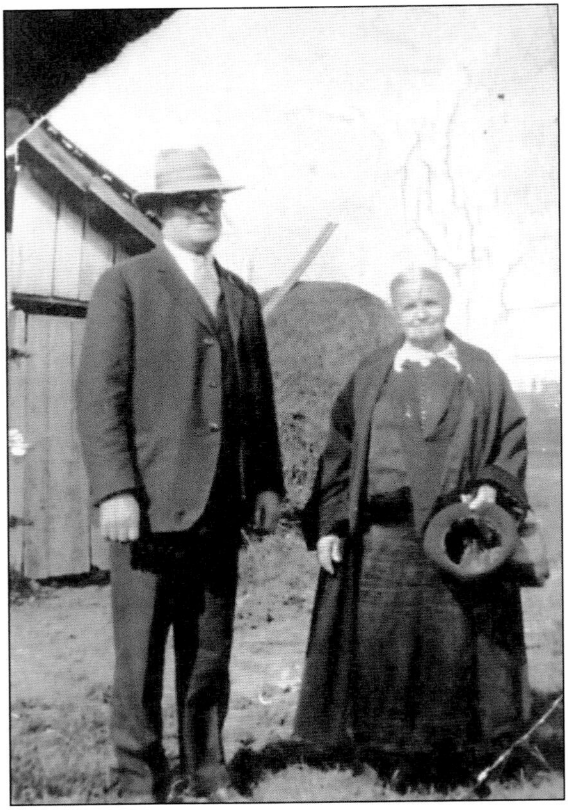

John Masengill was born at Rocky Mount on December 17, 1882, and is shown here with his mother, Deborah Masengill. William Cobb, who originally settled Rocky Mount and built a home there in 1770, allowed governor William Blount to live in his home from 1790 to 1792. Rocky Mount was the first territorial capital of the Southwest Territory. (Courtesy of Rocky Mount Historical Association.)

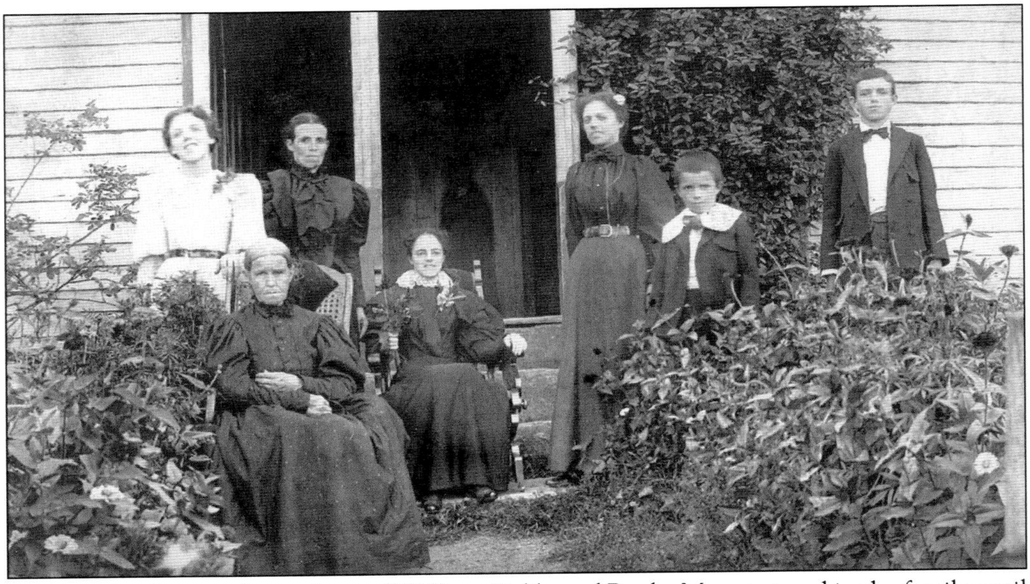

The Masengills were descendants of William Cobb, and Rocky Mount stayed in the family until the State of Tennessee purchased it in 1958. Here is the Masengill family in 1897. Identification with the photo says "from left to right are Maggie, Deborah, Lula, Jennie, Alex, and John Michael." This leaves out one of the women, but there is no way to know which one. (Courtesy of Rocky Mount Historical Association.)

Three

RAILROADS

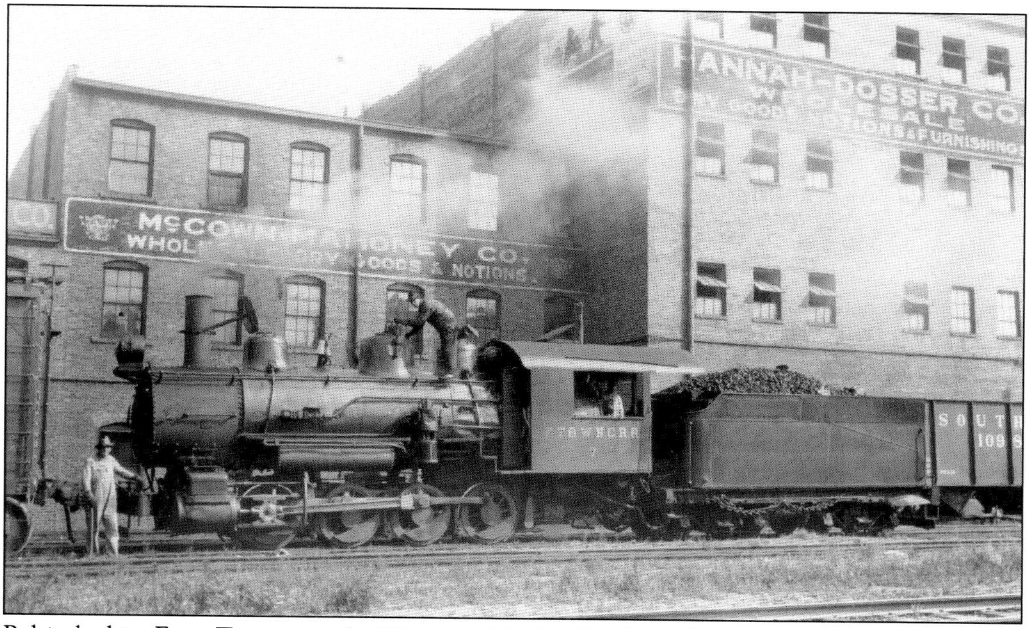

Behind this East Tennessee & Western North Carolina (ET & WNC) train engine, you can see the buildings of the McCown-Mahoney Company and Hannah-Dosser Company. This train yard was located near what is now Legion Street. (Courtesy of the James T. Dowdy Collection.)

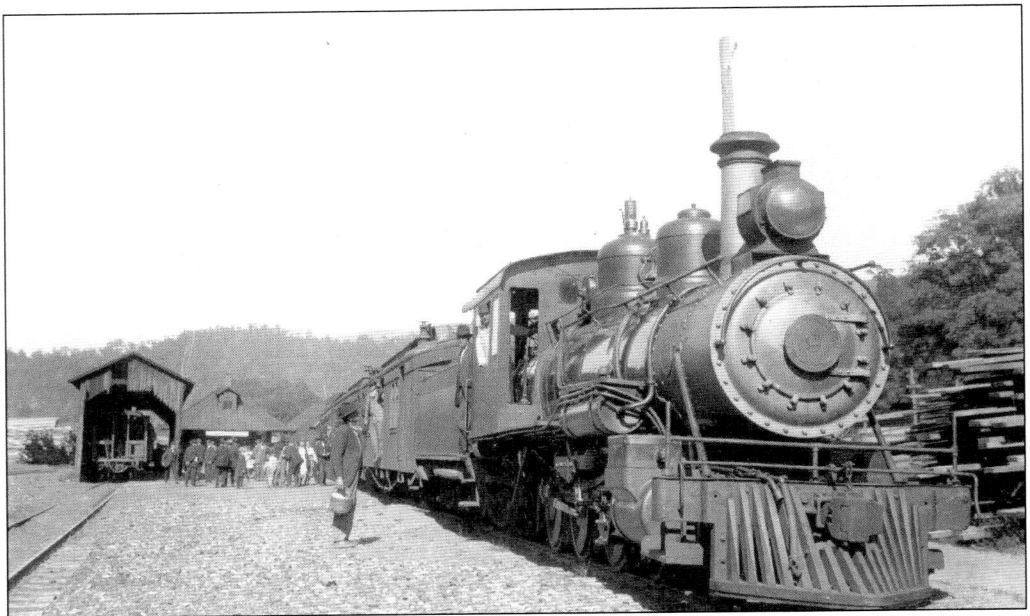

The railroad line was completed into Cranberry, North Carolina, on July 3, 1882, and transportation of iron ore, passengers, and freight began. ET & WNC used a narrow-gauge line because it was more economical to build and to operate through the rugged mountains of Tennessee and North Carolina. Shown here is the Cranberry, North Carolina, depot. (Courtesy of the James T. Dowdy Collection.)

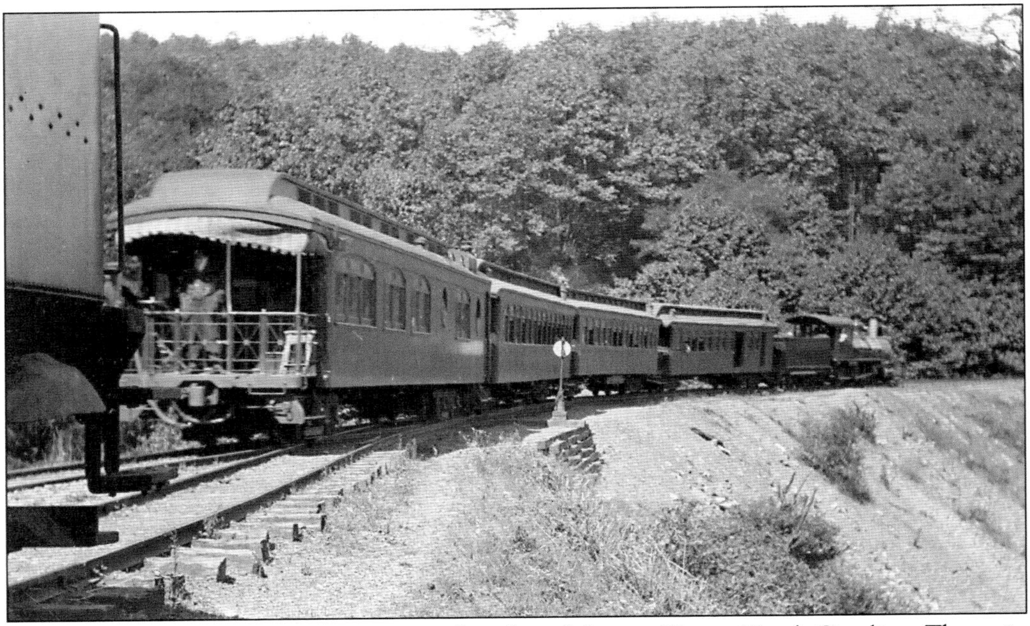

This is another view of the narrow-gauge line from Johnson City to North Carolina. The train is headed out to the gorge. Visitors to Doe River Gorge can still experience the joy of riding into the gorge today. (Courtesy of the James T. Dowdy Collection.)

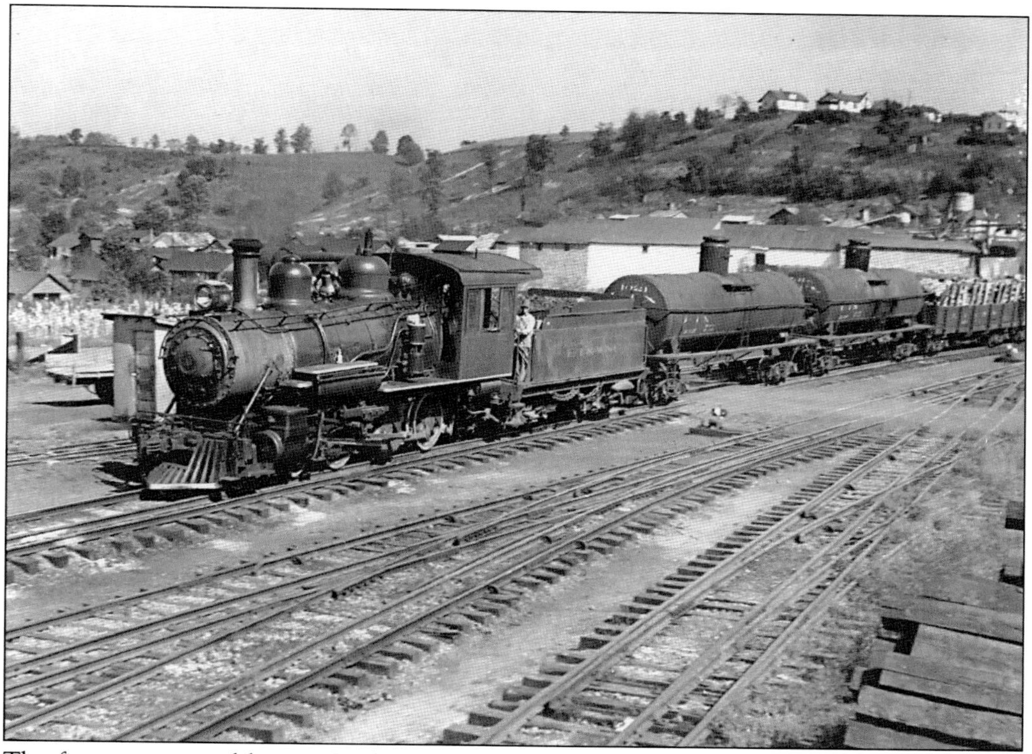

The fireman pictured here is Fred Helton with engine number 11. This engine was built in 1916, retired in 1950, and scrapped in 1952. With the exception of a few houses, buildings are scarce in the background of this Johnson City train yard photograph from the early 1900s. (Courtesy of the James T. Dowdy Collection.)

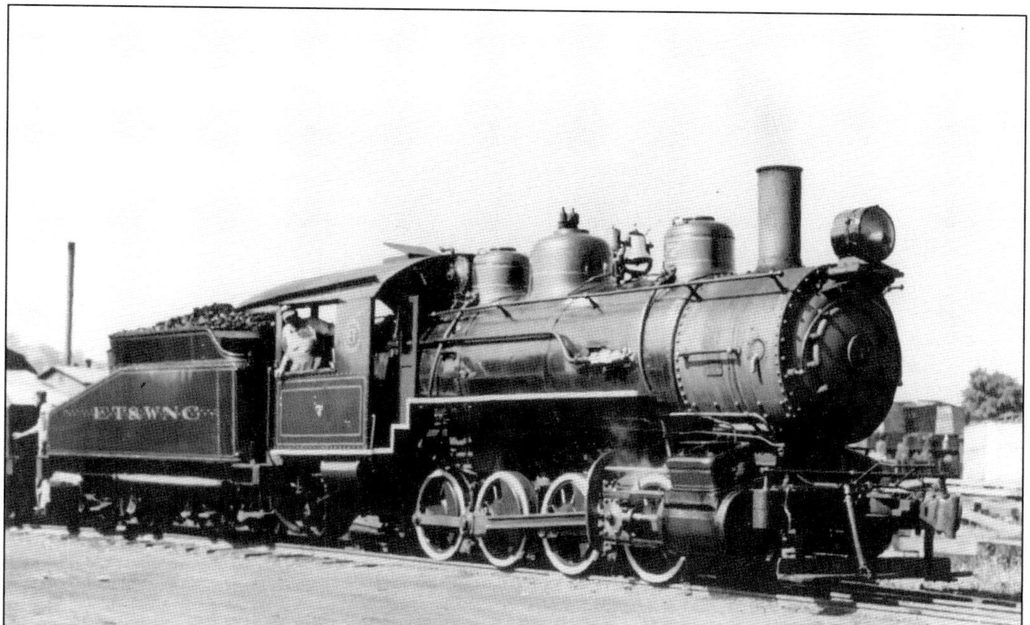

Engine number 7 was the largest narrow-gauge engine in the Johnson City yards. It was built in June 1906, rebuilt in 1925, and scrapped in 1939. (Courtesy of the James T. Dowdy Collection.)

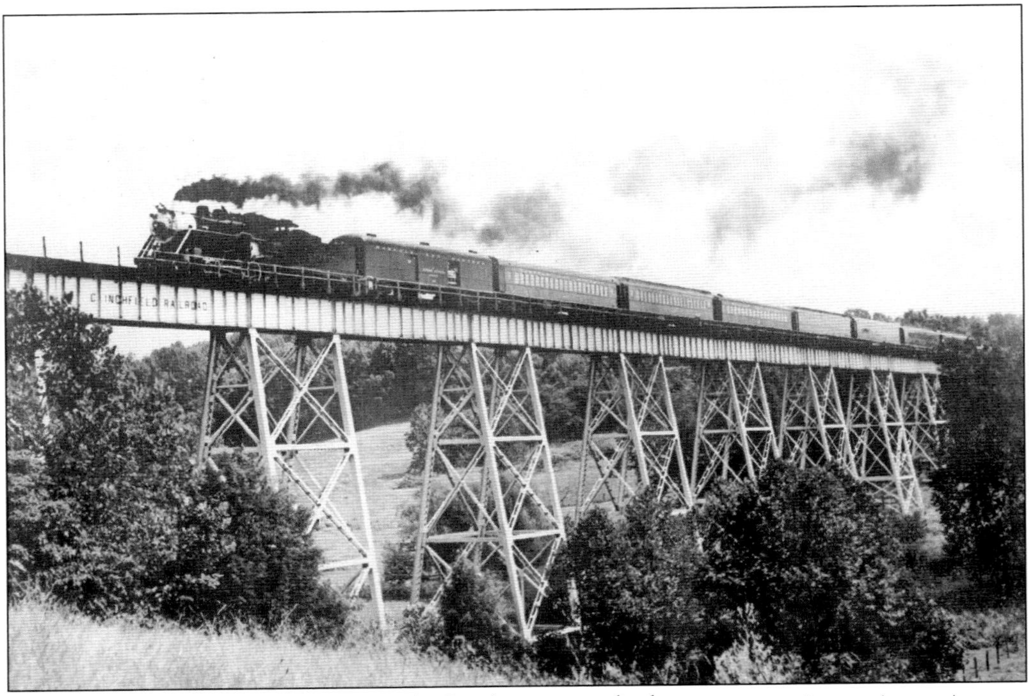

Shown here on the trestle in Boone's Creek is a standard-gauge excursion train on its way from Johnson City to Kingsport. These excursions were organized by the National Railroad Historical Society. (Courtesy of the James T. Dowdy Collection.)

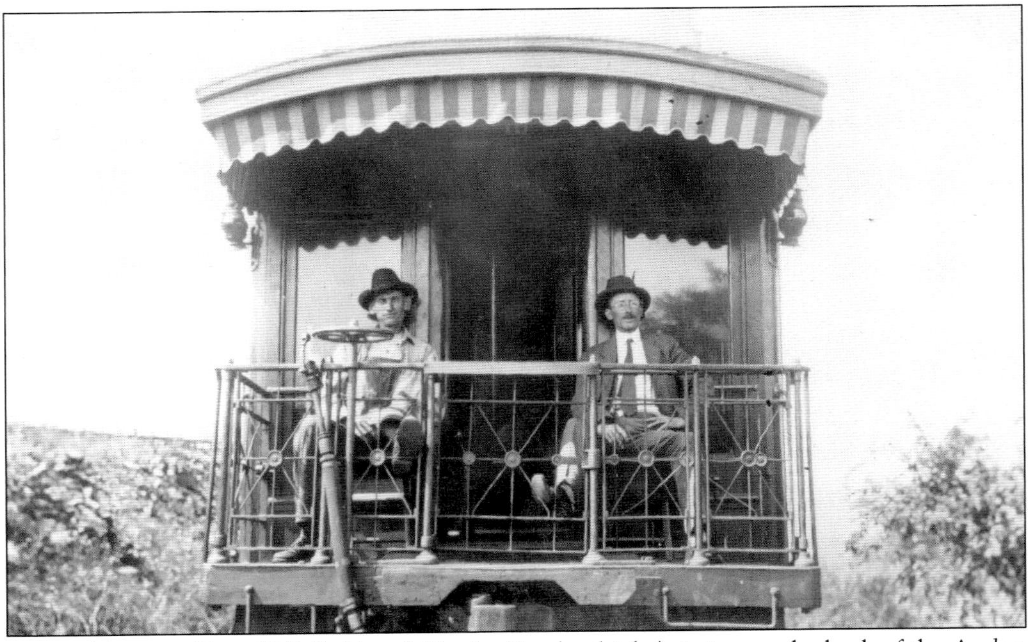

Pictured here are Dave Hill (left) and Charles Beasley (right) sitting on the back of the *Azalea*. This parlor car was purchased in May 1912, probably second-hand. It was retired in 1935, sold in 1936 to the Georgia Car & Locomotive Company, and it went to the United Fruit Company in the Dominican Republic. (Courtesy of the James T. Dowdy Collection.)

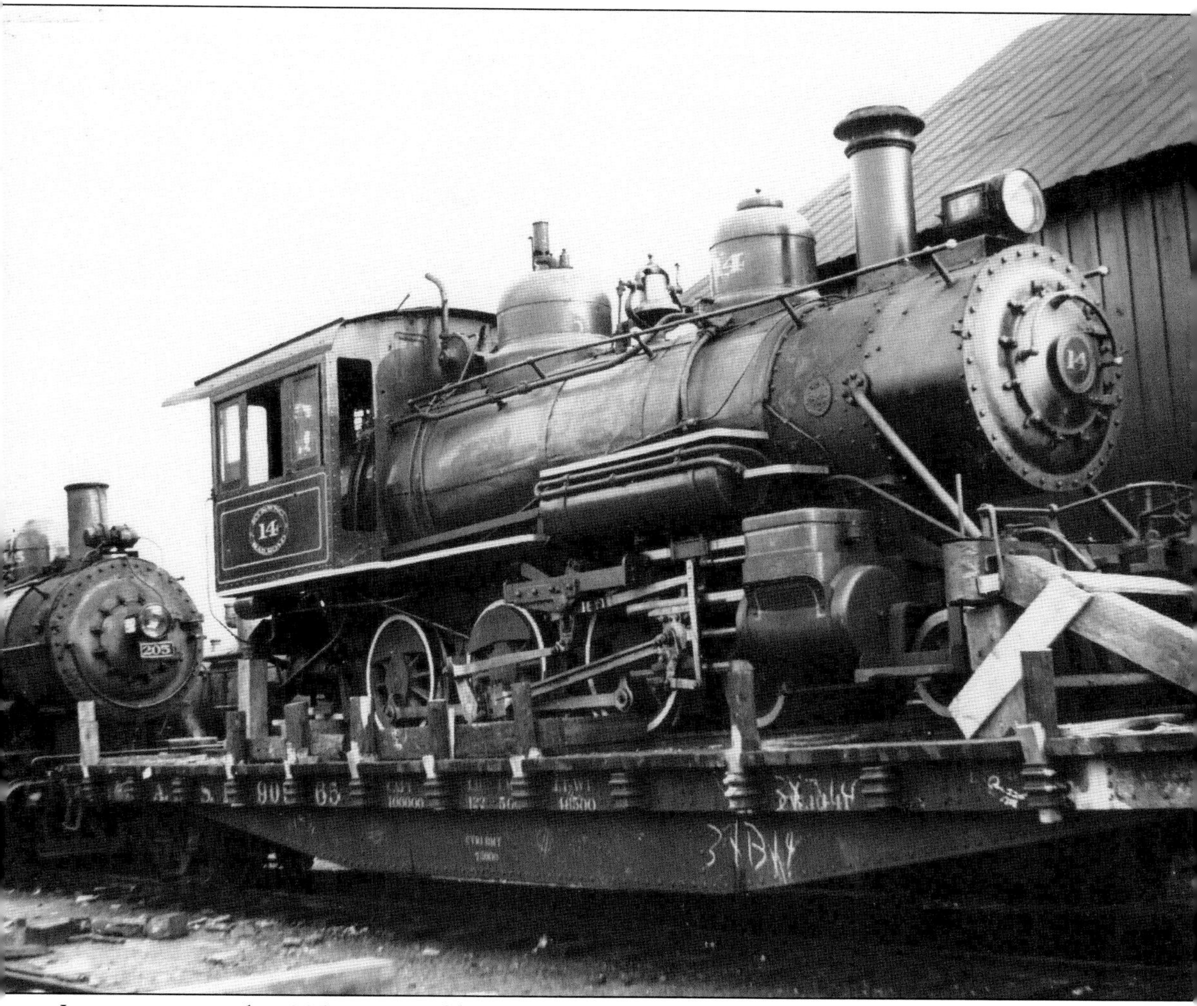

Locomotive number 205 is pictured here on the left moving a standard-gauge flatcar carrying narrow-gauge engine number 14. The narrow-gauge engine was being transported to Alaska in May 1942 to assist in the efforts of World War II. Engine number 14 was scrapped in Seattle, Washington, in 1945 after a fire. (Courtesy of the James T. Dowdy Collection.)

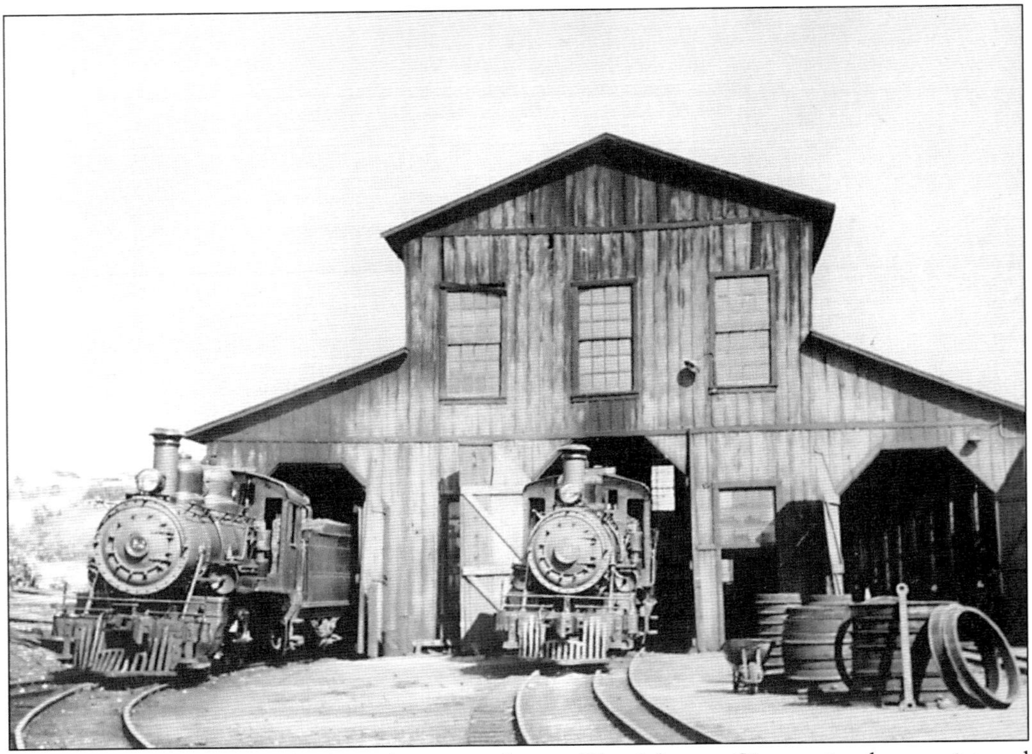

Trains are repaired and rebuilt at the engine house. The Johnson City engine house pictured here is located on what is now Legion Street. (Courtesy of James T. Dowdy Collection.)

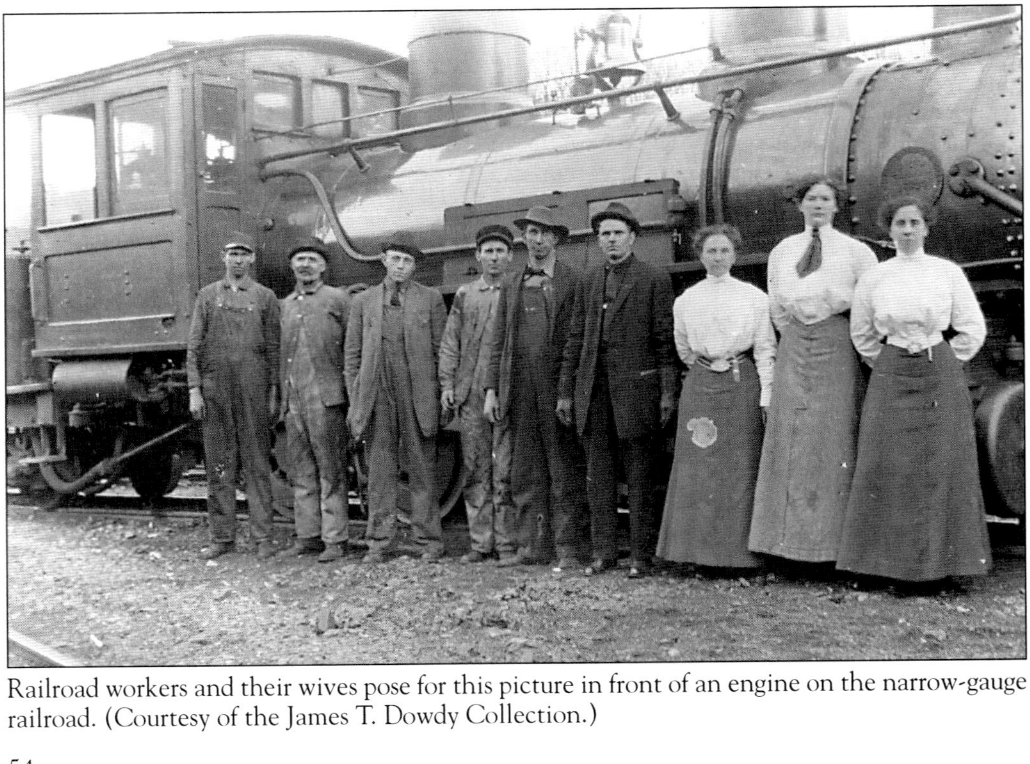

Railroad workers and their wives pose for this picture in front of an engine on the narrow-gauge railroad. (Courtesy of the James T. Dowdy Collection.)

2

EXPLANATION OF ABBREVIATIONS.

E. T. & W. N. C. R. R.—East Tennessee & Western North Carolina Railroad.
L. R. Ry.—Linville River Railway.

EXPLANATION OF REFERENCE MARKS.

•Reduction. **♦Advance.** (See Note A on title page.)

RULES.

Rule 1.—Sale of Tickets.

Agents must open their ticket offices for the sale of tickets at least thirty minutes before the departure of any train carrying passengers, and keep them open until the departure of such train. They must also see that all persons boarding trains at their stations purchase tickets, or are given an opportunity of purchasing them, before entering train.

All tickets sold must be stamped on back with the date of sale with dating stamp; care being taken to keep ribbons and type in good order so as to insure distinct impressions.

Tickets must not be sold to points at which trains do not stop, nor for extra trains without instructions to do so.

Agents will refuse to sell tickets to insane, drunken or other persons who are not in a condition to take care of themselves, or whose conduct would endanger their lives, or be a source of annoyance to other passengers, unless they are in charge of a responsible party.

Rule 2.—Stop-over on Tickets Not Allowed.

Tickets sold at rates shown herein are good only for continuous passage from starting point to destination, and no stop-over will be allowed.

Rule 3.—Conductors' Fare.

Passengers boarding trains at stations (where there are agents on duty) without buying tickets will be charged the fares shown herein as "Train Fare."

Where passengers board a train at a station where there is no ticket agent or when the ticket office for any reason is not opened for the sale of tickets, conductors will collect fare at the rates shown in column headed "Ticket Fare."

Rule 4.—Fares For Children.

No charge will be made for children under five years of age when accompanied by an adult. Children five years of age and under twelve will be charged half-fare, with a minimum charge of ten cents. (Add 2½ cents when necessary to make such fares terminate in "0" or "5"). Those twelve years and over, full fare.

Rule 5.—Fares For Ministers of the Gospel.

Ministers holding clergy reduced fare permits of these companies will be charged at the rate of two (2) cents per mile with minimum of ten (10) cents (add 2½ cents when necessary to make such fares terminate in "0" or "5.") (**Reduction** when from or to points on Linville River Railway).

Rule 6.—Baggage, Checking and Weighing of.

Rates, rules and regulations governing checking, handling and weighing of baggage formerly carried in I. C. C. No. P-58, are cancelled. For rates, rules and regulations to apply, see Joint and Local Baggage Tariff 1, I. C. C. No. P-334, supplements thereto and reissues thereof.

Rule 7.—Baggage, Transfer of, at Johnson City, Tenn.

Charges for transfer of baggage at Johnson City, Tenn., formerly carried in I. C. C. No. P-58 are cancelled. For charges to apply, see Joint and Local Baggage Tariff 1, I. C. C. No. P-334, supplements thereto and reissues thereof.

Rule 8.—Baggage, Excess, Rates to Apply.

Excess baggage rates formerly carried in I. C. C. No. P-58, are cancelled. For rates to apply, see Joint and Local Baggage Tariff 1, I. C. C. No. P-334, supplements thereto and reissues thereof.

Rule 9.—Corpse, Transportation of.

Rates, rules and regulations governing transportation of corpse formerly carried in I. C. C. No. P-58, are cancelled. For rates, rules and regulations to apply, see Joint and Local Baggage Tariff 1, I. C. C. No. P-334, supplements thereto and reissues thereof.

Rule 10.—Bicycles, Baby Carriages, Go-carts, Baby Sleighs and Tricycles, Checking of.

Rates, rules and regulations governing checking of bicycles, baby carriages, go-carts, baby sleighs and tricycles formerly carried in I. C. C. No. P-58, are cancelled. For rates, rules and regulations to apply, see Joint and Local Baggage Tariff 1, I. C. C. No. P-334, supplements thereto and reissues thereof.

Rule 11.—Dogs and Birds, Transportation of.

Rates, rules and regulations governing transportation of dogs and birds formerly carried in I. C. C. No. P-58, are cancelled. For rates, rules and regulations to apply, see Joint and Local Baggage Tariff 1, I. C. C. No. P-334, supplements thereto and reissues thereof.

CANCELLATION.

Additional fares for parlor and chair car seat accommodations formerly published in Supplement No. 4 (Special Supplement) to I. C. C. No. P-58 and not brought forward herein, are cancelled. Apply fares named in I. C. C. No. P-329, supplements thereto or reissues thereof. **Reduction.**

A page from the ET & WNC Railroad Company Linville River Railway explains the rules of the railway, addressing issues such as the transportation of a corpse, fares for ministers of the gospel, excess baggage, and the transportation of animals. Notice under Rule 1, it states that "Agents will refuse to sell tickets to insane, drunken or other persons who are not in a condition to take care of themselves, or whose conduct would endanger their lives, or be a source of annoyance to other passengers, unless they are in charge of a responsible party." These particular rules were issued December 16, 1918, and became effective February 1, 1919. (Courtesy of the James T. Dowdy Collection.)

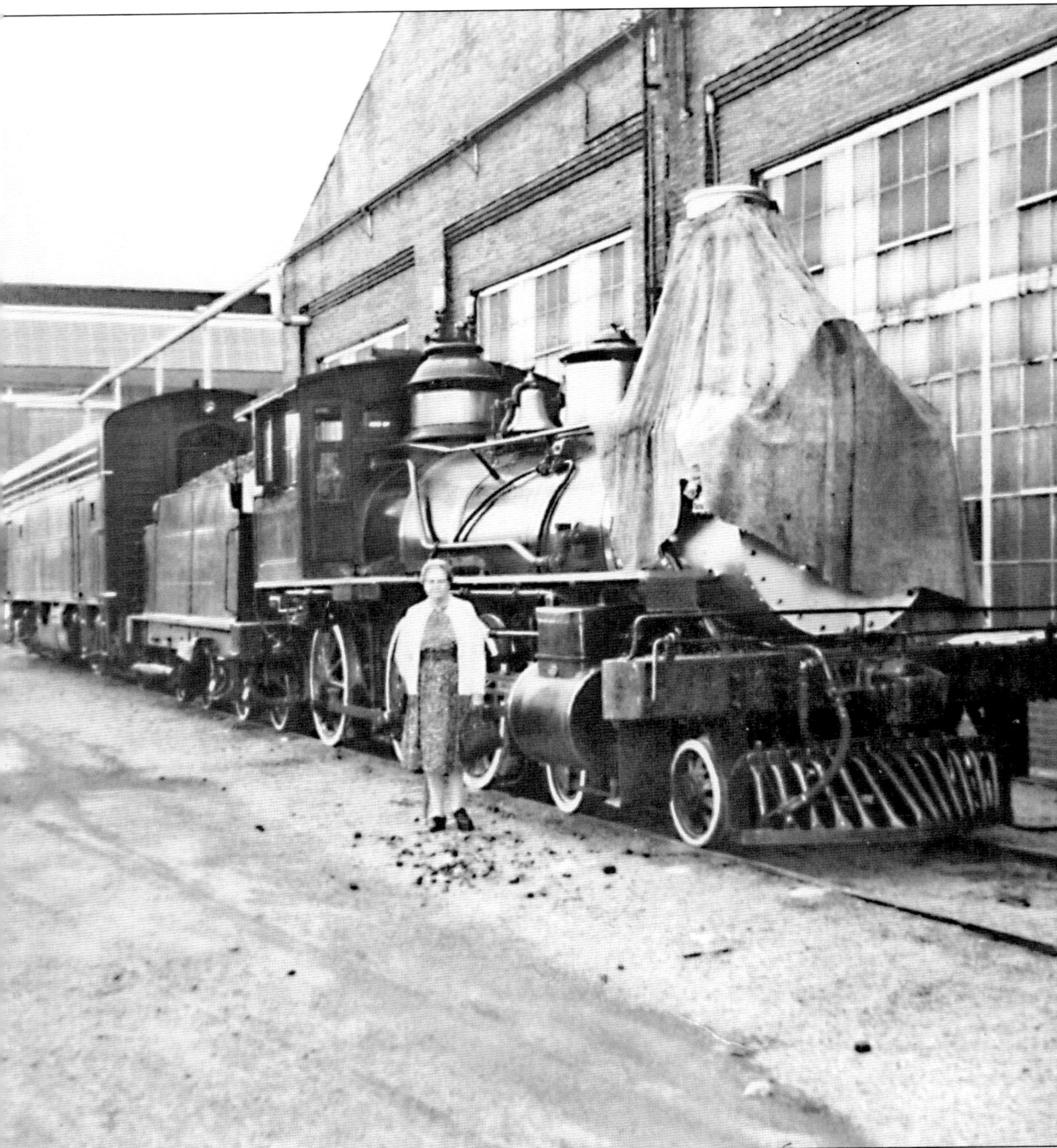

This train was dubbed "the Santa Train" because each year at Thanksgiving, train workers would travel up into rural areas of Virginia, tossing candy and presents from the train for children. Merchants in the Tri-Cities area would donate goods to be placed on the train. (Courtesy of Terry and Kim Jones.)

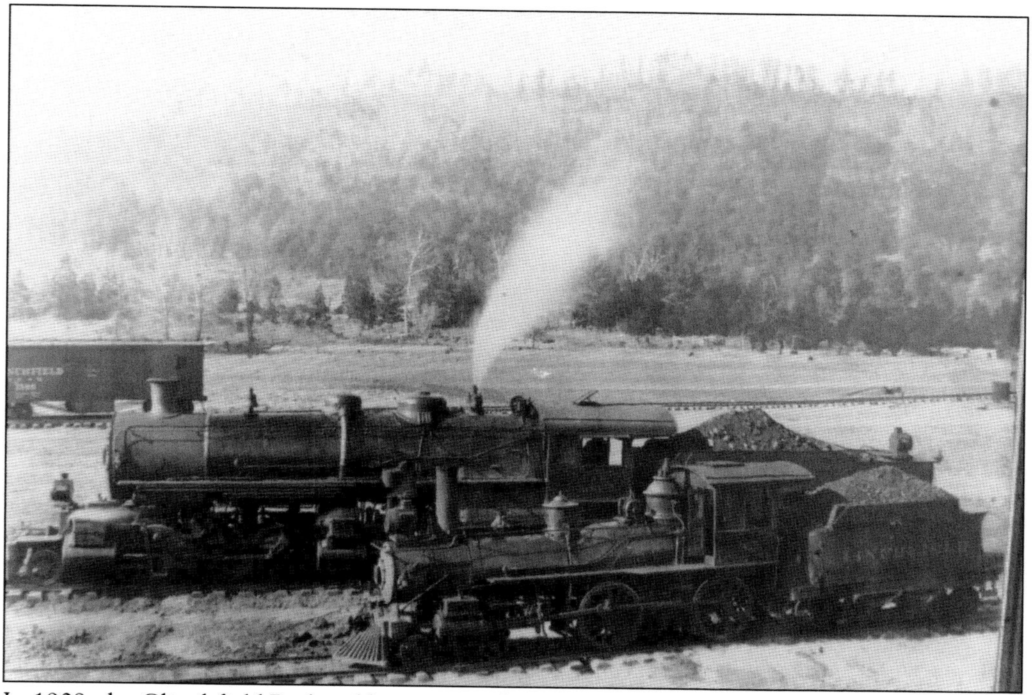

In 1908, the Clinchfield Railroad began providing service from Johnson City to Marion, North Carolina. Johnson City was a major hub, with three railroads servicing the area. As automobiles became more popular, trains were used less often for travel; the last passenger train of the Clinchfield Railroad traveled through Johnson City in 1954. (Courtesy of William Jones.)

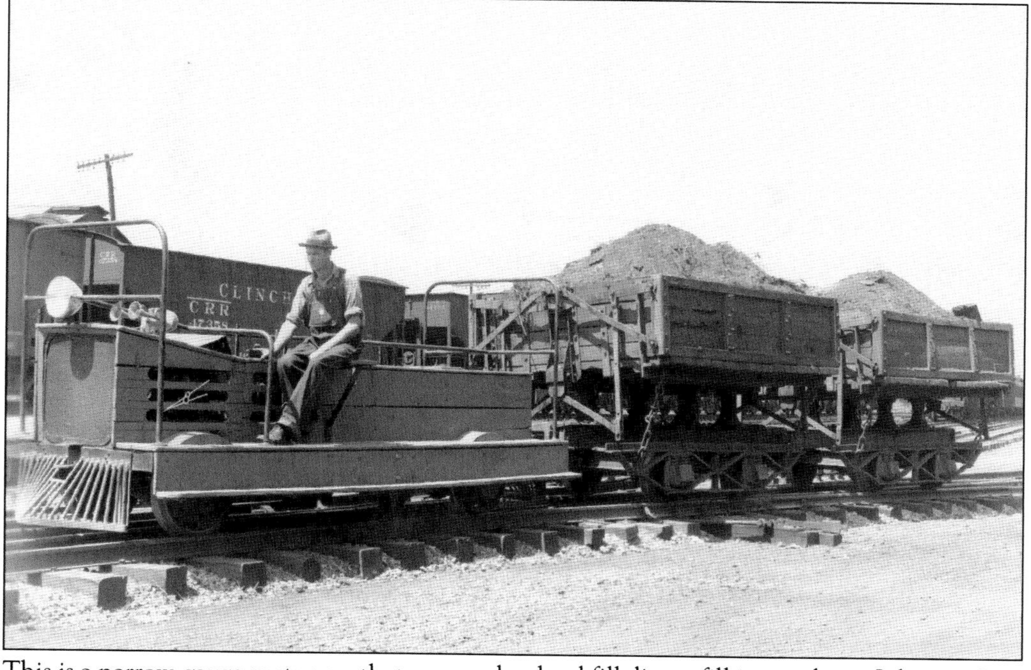

This is a narrow-gauge motor car that was used to haul fill dirt to fill in trestles in Johnson City. As can be seen here, these were very small cars, simply used to transport dirt and other supplies back and forth. (Courtesy of Bruce and Mildred Kidd.)

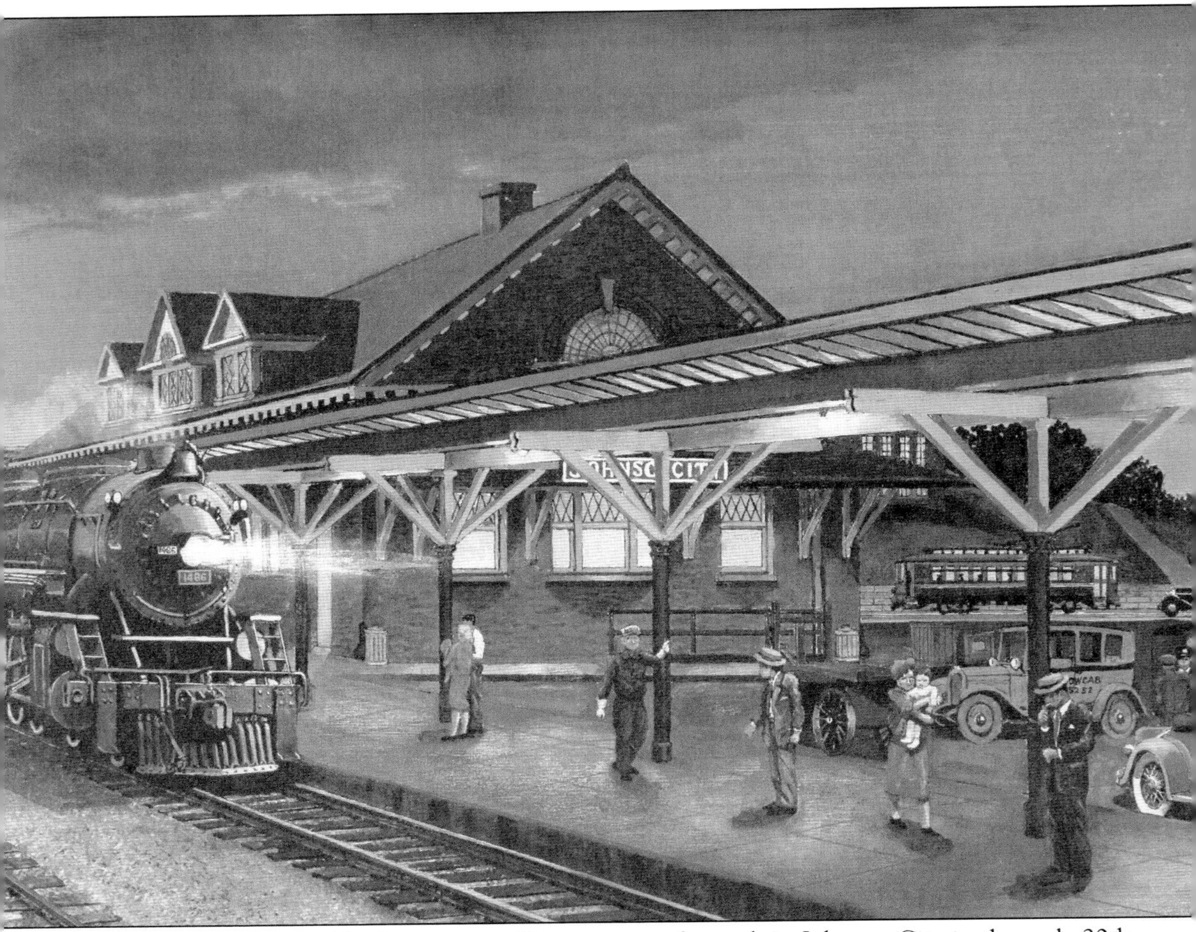

Railroads were arguably the most significant aspect of growth in Johnson City in the early 20th century. This painting by Ted Laws Sr. portrays the Southern Railway depot, which was destroyed in 1973 to make way for the Downtown Traffic Loop. (Courtesy of Lewis Wexler Sr.)

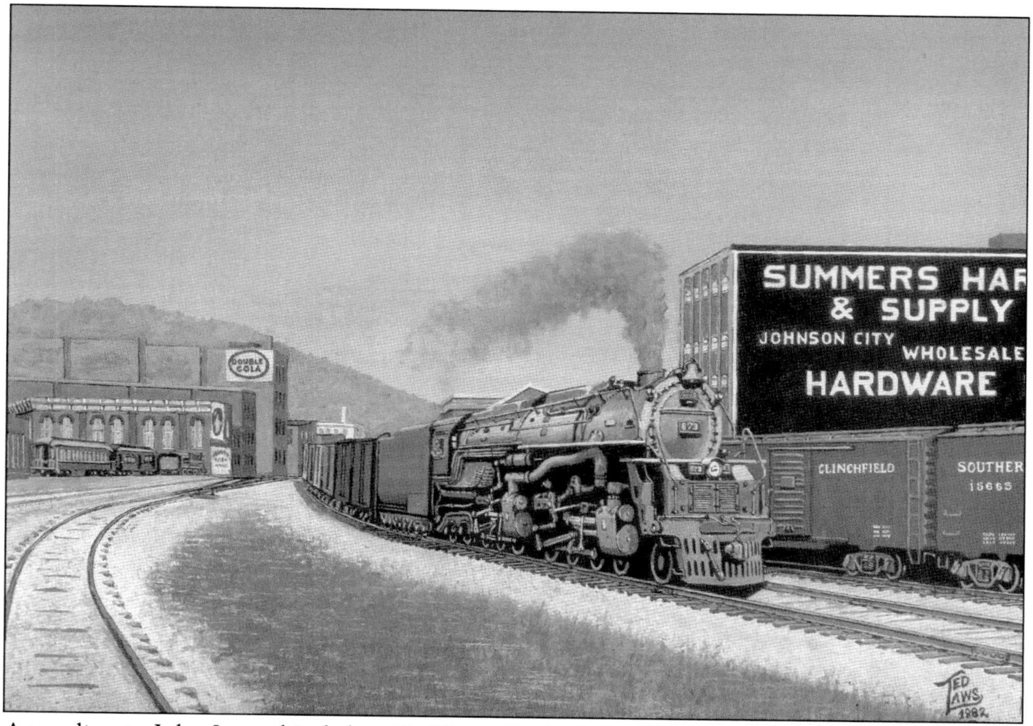

According to John Laws, his father, Ted Laws Sr., had always been interested in area railroads. Ted Laws Sr. (1910–1992) was a lifelong resident of Johnson City and had helped build a lot of the depots depicted in his paintings. The prints shown on these two pages were painted in 1982, around the time of Laws's other works. (Courtesy of Lewis Wexler Sr.)

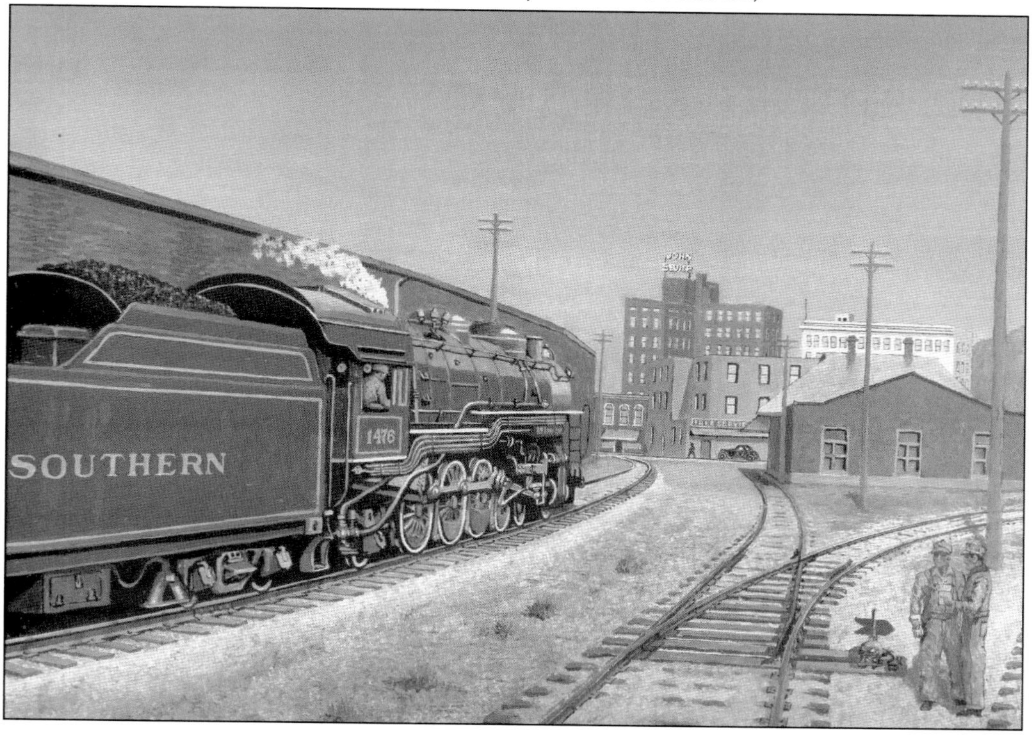

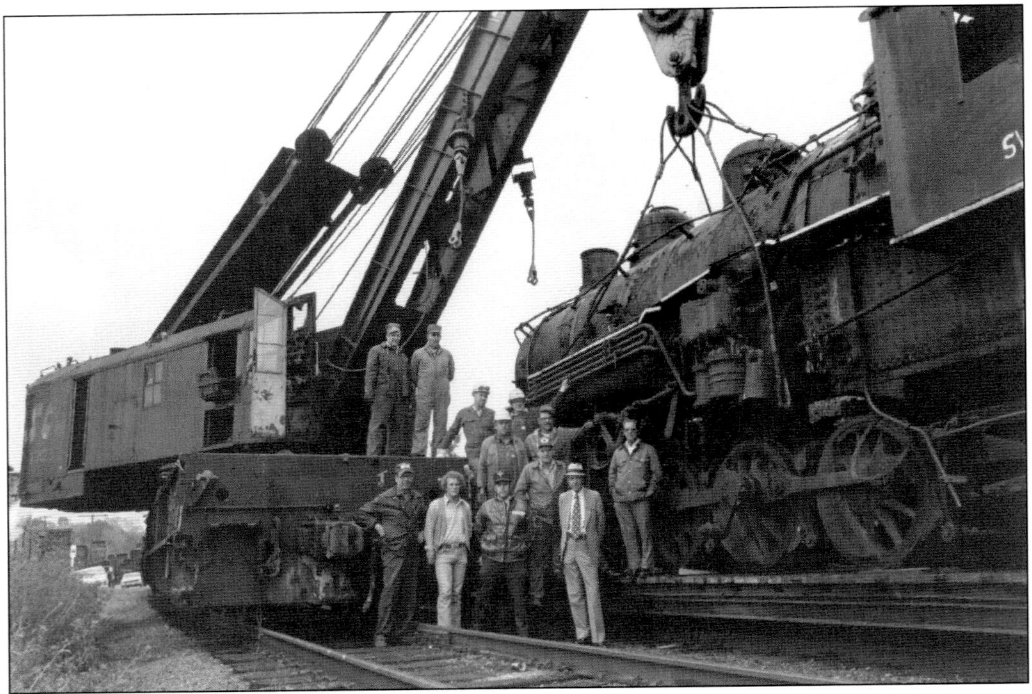

Workers for the Clinchfield Railroad are using a wreck train to lift a steam locomotive onto a flatbed car for transportation. It is possible that the engine had been derailed and damaged. (Courtesy of William Jones.)

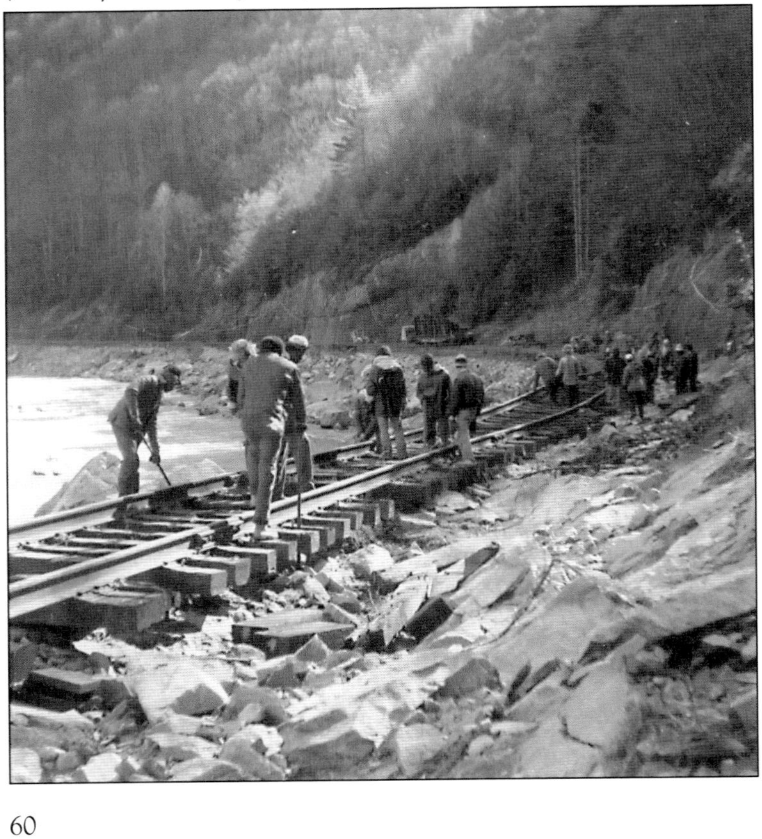

Men from the Clinchfield Railroad are fixing a portion of the line that had been washed out. The steep inclines above the track that allowed rock to slide and the Nolichuckey River below the track made frequent repairs necessary. (Courtesy of William Jones.)

Four

RELIGION

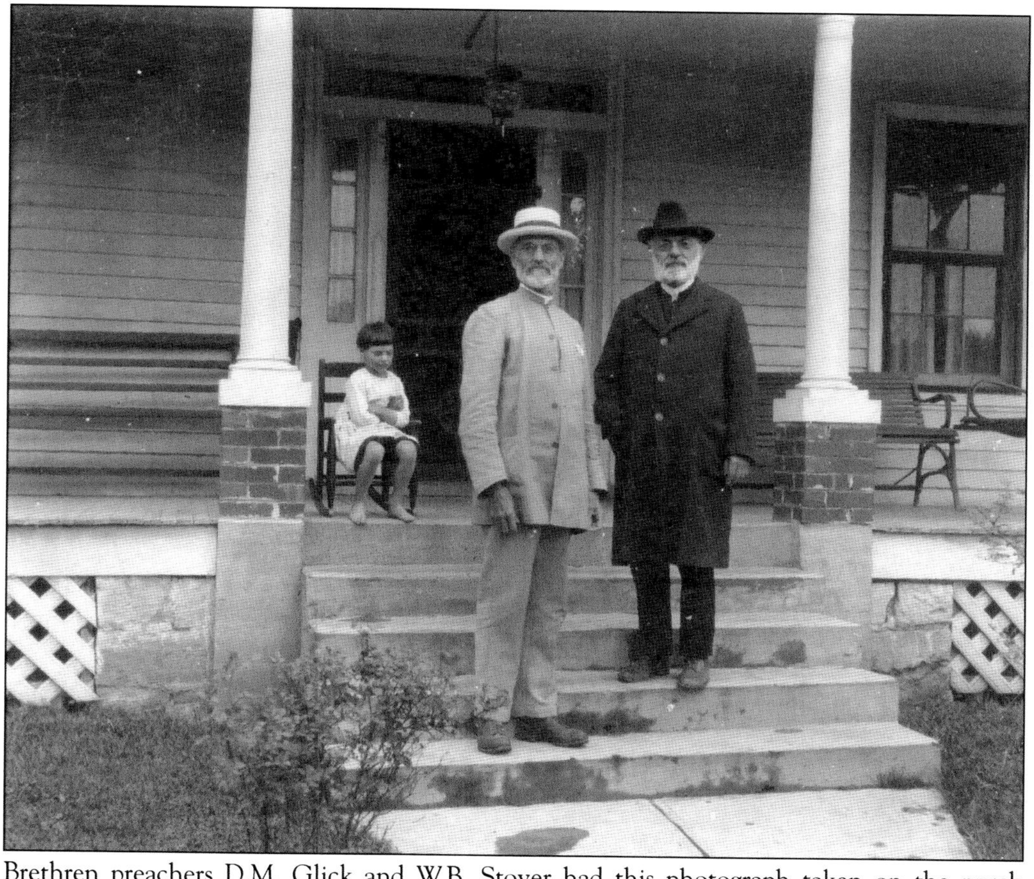

Brethren preachers D.M. Glick and W.B. Stover had this photograph taken on the porch of the Peter Bowman residence in the Knob Creek community. (Courtesy of George and Margaret Holley.)

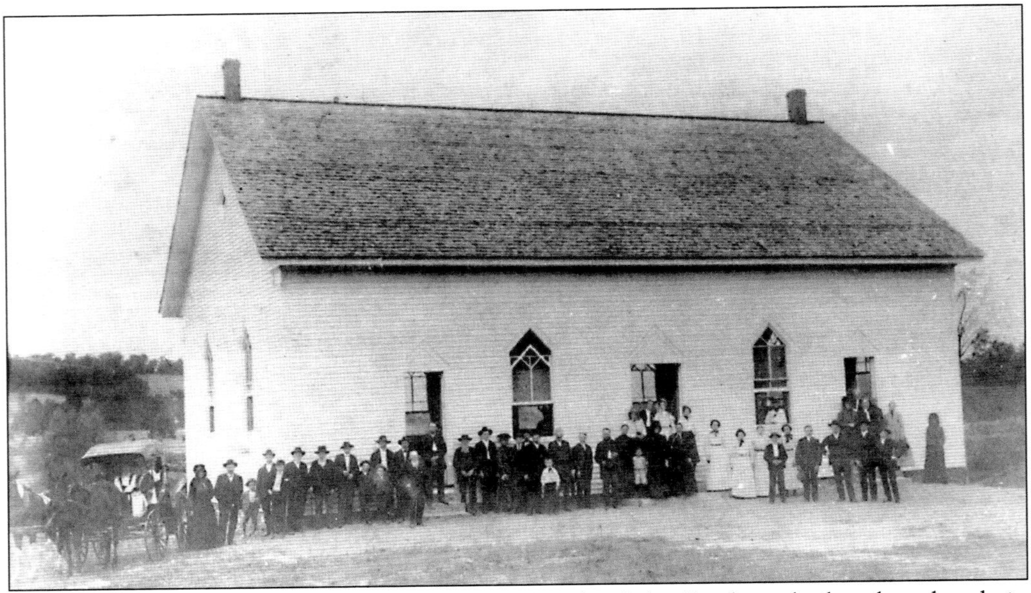

After being organized in 1799, Knob Creek Church of the Brethren built a log church in 1834. In a new sanctuary in 1905, members celebrated the first Love Feast. During this event, members wash each other's feet and share communion. This is still an ordinance celebrated in the Brethren church, along with anointing and Triune Immersion. (Courtesy of George and Margaret Holley.)

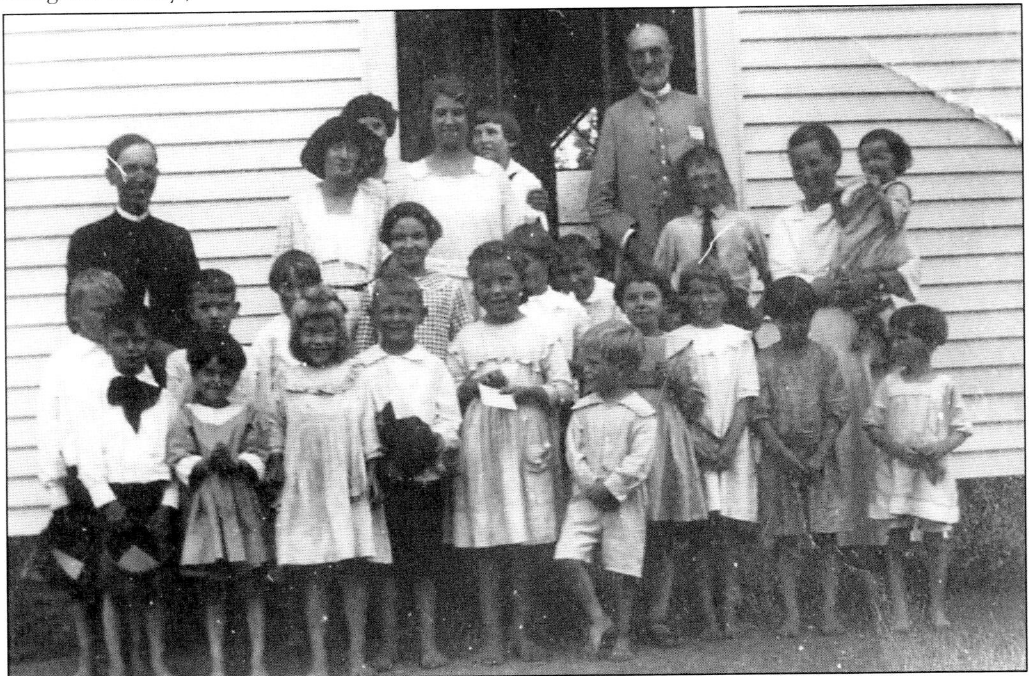

Vacation bible schools, like this one of the 1920s, ministered to young and old. Though they are still popular in Johnson City today, vacation bible schools were even more anticipated events in a time when there were no televisions or computers. On the far left is Will Swadley. The man on the far right is D.M. Glick. The woman on the right holding the child is Laura Swadley. (Courtesy of George and Margaret Holley.)

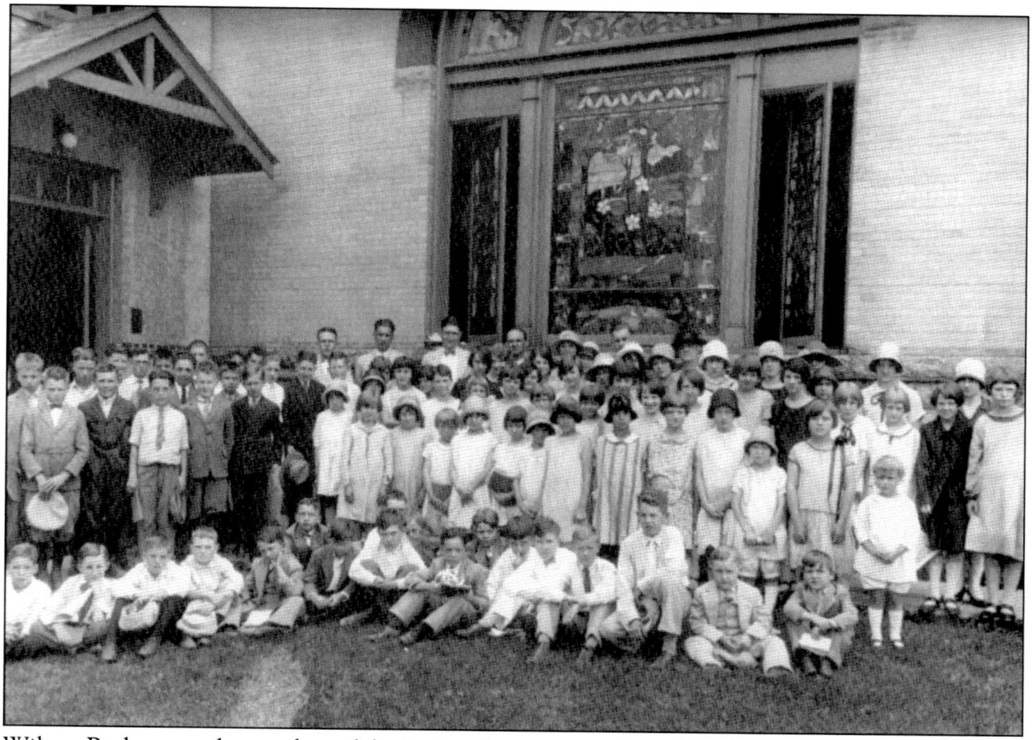

Wilson Barker was the teacher of the junior department when this photograph was taken in the early 1900s. (Courtesy of First Christian Church.)

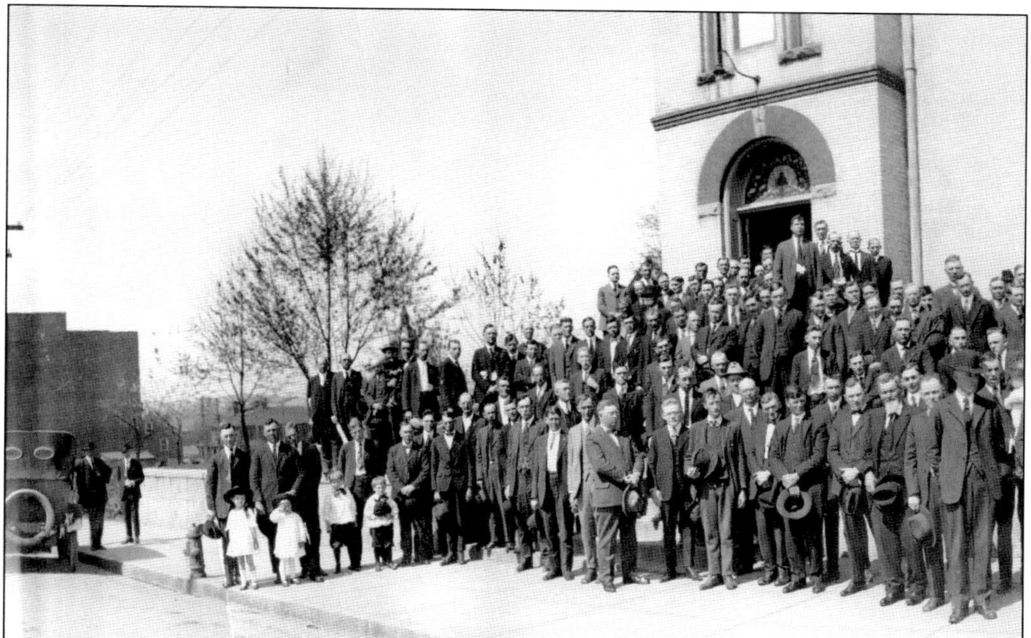

The "Loyal Men's Bible Class" had 210 present on March 27, 1921, when this photograph was taken. The top and bottom portions of the photograph on this page were actually part of a beautiful panoramic shot produced by Tunnell's Studio. (Courtesy of First Christian Church.)

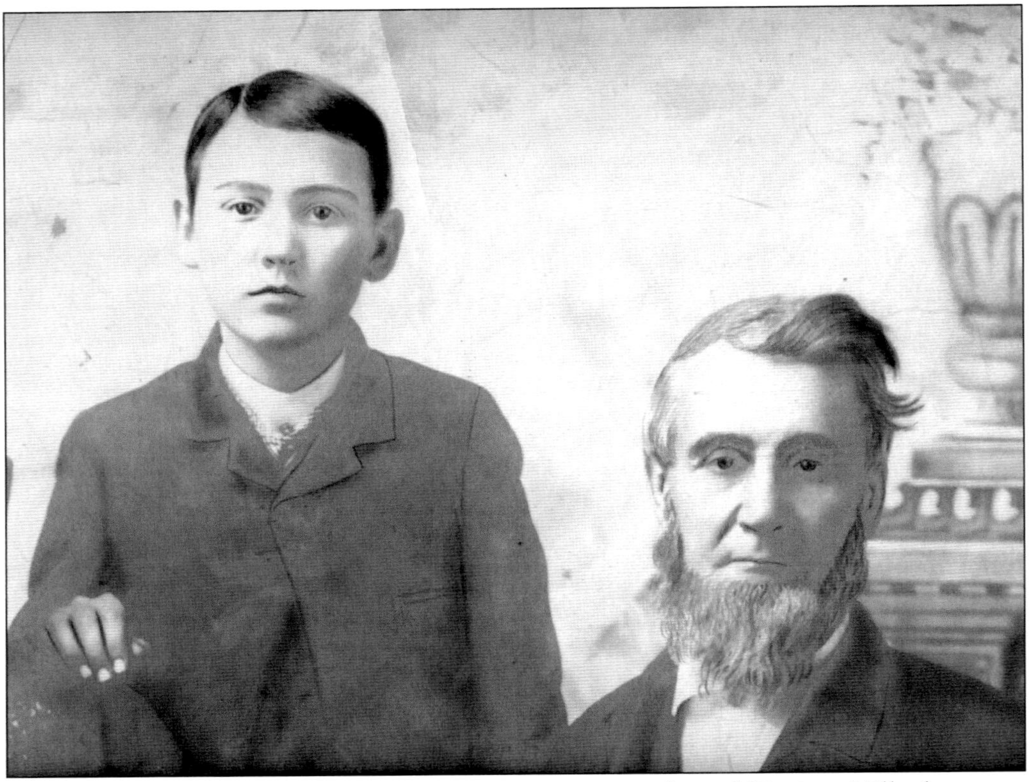

Samuel Harrison Millard came to Johnson City in the fall of 1878. He served as preacher of the First Christian Church in the 1880s and from 1895 to 1896. Millard is pictured here with his son, Samuel T. Millard, c. 1890. The family built a beautiful home on Millard Street where the Johnson City Public Library is now located. (Courtesy of First Christian Church.)

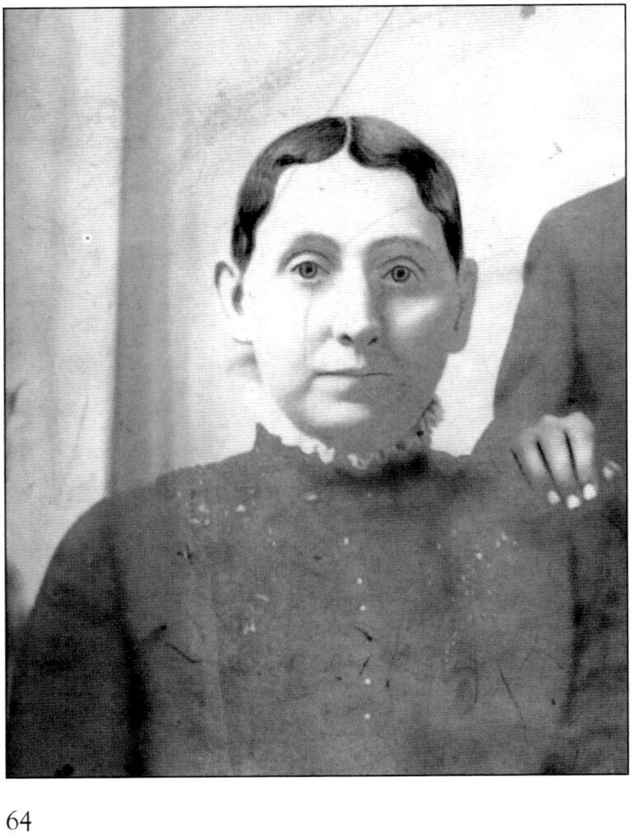

Mary Jane Taylor Kitzmiller, a widow, married widower Samuel H. Millard in the fall of 1873. They brought a total of five children to the marriage, then Samuel T. Millard, pictured above with his father, was born December 20, 1874. Mary Jane served as the first president of the Ladies Aid Society, organized on February 2, 1887. (Courtesy of First Christian Church.)

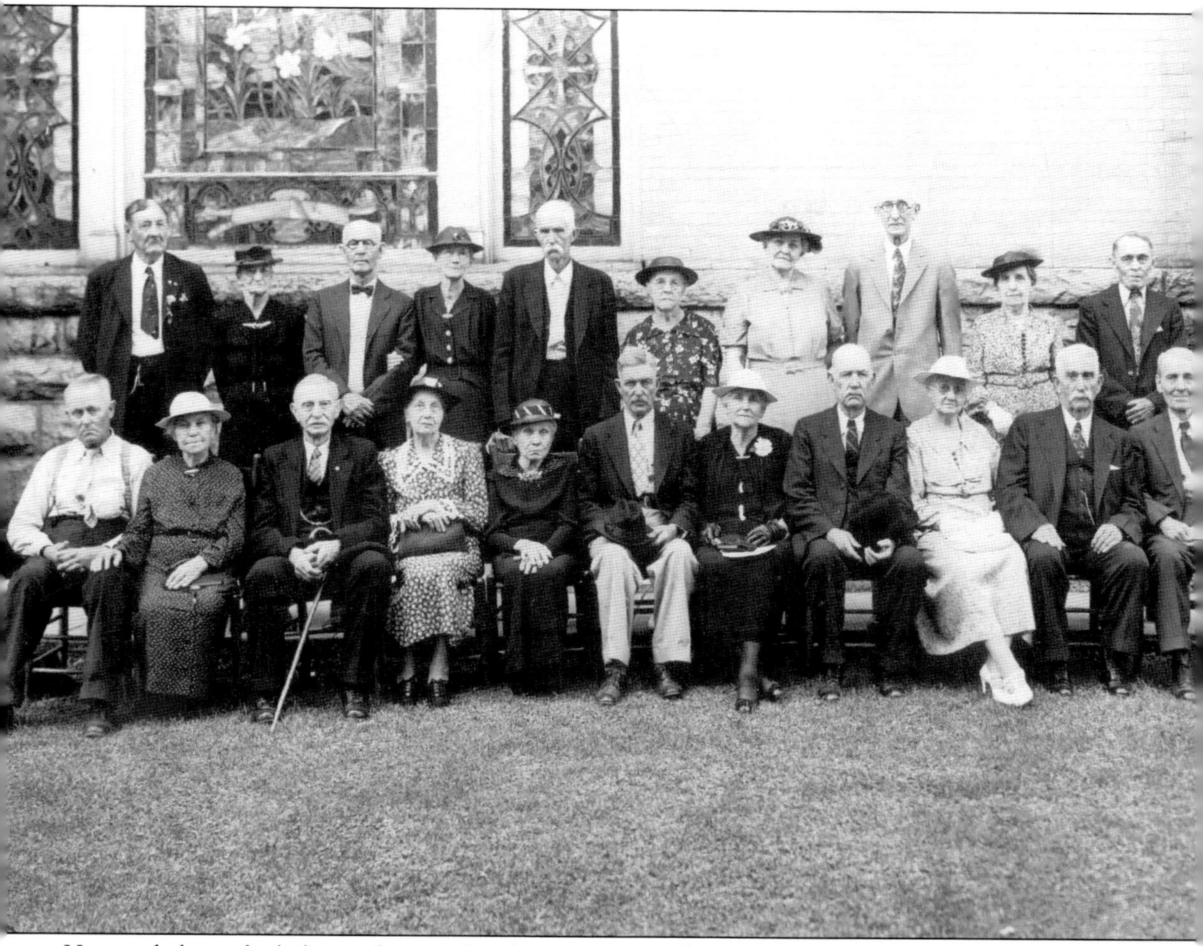

Hats and gloves for ladies and mustaches for men were still common when this photograph was taken c. 1939 to commemorate couples who had been married 50 years or more. (Courtesy of First Christian Church.)

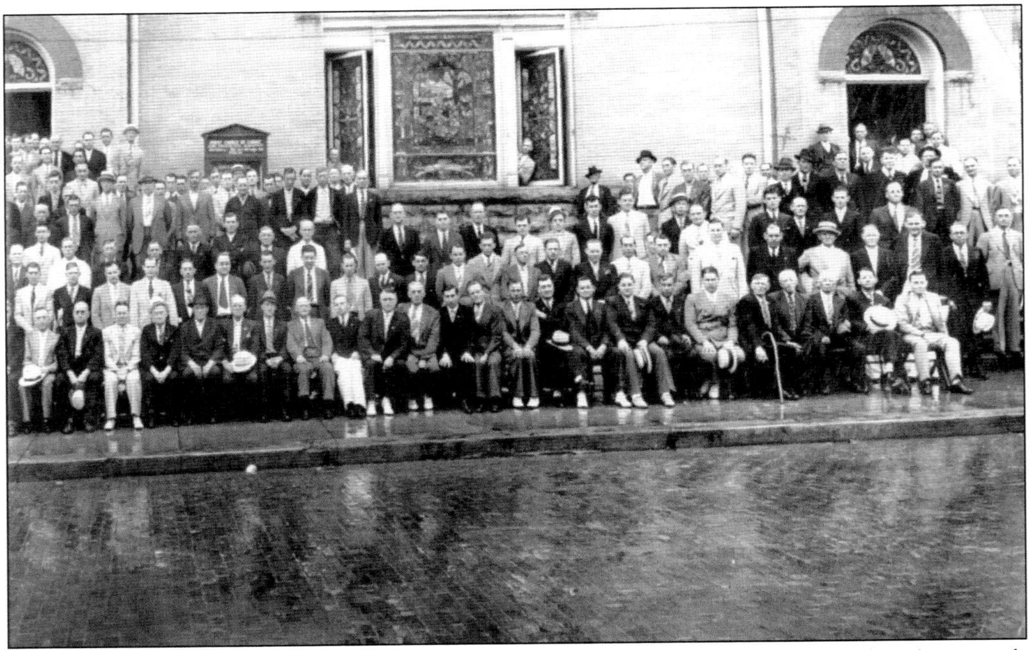

Notice the brick road in front of what is now Downtown Christian Church when this photograph was taken of the "Ninety and Nine" men's class, *c.* 1938. (Courtesy of First Christian Church.)

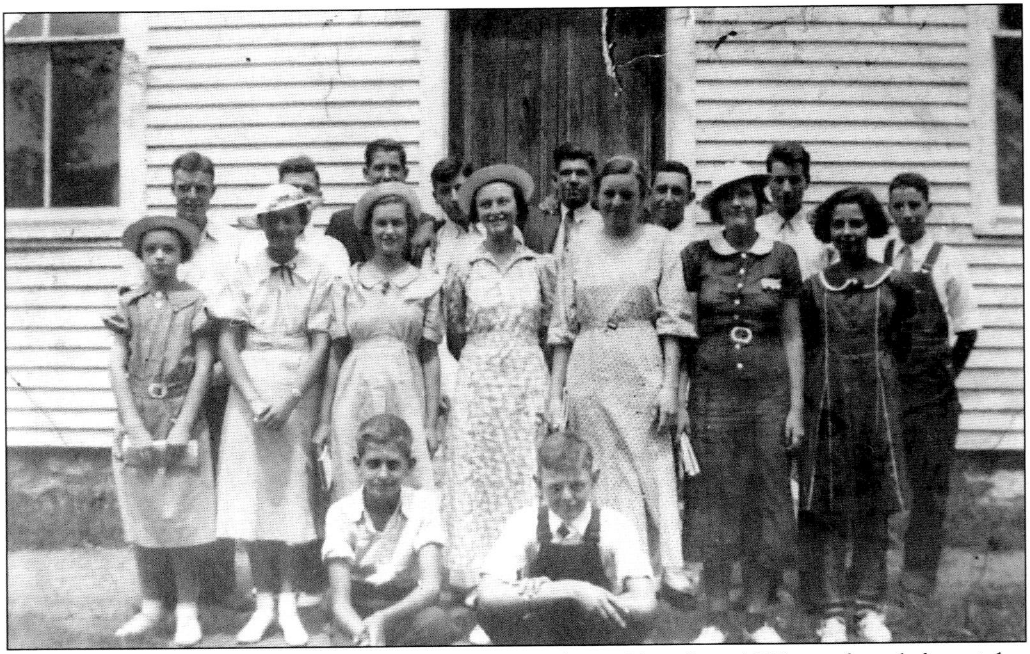

Knob Creek youth pictured here in front of the Brethren Church in 1938 are, from left to right, as follows: (kneeling) L.D. Simmons and Howard Tester; (front row) Margaret Sherfey, Dorothy Sells, Ruth Krouse, Helen Sherfey, Dorothy Tester, Bertha Burgess, and Sammy Bowman; (back row) Raymond Tester, Ray Bowman, Howard Simmons, Ralph Bowman, Reynolds Simmons, Tom Douglas, Grady Stines, and Harmon Bond. (Courtesy of George and Margaret Holley.)

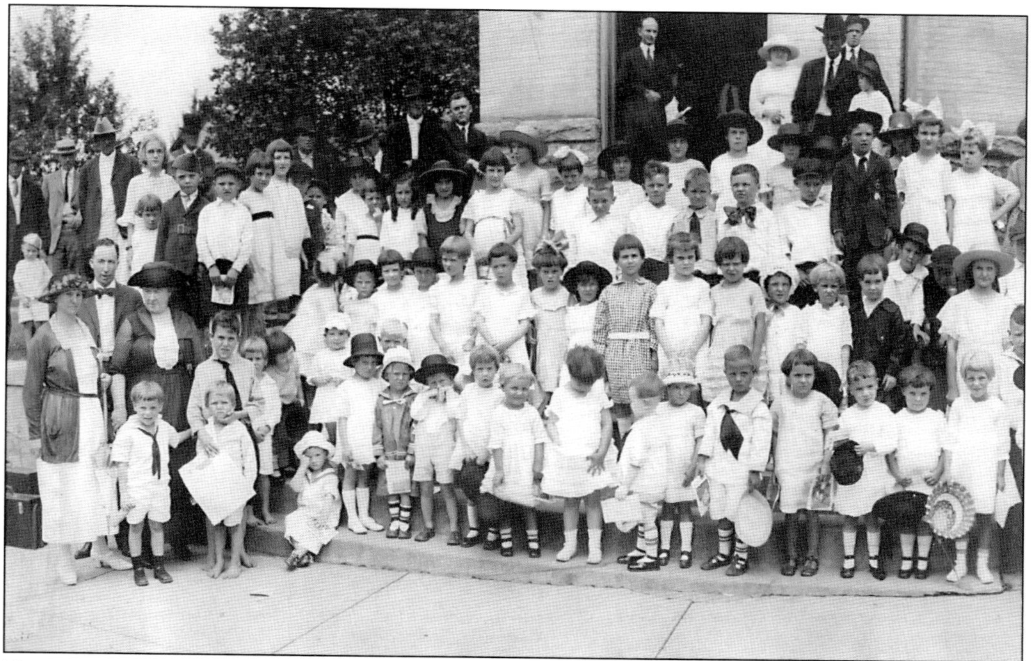

Notice several of the children are without shoes in this split panoramic photo of the primary department of the First Christian Church taken on August 7, 1921, by Tunnell's Studio. Hats were also popular. (Courtesy of Grandview Christian Church.)

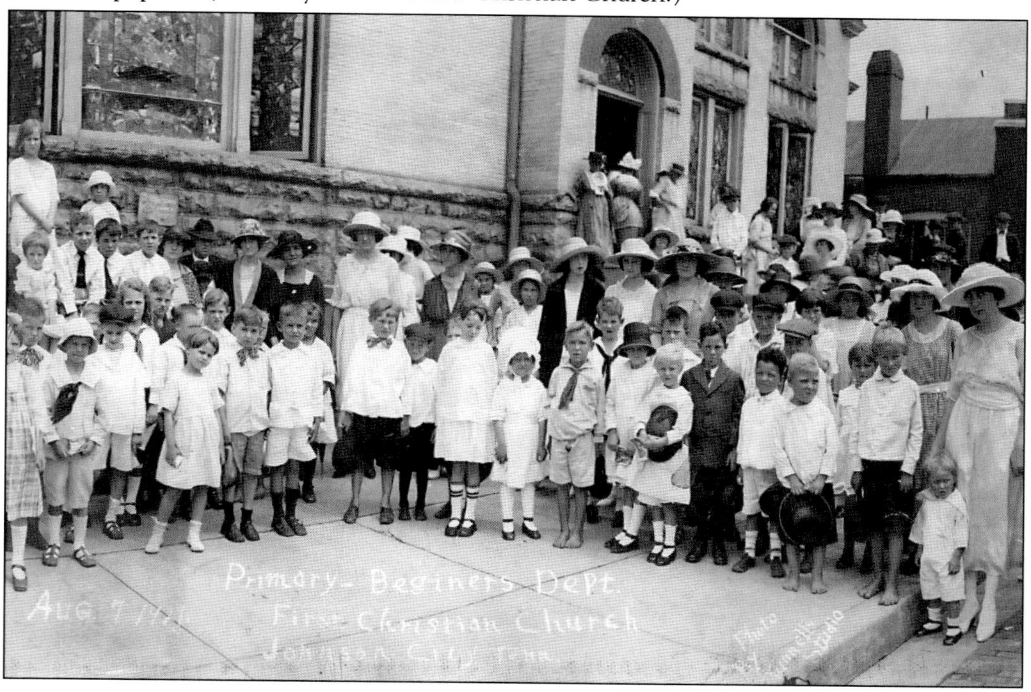

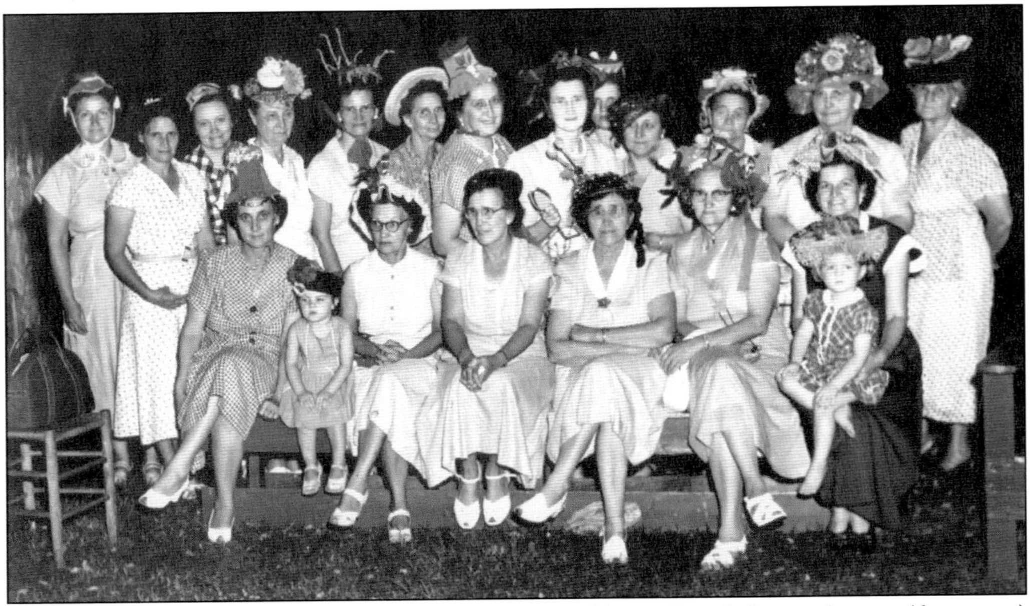

The Ladies Aid Society hosted a hat contest. Pictured here, from left to right, are (front row) Golda Hayes, Phyllis Gray's daughter (name unknown), ? McNeil, Bertie Miller, Nora Bailey, ? Hicks, and Thelma Loggans holding Vikki White; (back row) ? Miller, Dixie Campbell, Mildred Dulaney, Carrie Reed, Mildred Randolph, ? York, Tanny Miller, Katie Lilly, Katherine Lilly, B.N. Collis, Ida Dulaney, Ina Leonard, and Lucy White. (Courtesy of Grandview Christian Church.)

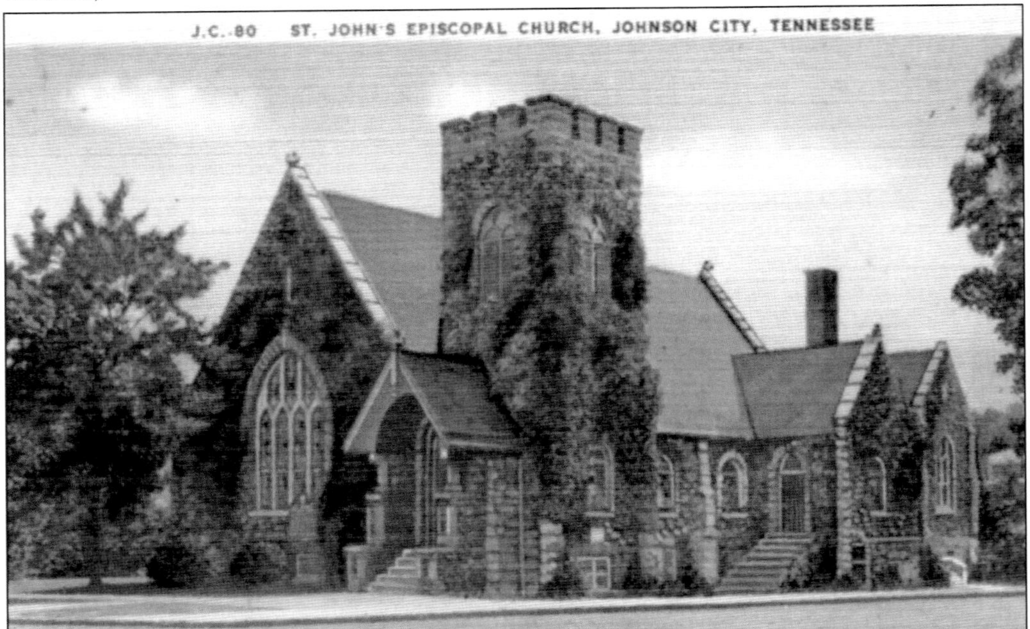

The first corporate Episcopal service held in Johnson City took place June 26, 1889, with Rev. Dr. Samuel Ringgold of Knoxville. Early Episcopalians used lamps and candles and met in schools and unused rooms of stores. The cornerstone of the beautiful stone church pictured here was laid on September 7, 1905. (Courtesy of St. John's Episcopal Church.)

Rev. Harry F. Keller served St. John's Parish from 1922 until his death in 1949. (Courtesy of St. John's Episcopal Church.)

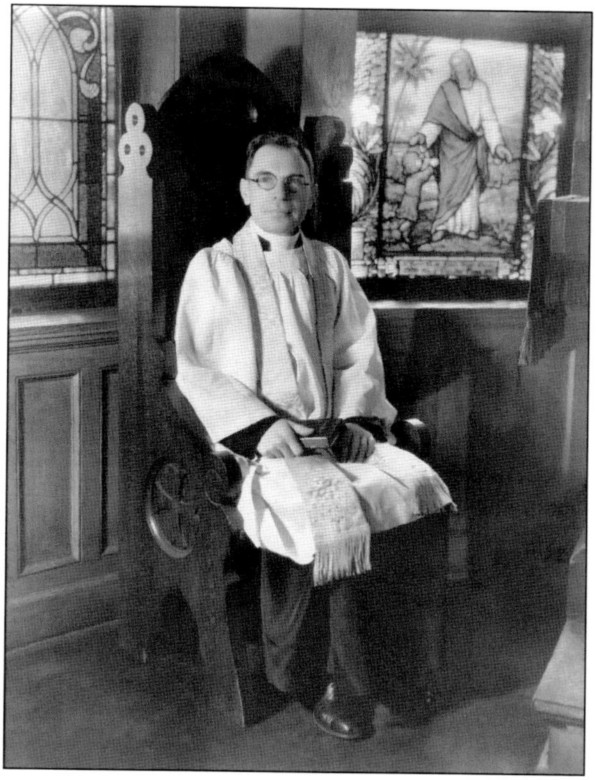

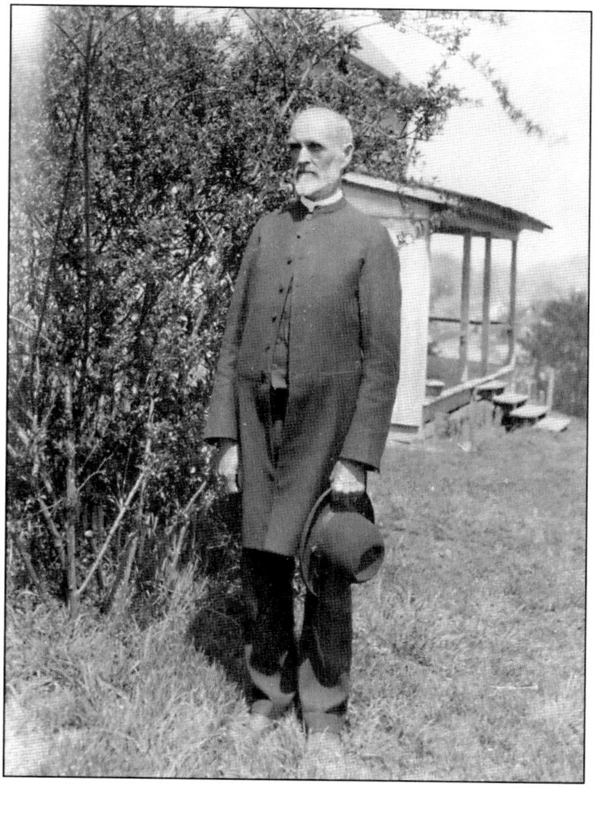

D.M. Glick served as a preacher with the Brethren Church during the early 1900s. This photograph was taken on April 16, 1923, at the Sherfey house in the Knob Creek community. (Courtesy of George and Margaret Holley.)

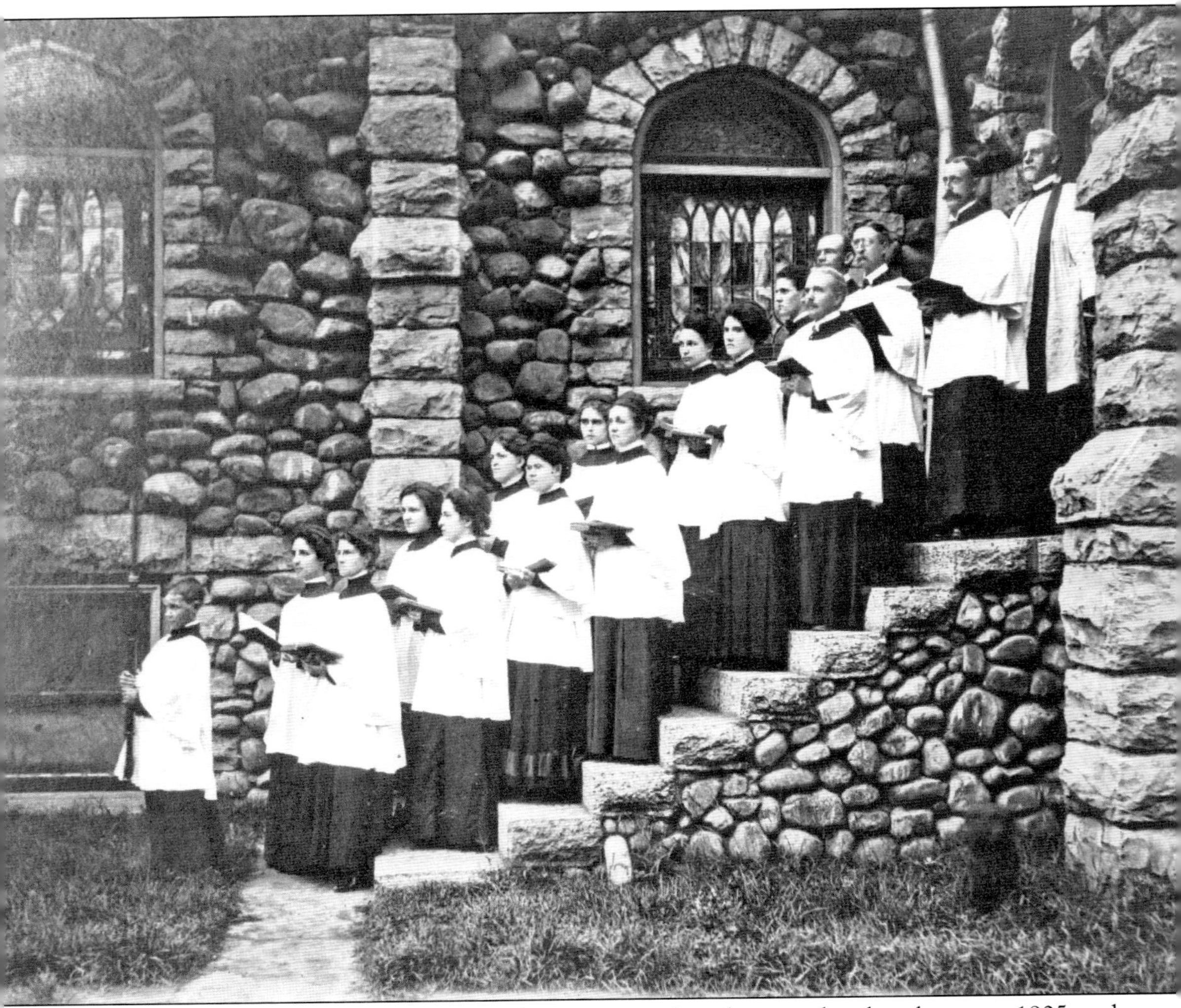

The St. John's choir hold a striking formation in this photograph taken between 1905 and 1911. (Courtesy of St. John's Episcopal Church.)

Five

Children

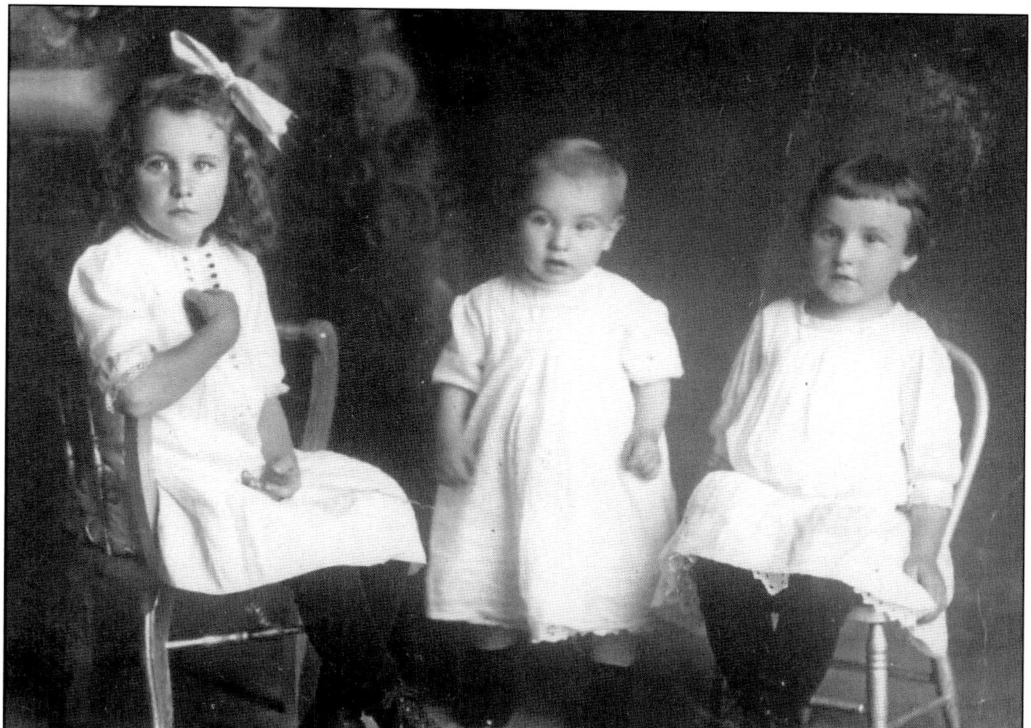

Pictured here c. 1913 are three of Philip and Ella Crumley's nine children. From left to right are Goldie (1907–1999), Robert (b. 1912), and Frances (1909–2000). As was customary for the early 20th century, Robert is wearing a dress. (Courtesy of Don and Sarah Walters.)

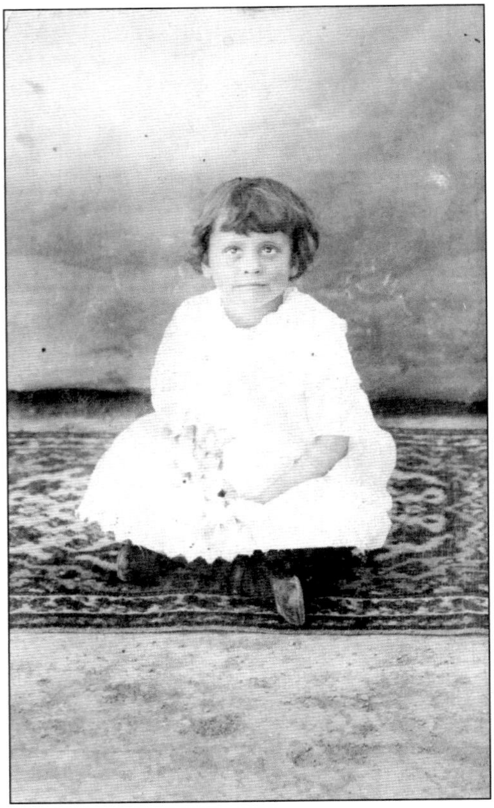

Lena Mae Tyree, the daughter of Joe and Carrie Tyree, is pictured here *c.* 1924. (Courtesy of Barbara S. Hilton.)

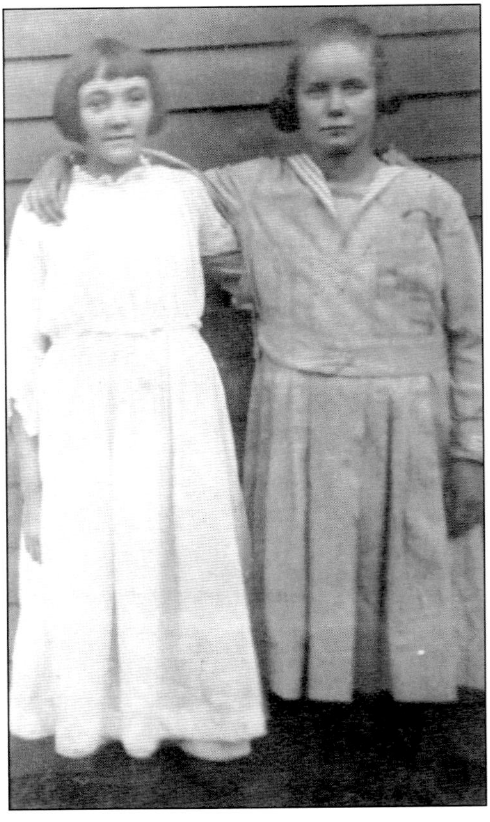

Cora Tapp Bowman (on the right) is pictured here with an unidentified friend in the early 1900s. (Courtesy of Barbara S. Hilton.)

Otta and Gladys Leach are pictured here in the early 1900s. Otta is holding her doll and the family cat. The girls were the children of John and Axie Leach of the Cherokee community. Otta's husband Sam Lecka ran a restaurant in Johnson City in the 1930s. Gladys married Ben Hoss. (Courtesy of Elaine Cantrell.)

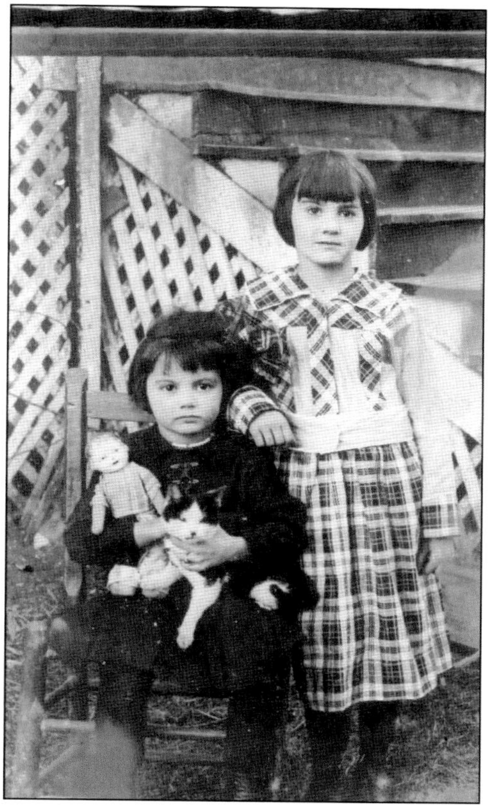

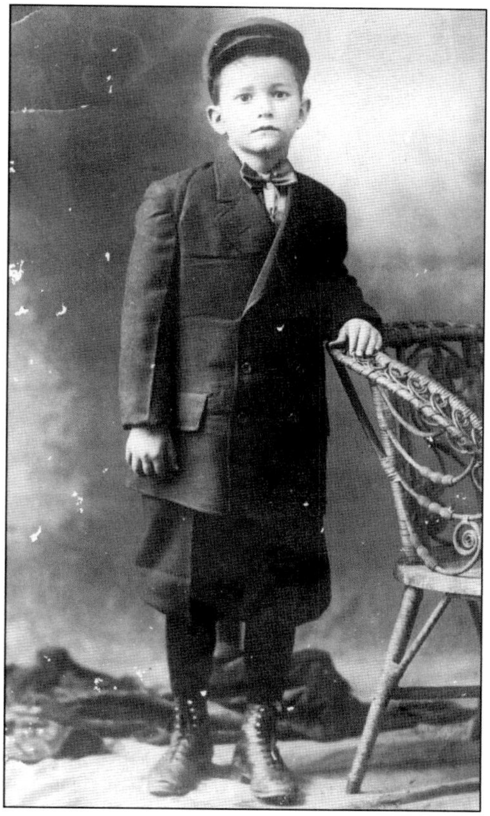

Hugh Huffine looks about five years old in this photograph of the early 1900s. (Courtesy of Elaine Cantrell.)

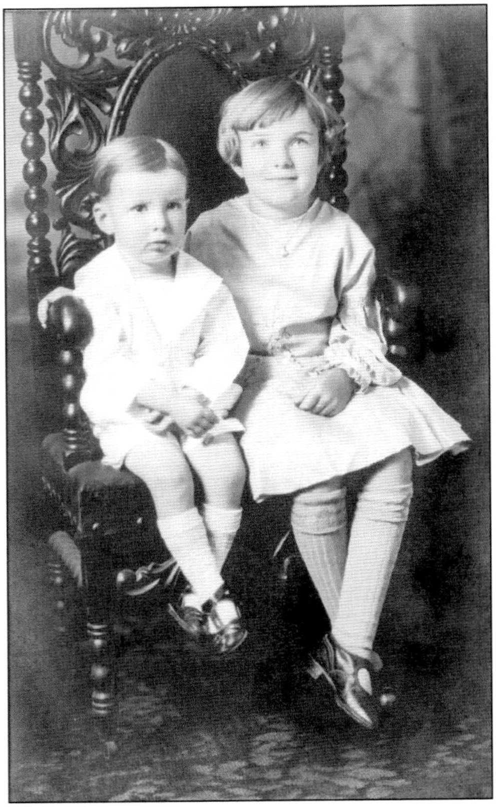

Joe and Elna Huffine were the children of Buford and Blanche Huffine. When she grew up, Elna married Lurie Barnett and was a hairdresser for more than 50 years at the Elite Beauty Shop and the Bonnie Kate Beauty Shop. (Courtesy of Elaine Cantrell.)

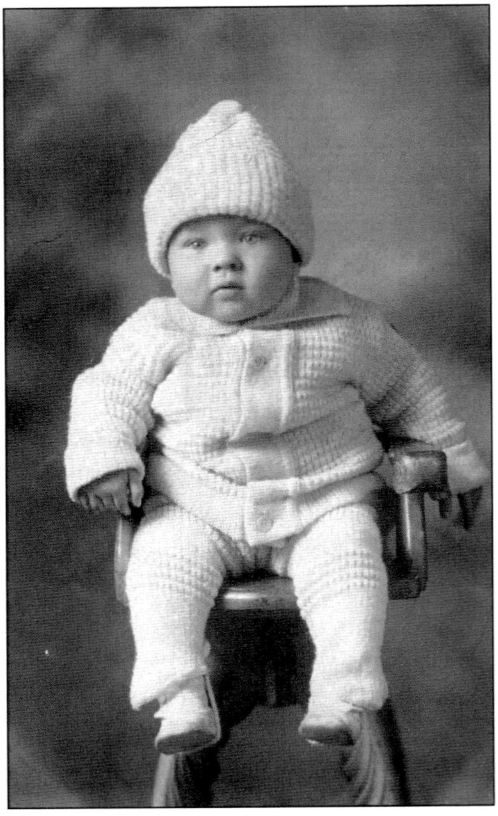

Ralph Eugene Scott Jr. was born in 1924. He grew up on Route 1 in Johnson City, which is now Greenwood Drive. Ralph's father worked at the National Soldiers' Home. (Courtesy of Elaine Cantrell.)

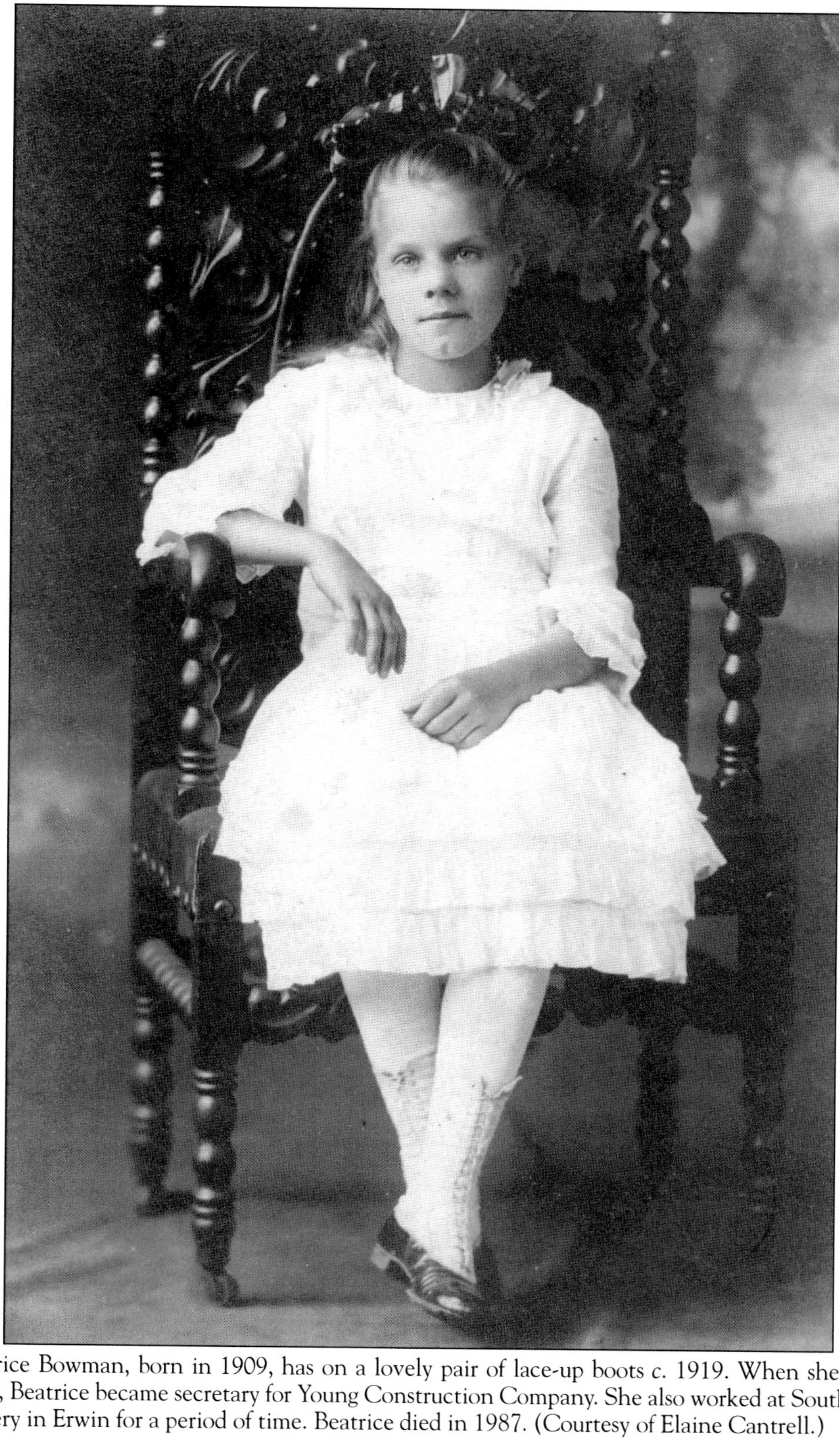

Beatrice Bowman, born in 1909, has on a lovely pair of lace-up boots c. 1919. When she was older, Beatrice became secretary for Young Construction Company. She also worked at Southern Pottery in Erwin for a period of time. Beatrice died in 1987. (Courtesy of Elaine Cantrell.)

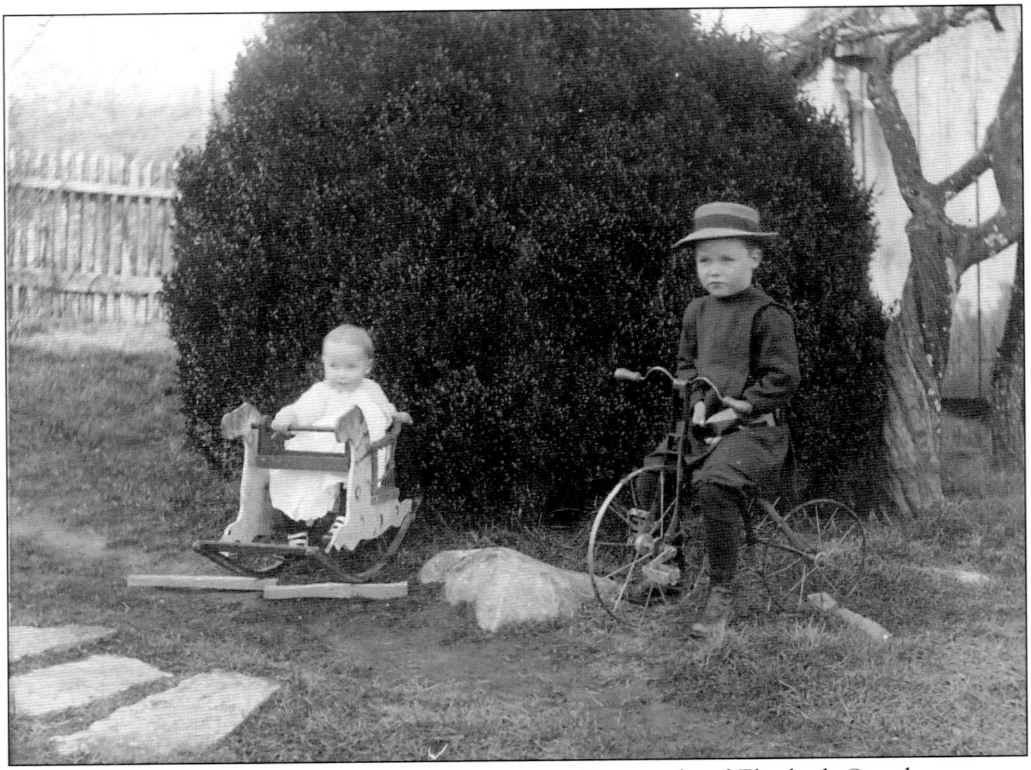

Raymond and Elizabeth Carathers grew up in the Knob Creek community during the early 1900s. Like many other children their ages, they enjoyed playing outside with a rocking horse and tricycle. (Courtesy of George and Margaret Holley.)

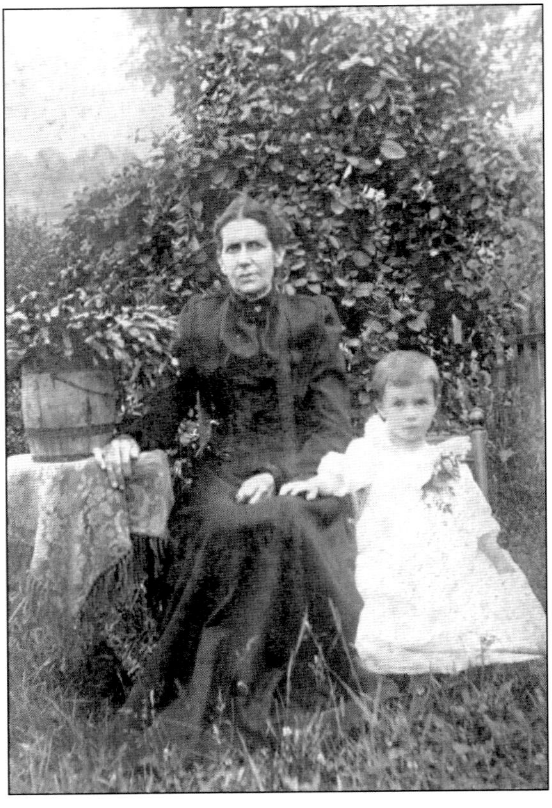

George Luther Crumley (November 30, 1897–February 7, 1984) is shown here in a very girlish dress *c.* 1900 with his aunt, Mary E. Crumley (December 3, 1842–March 20, 1911). The photograph was taken at the Crumley home in the Knob Creek community. (Courtesy of Don and Sarah Walters.)

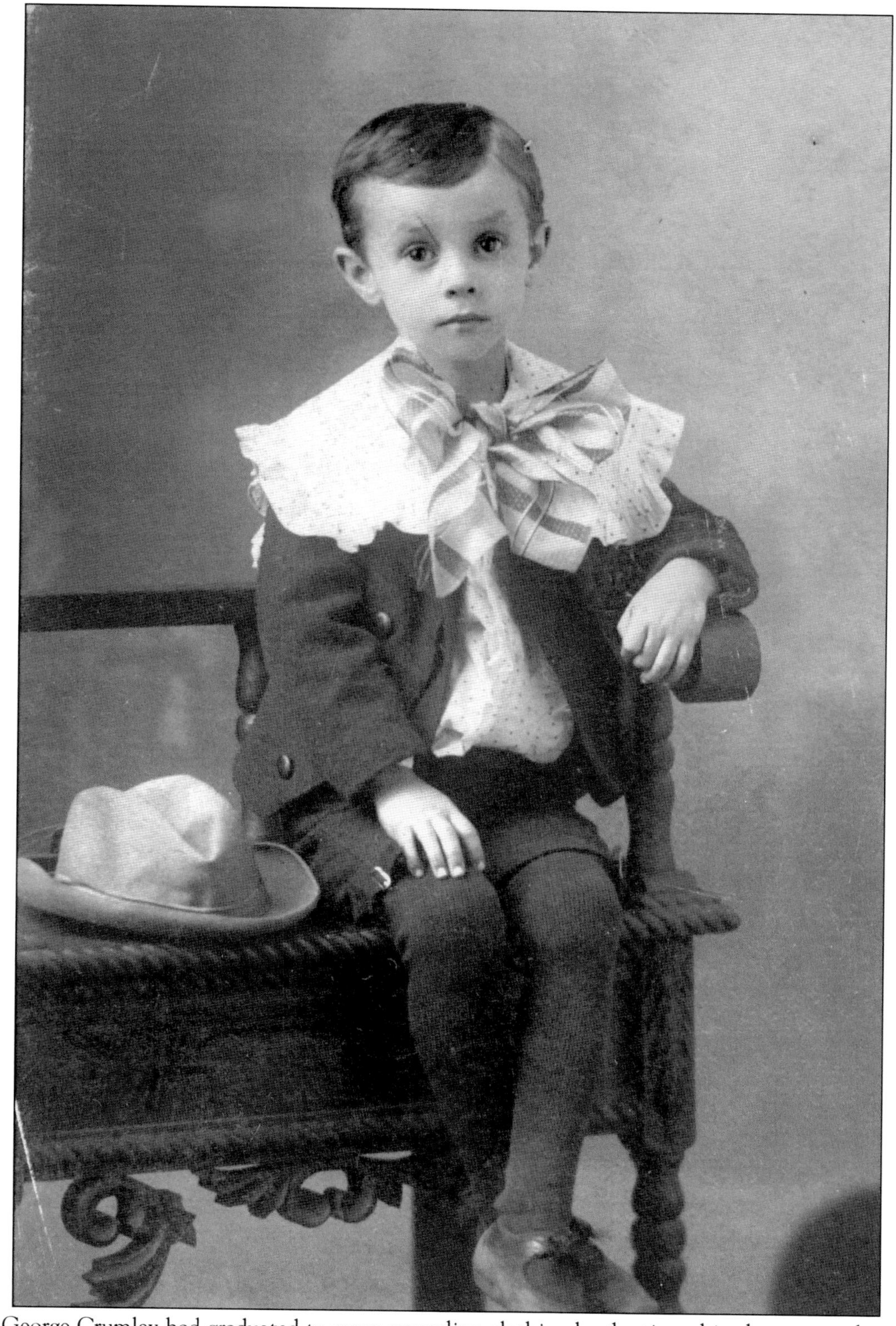

George Crumley had graduated to more masculine clothing by the time this photo was taken around 1902. (Courtesy of Don and Sarah Walters.)

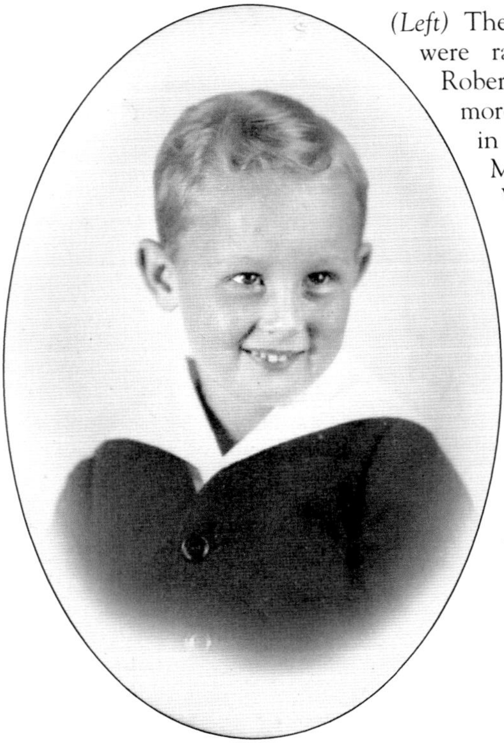

(Left) The children of Robert N. and Mildred Wilson were raised on the Willow Springs Dairy farm. Robert N. purchased approximately 45 acres (of more than 200) from his father, Millard Wilson, in 1948 for $5,000. Robert D. Wilson was born March 14, 1941. He died in 1981. (Courtesy of William E. Wilson.)

(Below, left) William E. Wilson, son of Robert N. and Mildred Wilson, was born March 29, 1944. He was raised on the Willow Springs Dairy Farm and now lives across the road. (Courtesy of William E. Wilson.)

(Below, right) Joe L. Wilson was born February 2, 1946. The youngest son of Robert N. and Mildred Wilson, Joe still lives in Johnson City and serves as a family historian. (Courtesy of William E. Wilson.)

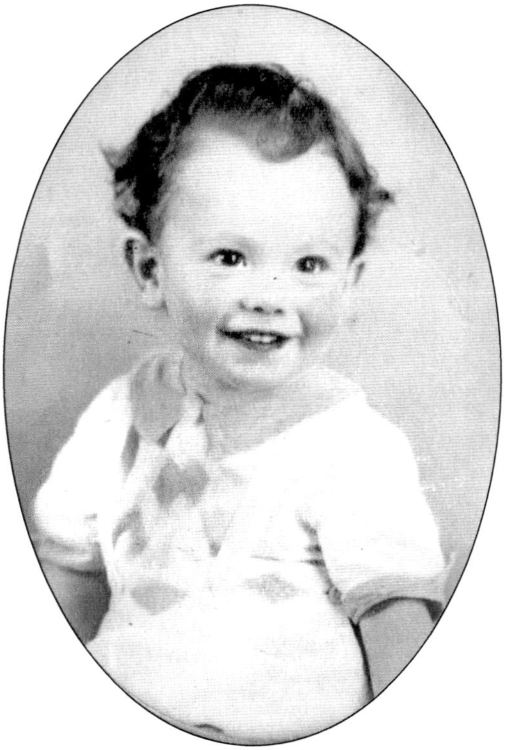

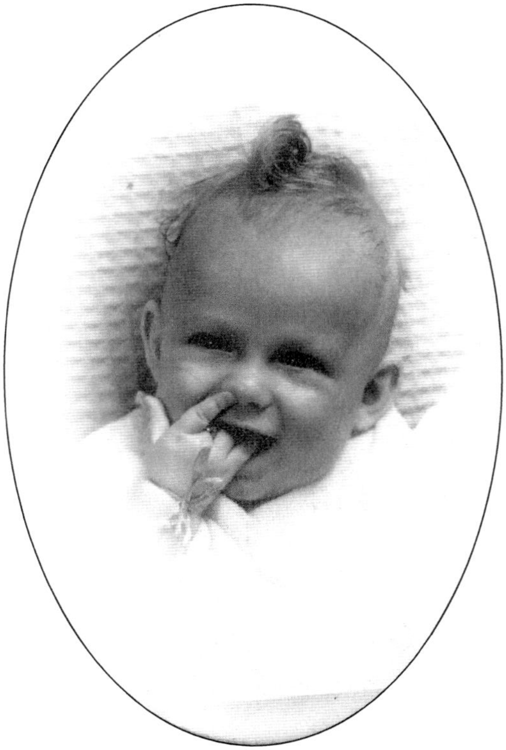

British lord Robert Baden-Powell founded the Boy Scout movement in 1908. Though troops were already operating in the United States, millionaire Chicago publisher William Dickson Boyce popularized the group here in 1910. Pictured here are boys from Scout Troop 61 of Erwin, Tennessee, c. 1950. (Courtesy of Terry and Kim Jones.)

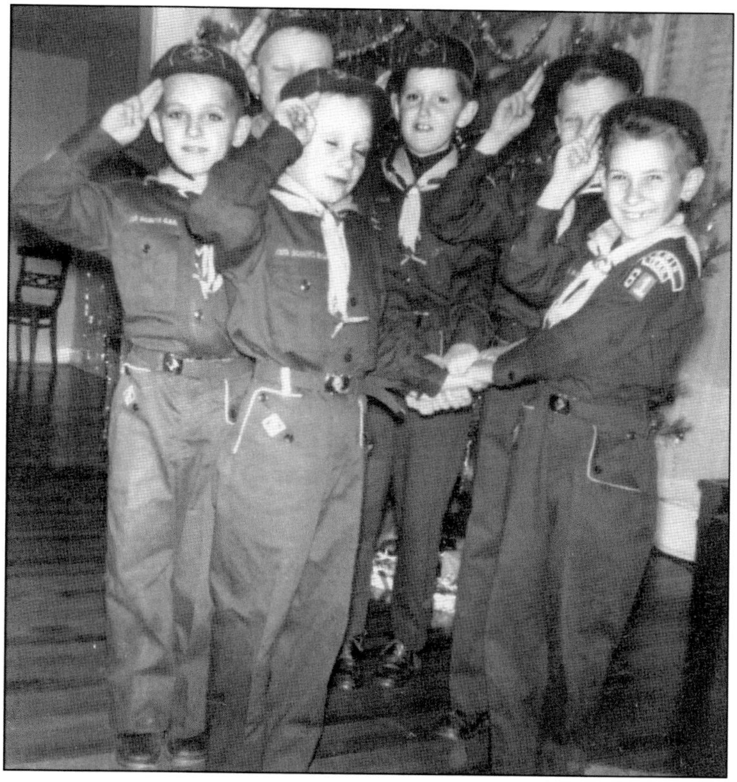

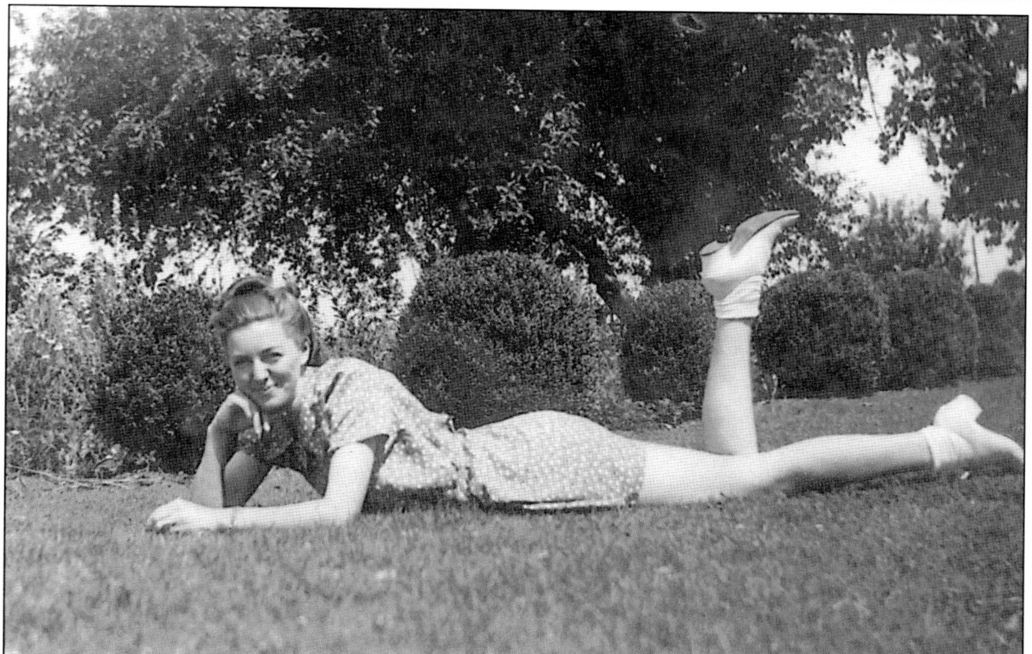

Grace Brown was about 17 years old when she and her friend Elsie Reeves took this picture c. 1920. There was a skirt that went around the bottom part of this outfit, but Grace took it off for the picture. Grace still emphasizes that she never would have shown her legs in public that way, but Elsie enjoyed kidding her about the photo. (Courtesy of Grace Brown Miller.)

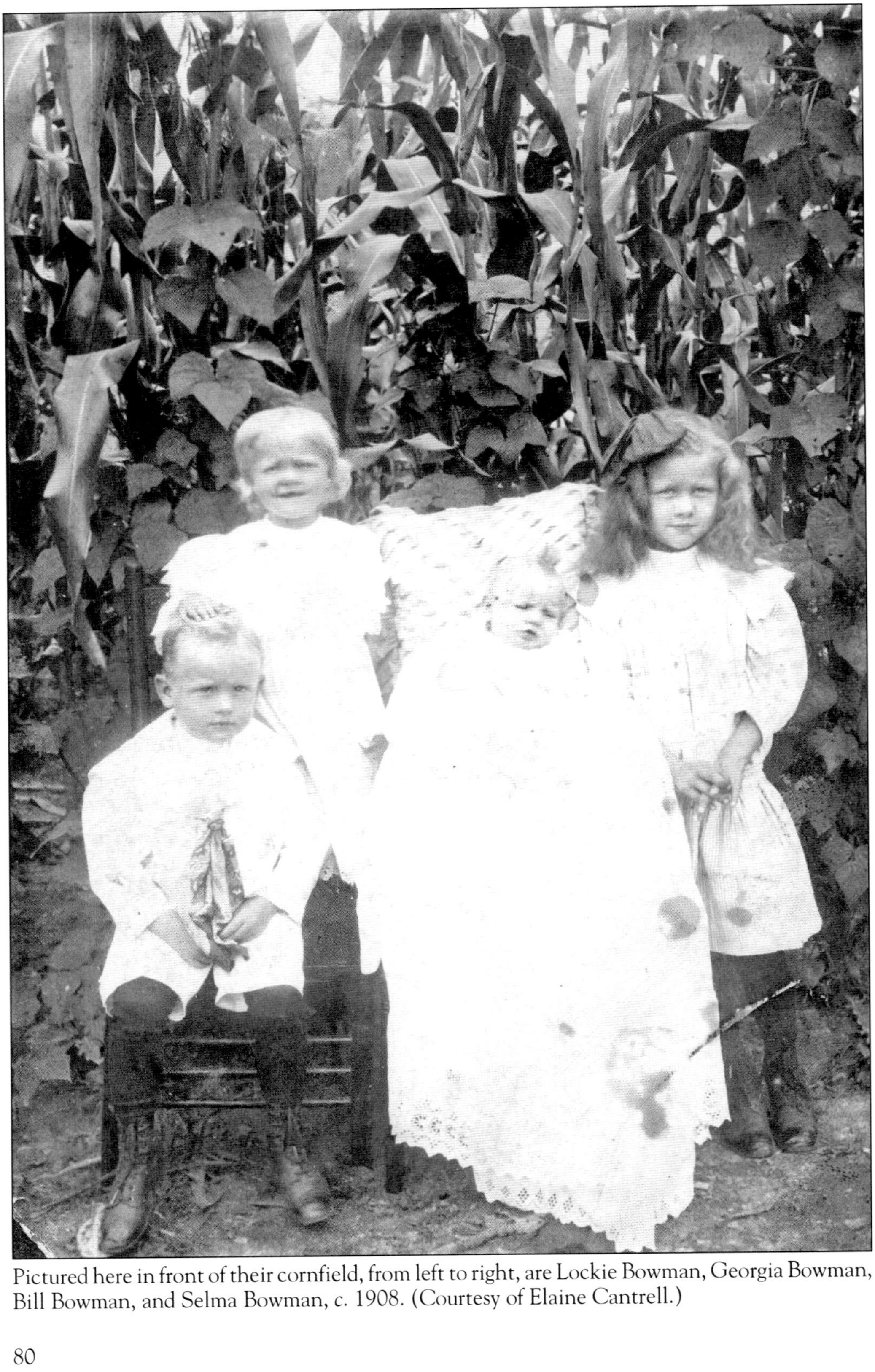

Pictured here in front of their cornfield, from left to right, are Lockie Bowman, Georgia Bowman, Bill Bowman, and Selma Bowman, c. 1908. (Courtesy of Elaine Cantrell.)

Six

EDUCATION

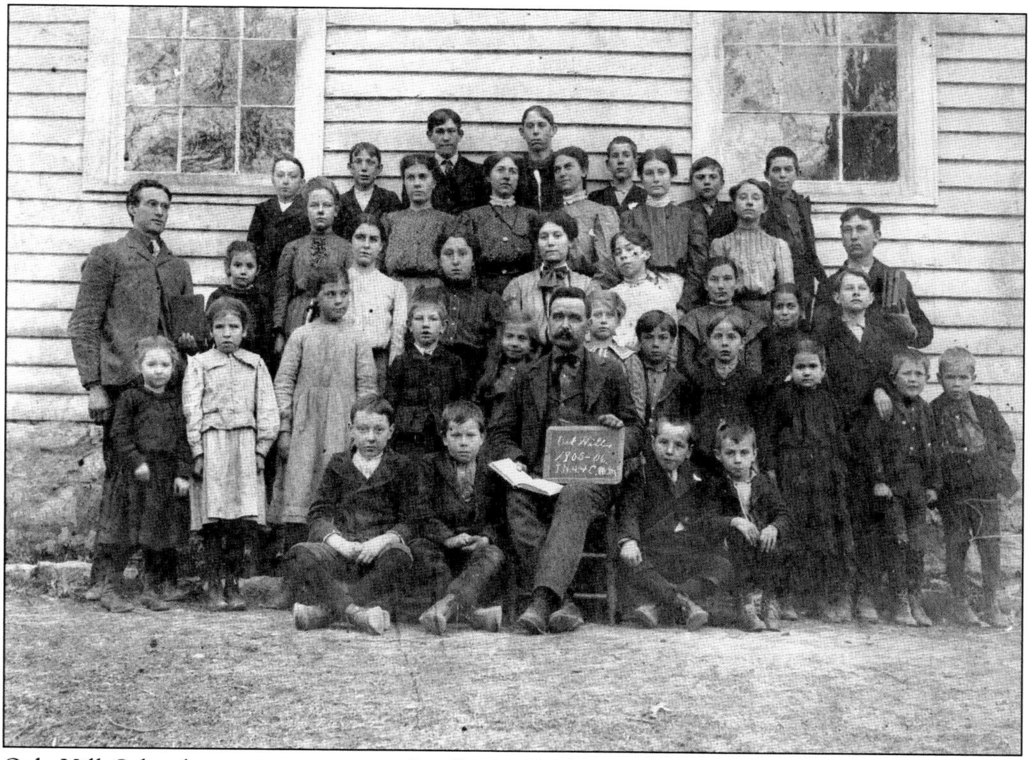

Oak Hill School was a one-room schoolhouse built in 1886. It sat on the property where Fuddruckers is now. Before the construction of Fuddruckers, the school building was moved to Jonesborough, where visiting students can do lessons, share books, and read out of McGuffey Readers as did the children in this photograph c. 1906. (Courtesy of Don and Sarah Walters.)

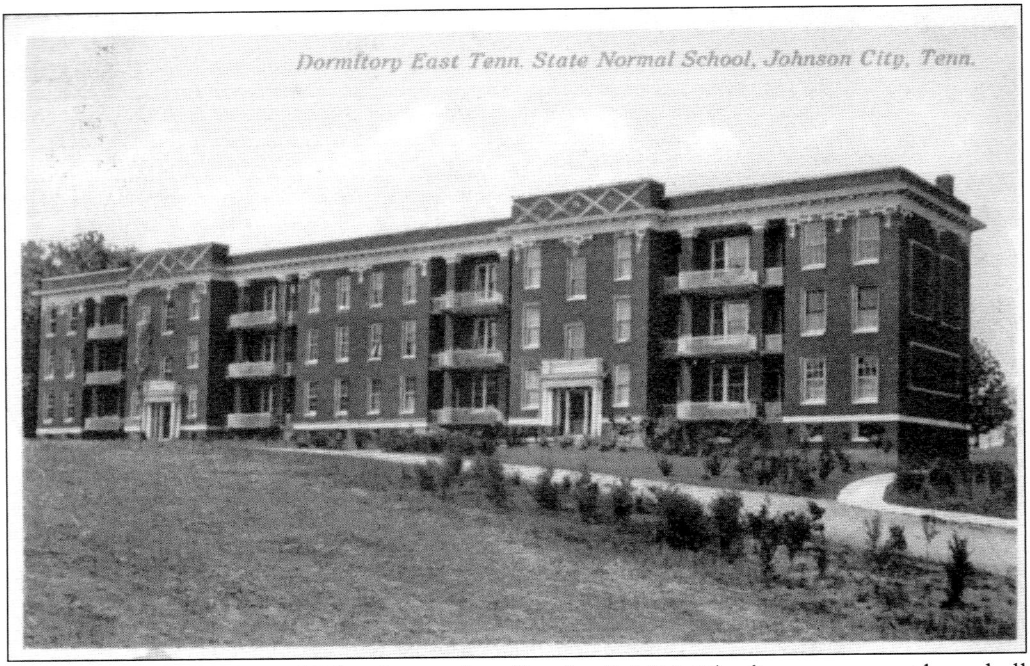

The East Tennessee Normal School opened on October 2, 1911. The first campus residence hall was named for Mayetta Wilkinson Carter, whose husband donated the 120 acres of land that helped ensure that the normal school would be established in Johnson City. (Courtesy of Betty Jane Hylton.)

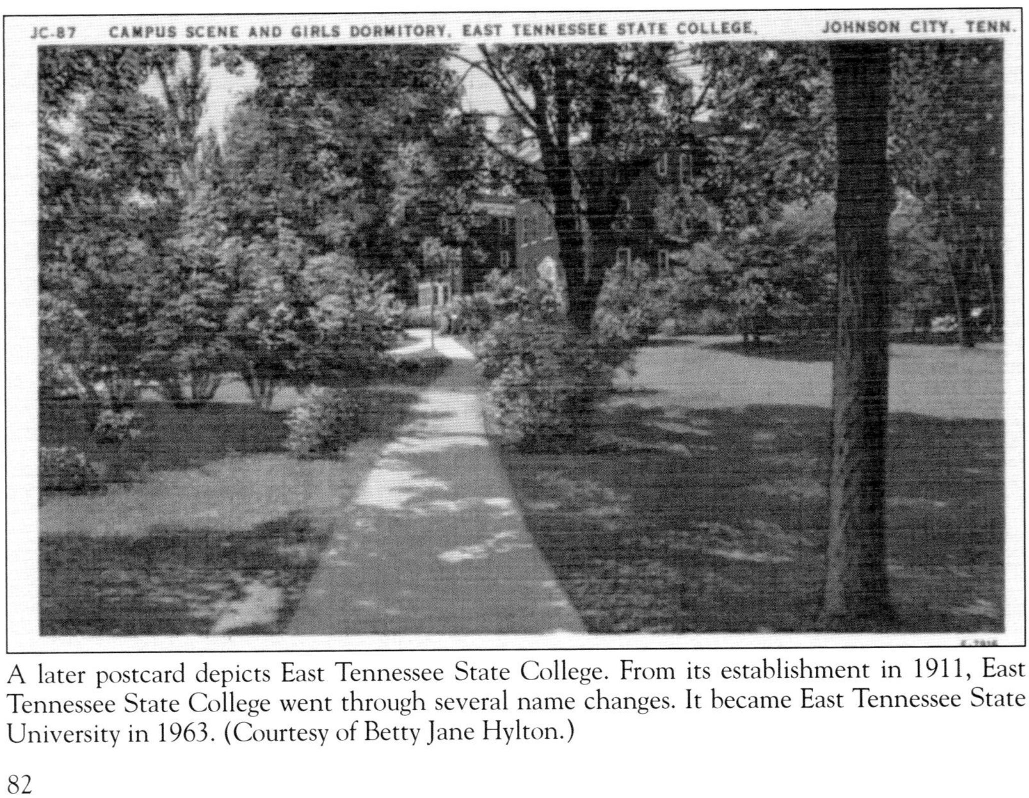

A later postcard depicts East Tennessee State College. From its establishment in 1911, East Tennessee State College went through several name changes. It became East Tennessee State University in 1963. (Courtesy of Betty Jane Hylton.)

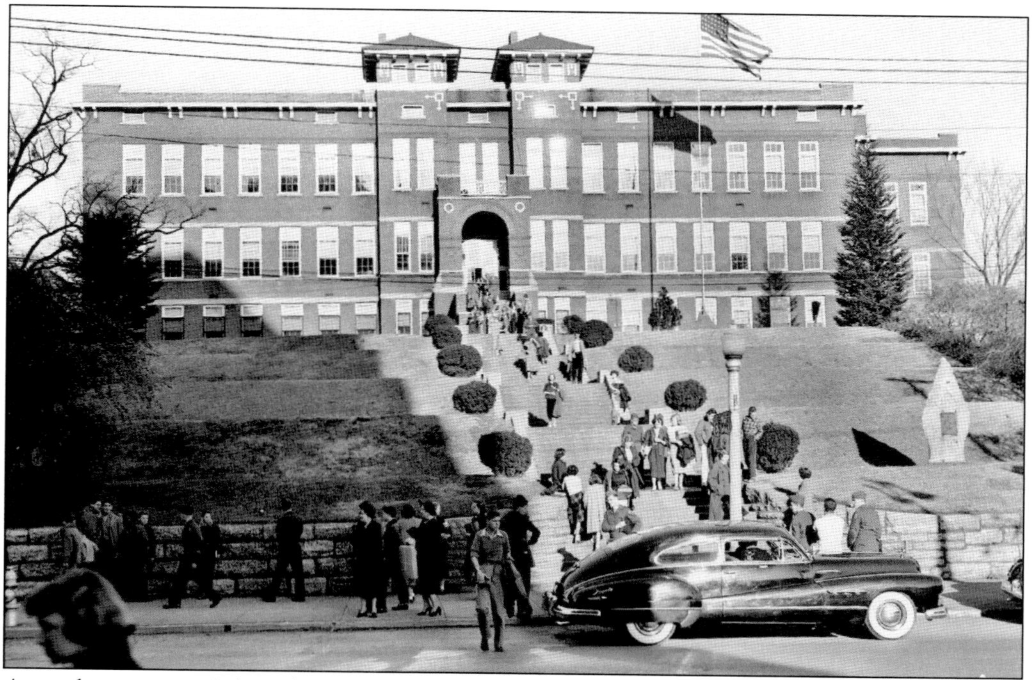

An enlargement of this photograph reveals several young men who are dressed in military uniform in this photo of Science Hill High School in 1952. The school was originally chartered as the Science Hill Male and Female High School in 1866, but it did not open until 1868. Tipton Jobe, who also constructed Jobe's Opera House, donated the land where Science Hill is located. (Courtesy of Doug Thompson.)

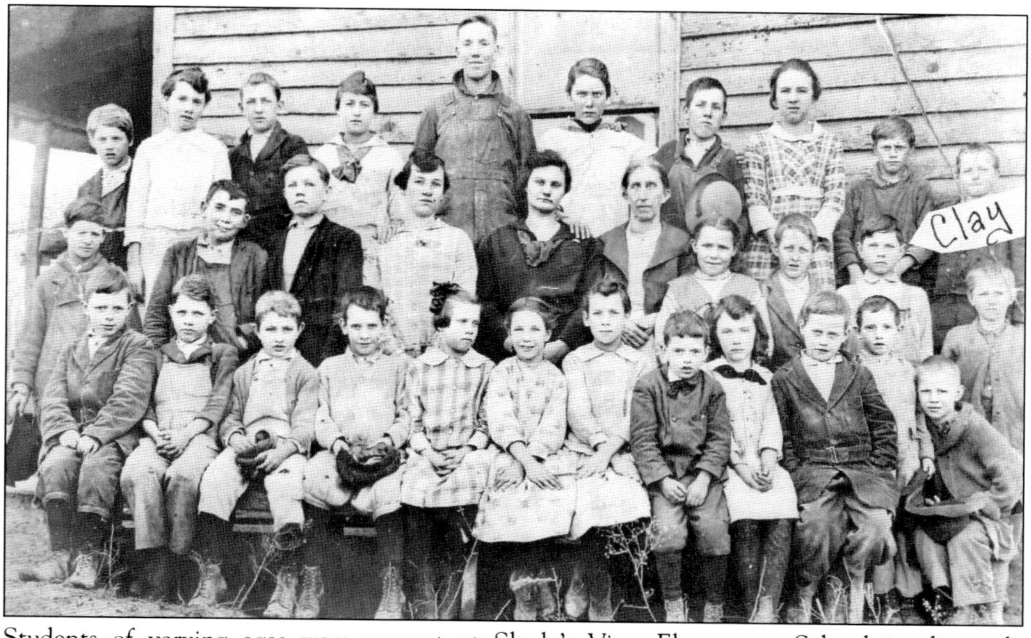

Students of varying ages were present at Slagle's View Elementary School in the early 1900s. The school was located at the corner of Dry Creek Road and Sinking Creek. The identified child, Clay Slagle, was born July 7, 1907, and died July 7, 2000. (Courtesy of Betty Jane Hylton.)

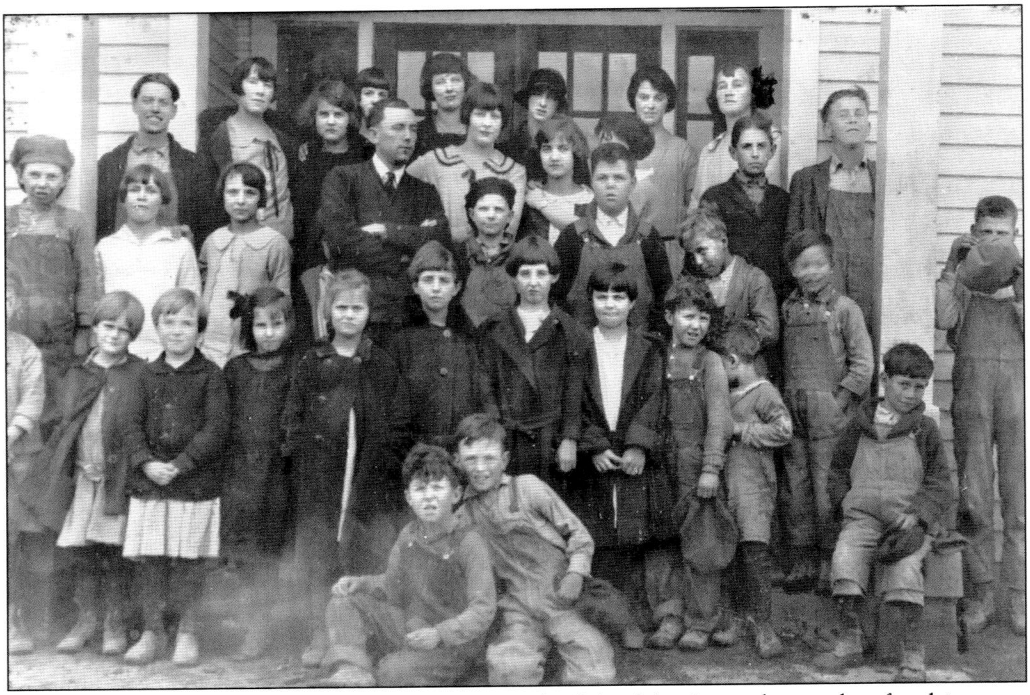

According to notes on the back of the photograph, "Miss Matt" was the teacher for this group of students in the Cherokee community in 1922. (Courtesy of Elaine Cantrell.)

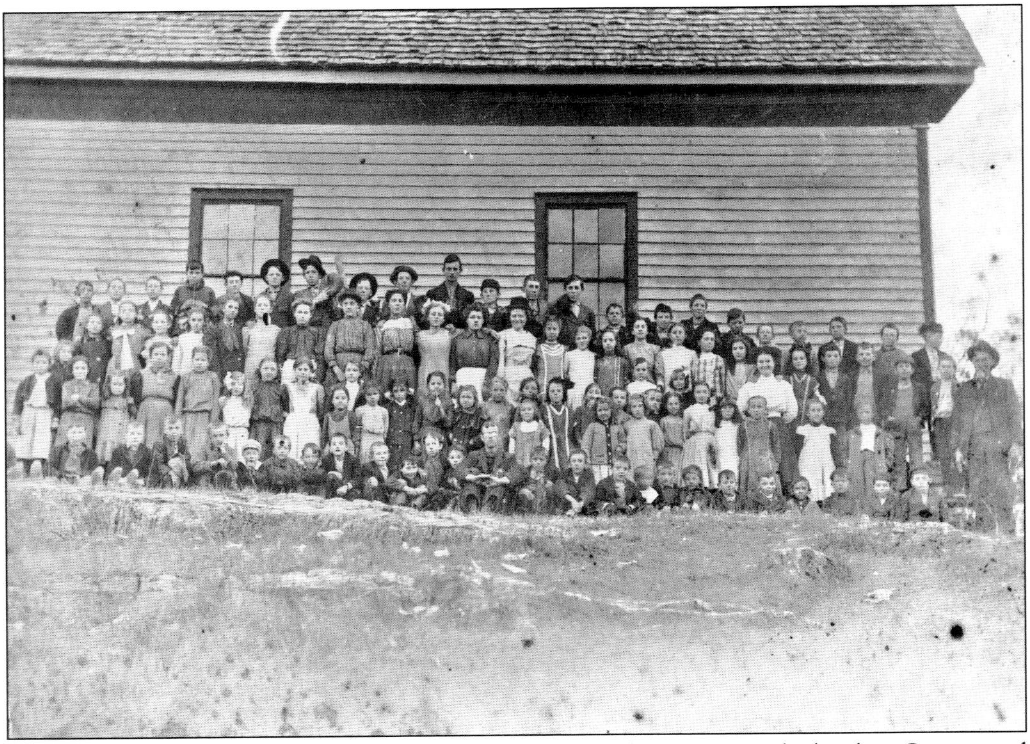

This multi-age school group is mostly likely of students at the Greenwood school on Greenwood Drive in the early 1900s. (Courtesy of Elaine Cantrell.)

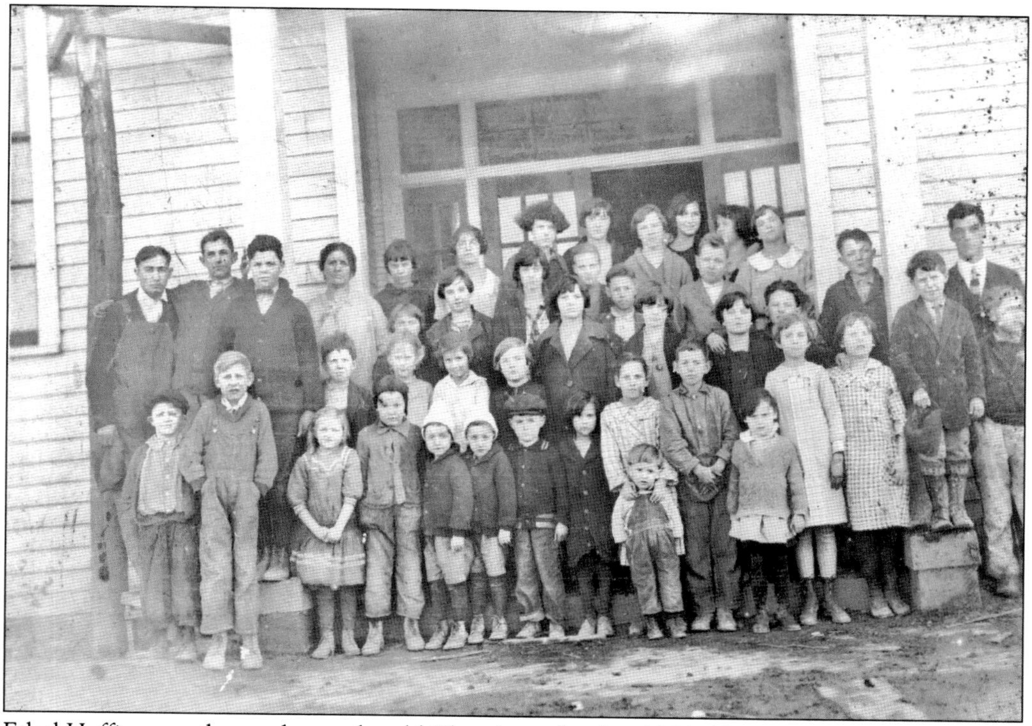

Ethel Huffine was the teacher at the old Cherokee school in 1908. (Courtesy of Elaine Cantrell.)

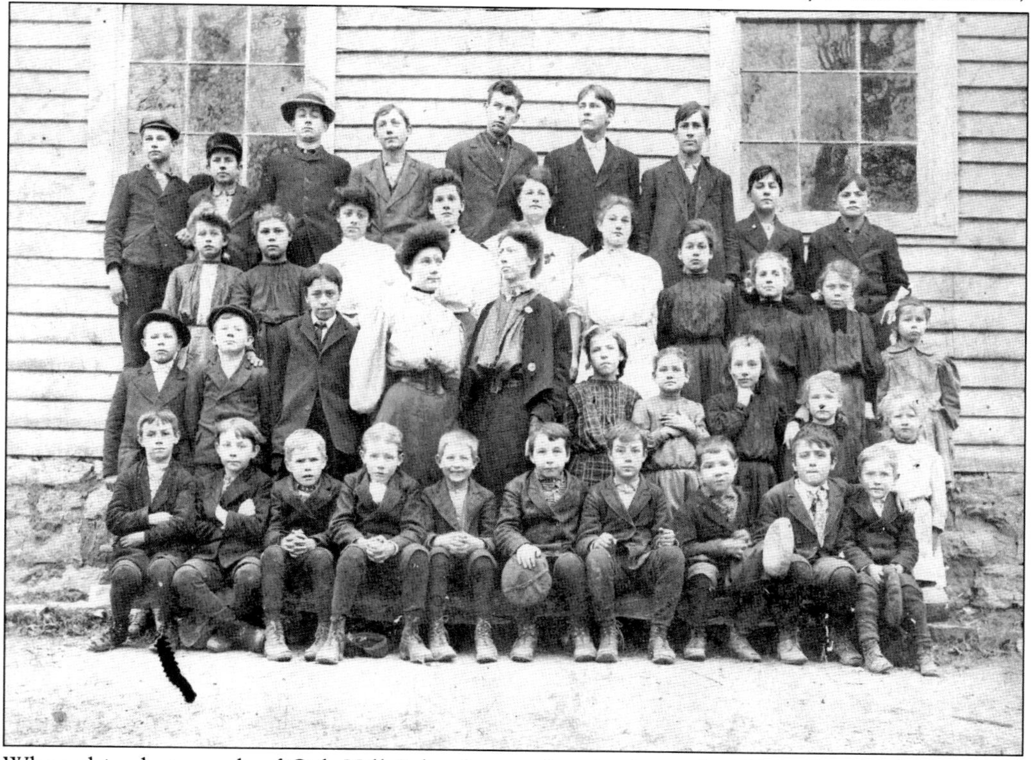

When this photograph of Oak Hill School was taken in the early 1900s, the teachers (in the center) were Cleo Miller and Ada Markwood. (Courtesy of Don and Sarah Walters.)

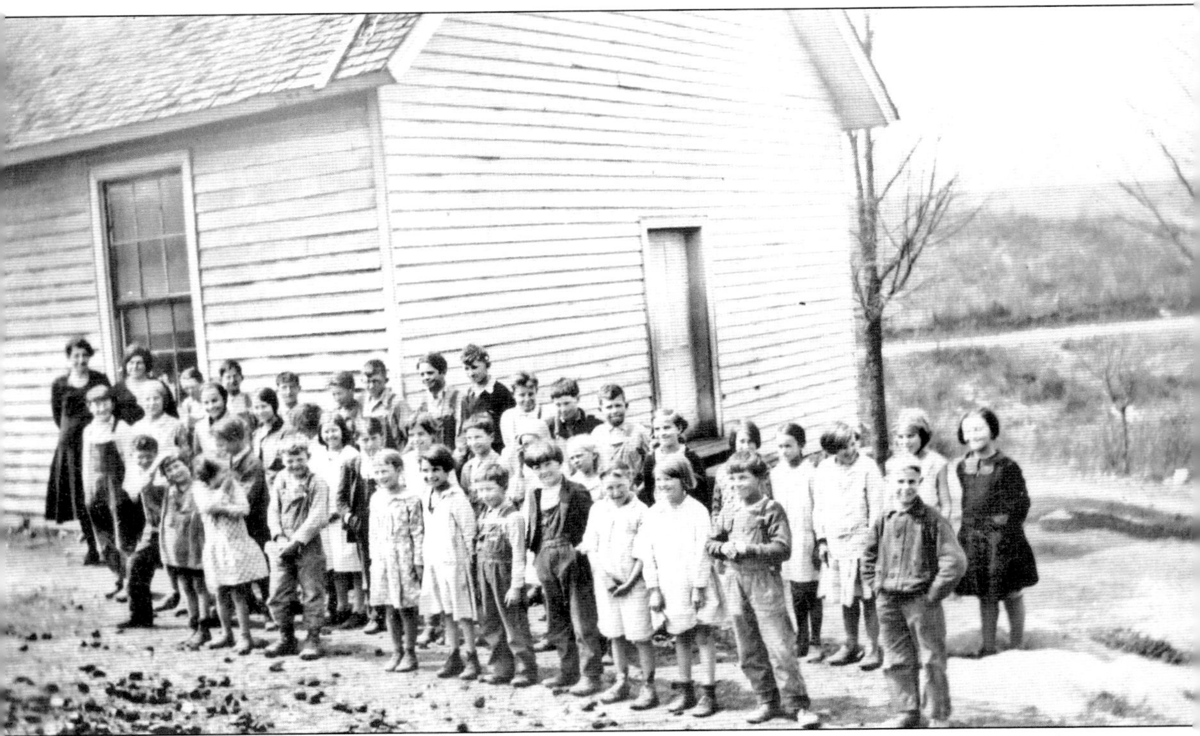

Oak Hill School was built in 1886 and served the Knob Creek community. When it was known that the area was going to be built upon, the school was donated to the Jonesborough–Washington County History Museum. To preserve local history and the history of one-room schoolhouses, the Heritage Alliance Museum conducts education programs in the building. Visiting students take lessons as though it were 1892, meaning that they share books and read out of McGuffey Readers, among other things. This photograph of Oak Hill School was taken c. 1905. (Courtesy of George and Margaret Holley.)

A 1907 public school report card for George Crumley in the fourth grade shows a completion of five months of school covering the subjects of reading, spelling, writing, arithmetic, geography, grammar, and U.S. history. The term began September 14 and the teacher was Laura Gibson. (Courtesy of Don and Sarah Walters.)

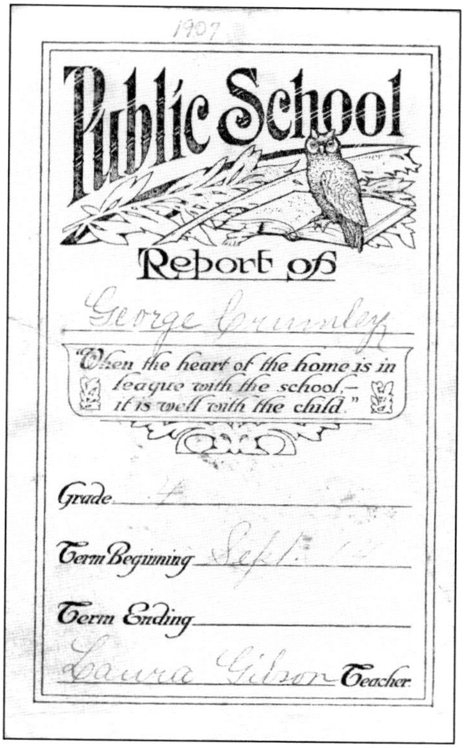

1907

Public School

Report of

George Crumley

"When the heart of the home is in league with the school,— it is well with the child."

Grade 4

Term Beginning Sept.

Term Ending

Laura Gibson Teacher

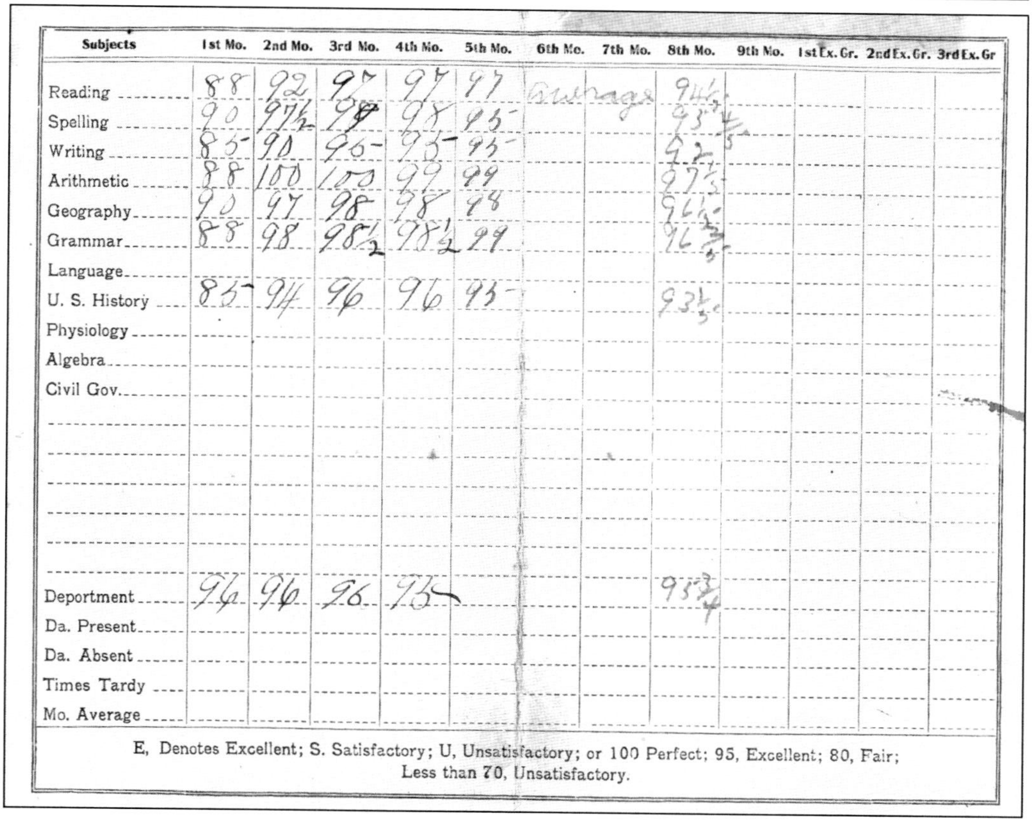

Subjects	1st Mo.	2nd Mo.	3rd Mo.	4th Mo.	5th Mo.	6th Mo.	7th Mo.	8th Mo.	9th Mo.	1st Ex. Gr.	2nd Ex. Gr.	3rd Ex. Gr.
Reading	88	92	97	97	97	Average		94 1/5				
Spelling	90	97½	99	98	95			93 4/5				
Writing	85	90	96	95	95			92				
Arithmetic	88	100	100	99	99			97 1/5				
Geography	90	97	98	98	98			96 1/5				
Grammar	88	98	98½	98½	99			96 3/5				
Language												
U. S. History	85	94	96	96	95			93 1/5				
Physiology												
Algebra												
Civil Gov.												
Deportment	96	96	96	95				95 3/4				
Da. Present												
Da. Absent												
Times Tardy												
Mo. Average												

E, Denotes Excellent; S. Satisfactory; U, Unsatisfactory; or 100 Perfect; 95, Excellent; 80, Fair; Less than 70, Unsatisfactory.

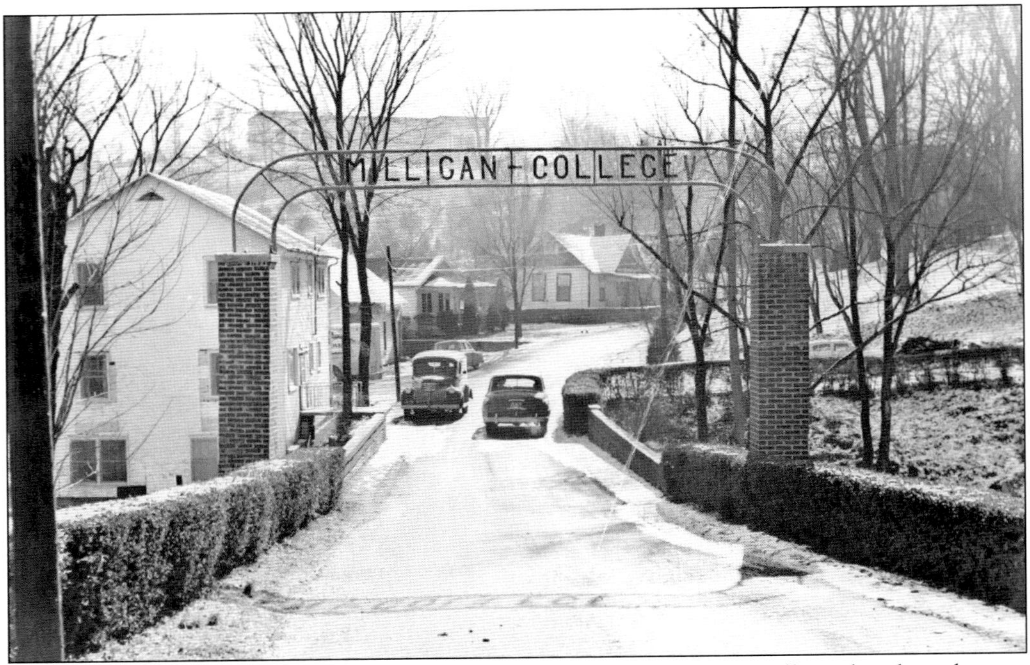

One of the oldest educational institutions in our region, Milligan College, has long been a leader in Christian higher education. Milligan College currently has around 900 students, more than 25 academic programs, and 3 master's degree programs. Recent years have brought major renovations to buildings and the campus. This is the Milligan College entrance as it appeared in 1957. (Courtesy of Milligan College.)

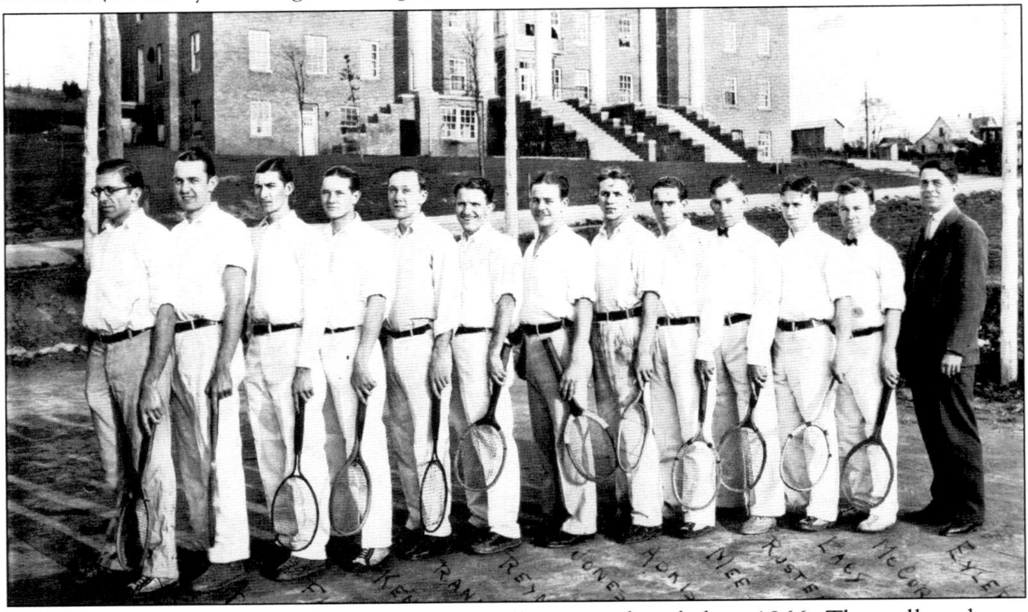

A Christian liberal arts college, Milligan College was founded in 1866. The college has a long-standing tradition of academic excellence and prepares students as servant leaders in various fields. Milligan has nationally recognized athletic teams that compete in the National Association of Intercollegiate Athletics's Appalachian Athletic Conference. Pictured here are members of the Milligan College tennis team in 1921. (Courtesy of Milligan College.)

Seven

Work

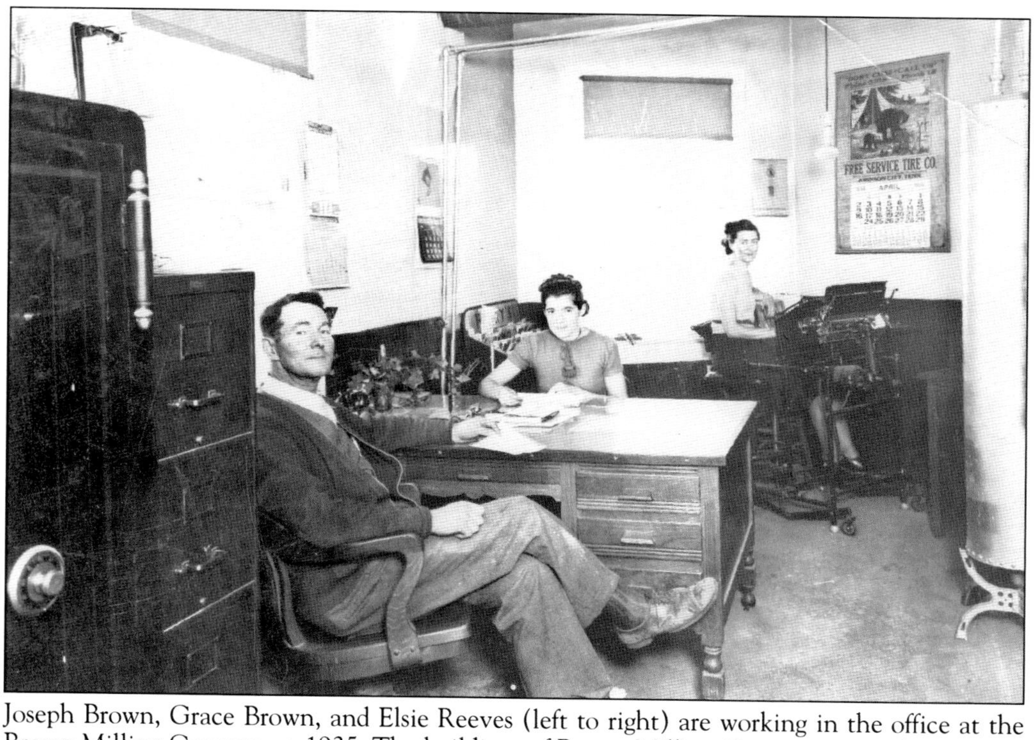

Joseph Brown, Grace Brown, and Elsie Reeves (left to right) are working in the office at the Brown Milling Company c. 1935. The buildings of Brown Milling Company were destroyed in a fire in 1955. (Courtesy of Grace Brown Miller and June Miller Gouge.)

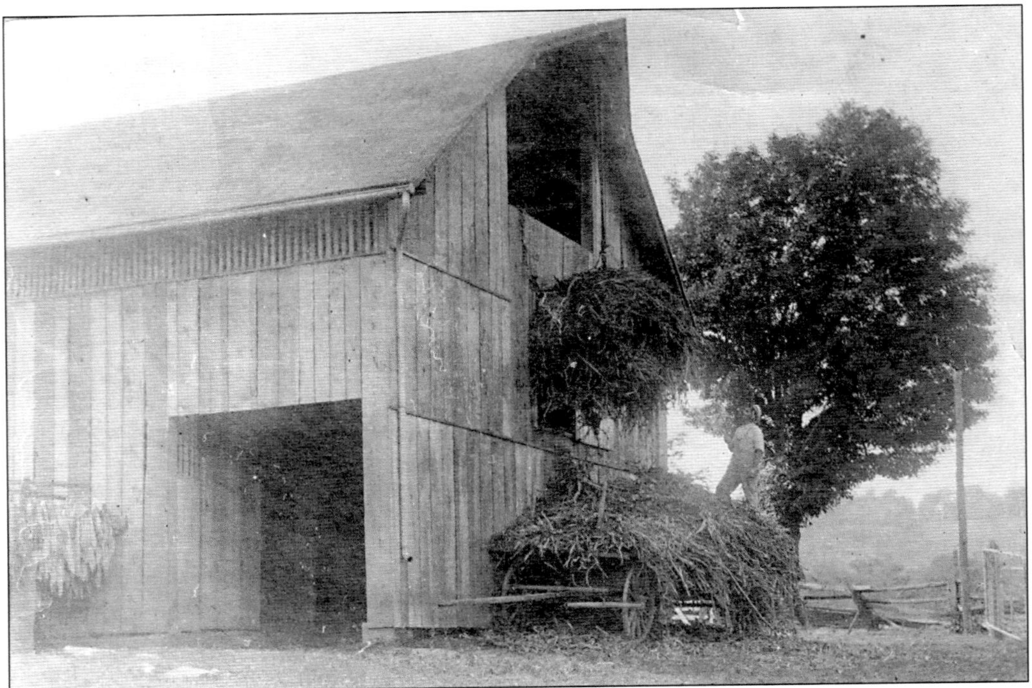

John A. Sherfey pulls hay into the barn he built in 1916. The barn still stands today on West Oakland Avenue and contains original hay pulleys, forks, and rope. (Courtesy of George and Margaret Holley.)

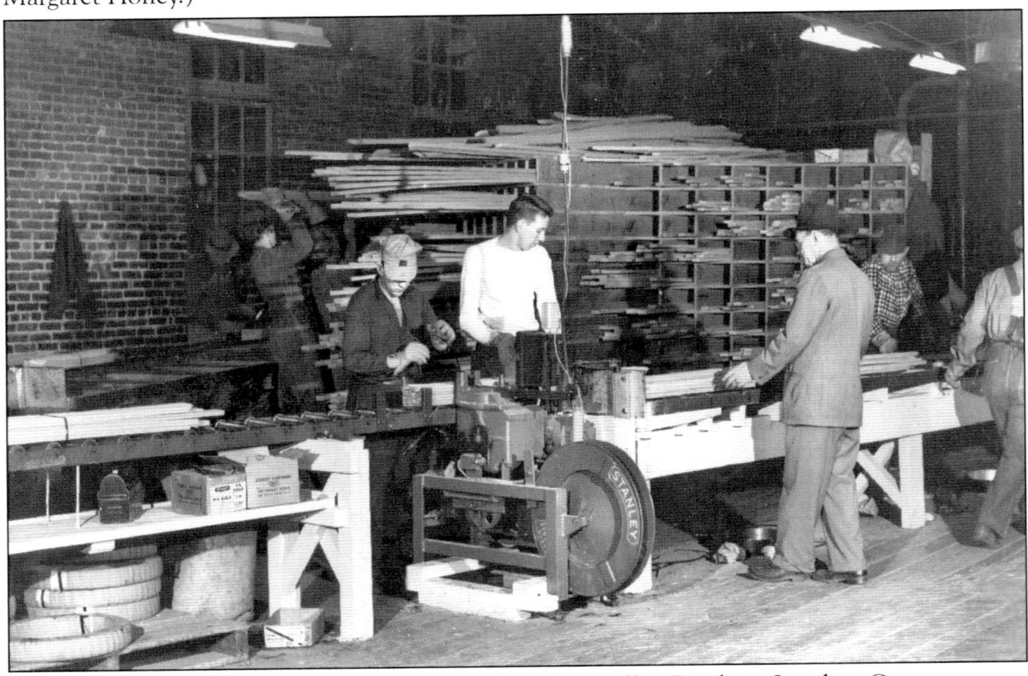

Perry O. Smith (center, in the suit) worked at the Miller Brothers Lumber Company as a general manager in the early 1900s. The Miller Brothers Lumber Company was a large lumber manufacturing plant that dried wood, processed it, and made flooring and other wood products. (Courtesy of Barbara G. Smith.)

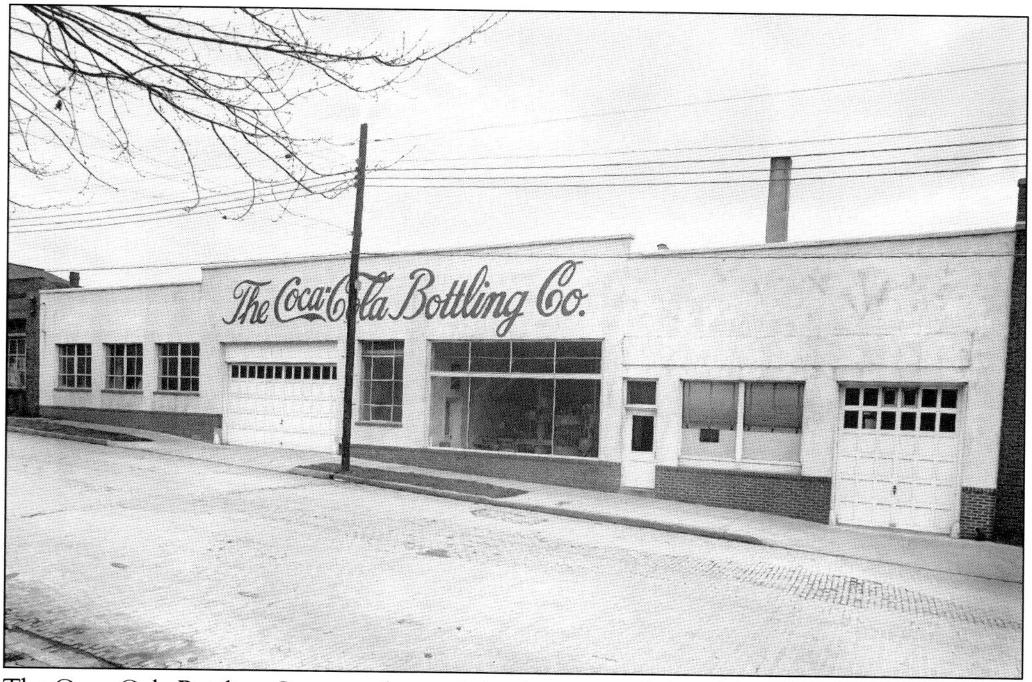

The Coca-Cola Bottling Company began doing business in Johnson City in February 1906 and has been at the current location on Wesley Street since 1970. This photograph of the Coca-Cola Bottling Company was taken *c.* 1940. (Courtesy of Doug Thompson.)

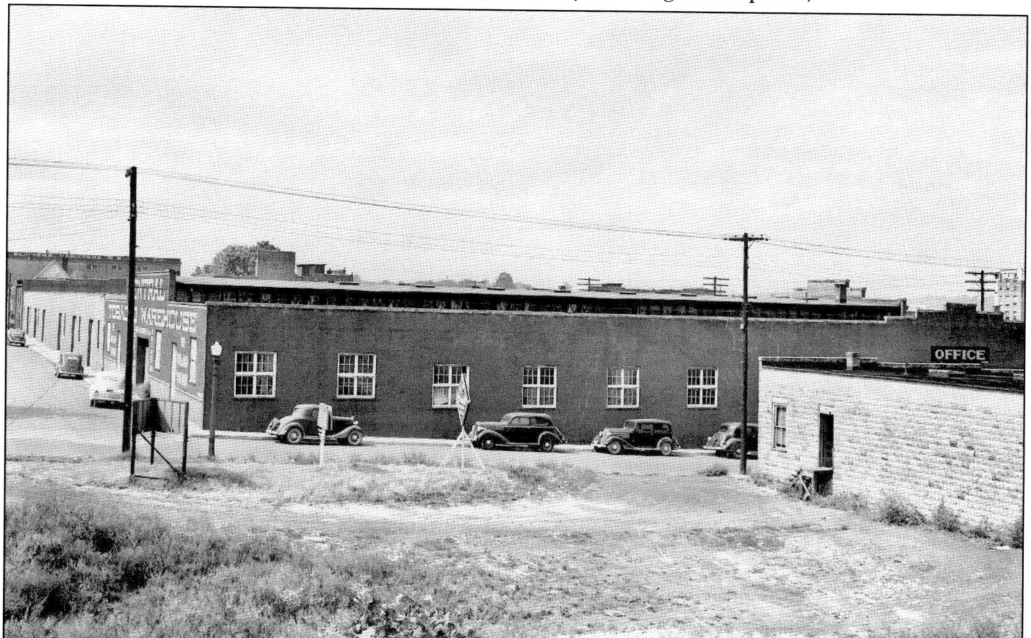

Summers Hardware & Supply Company started in Johnson City in 1893 at Fountain Square. It has been at this Buffalo Street location since 1910. While it was originally a wholesale hardware distributor, Summers Hardware & Supply Company now sells industrial and manufacturing supplies. The Central Tobacco Warehouse can be seen in the middle of the photo. (Courtesy of Doug Thompson.)

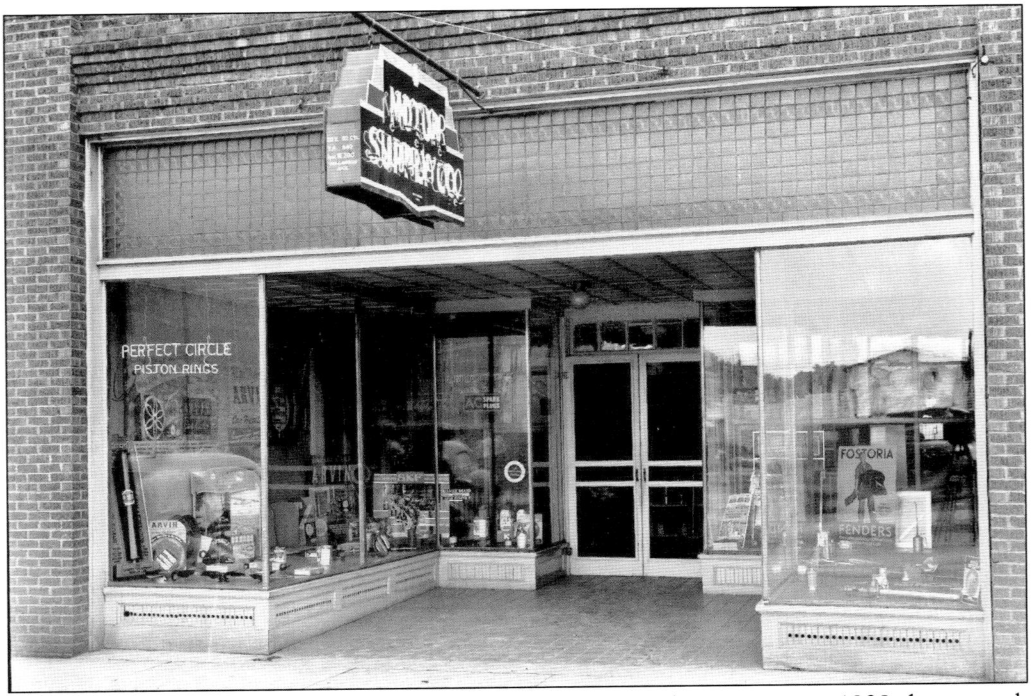

A close-up of the windows of the Johnson City Motor Supply Company *c.* 1938 shows spark plugs, Victor gaskets, mufflers, oil cans, Triangle brand axle shafts, and Fostoria fenders for "Fords, Chevrolets, Plymouths, and other popular cars." (Courtesy of Doug Thompson.)

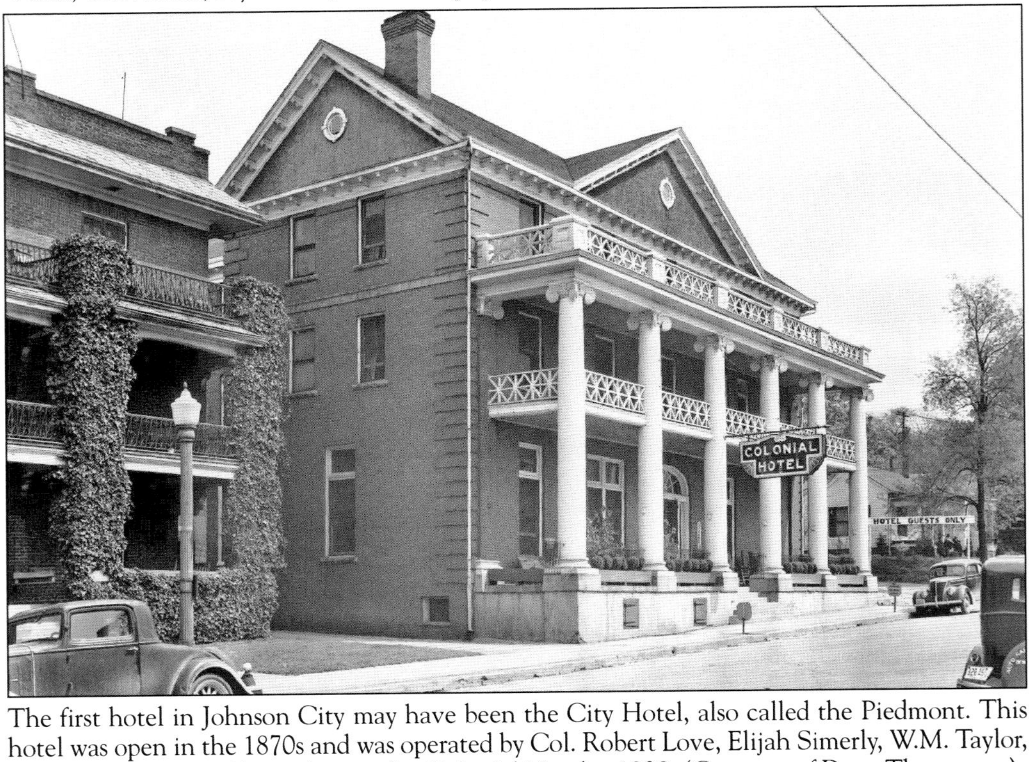

The first hotel in Johnson City may have been the City Hotel, also called the Piedmont. This hotel was open in the 1870s and was operated by Col. Robert Love, Elijah Simerly, W.M. Taylor, and other investors. Shown here is the Colonial Hotel *c.* 1938. (Courtesy of Doug Thompson.)

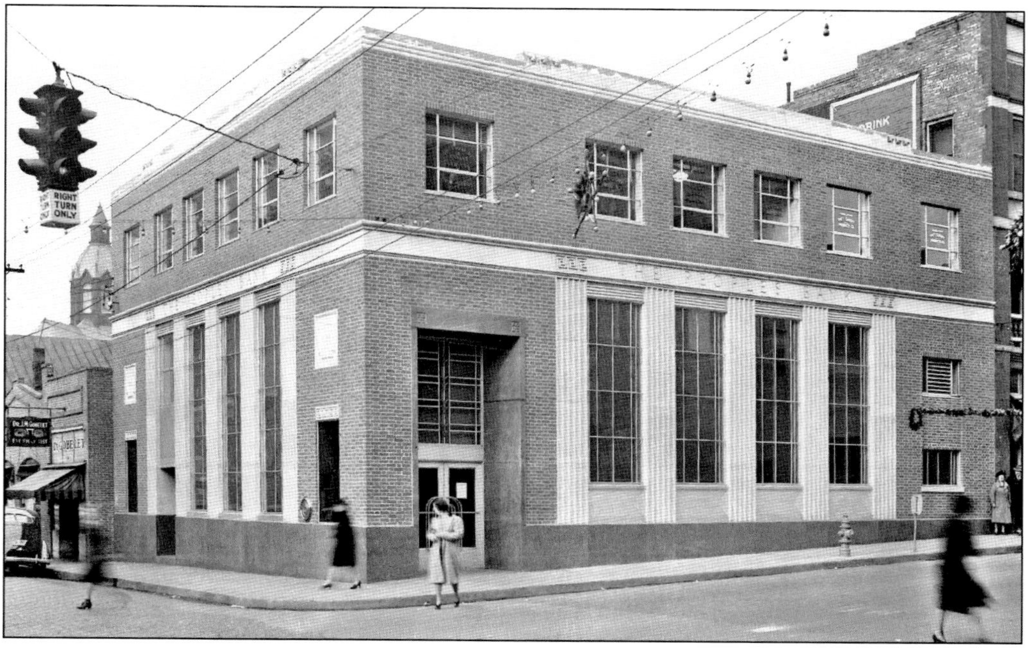

Vines, Hawkins, & Bryant and the Pet Dairy and Products Company were in the upstairs offices of the Peoples Bank building in downtown Johnson City. To the left is the office of Dr. J.M. Gobelet, eye specialist. (Courtesy of Doug Thompson.)

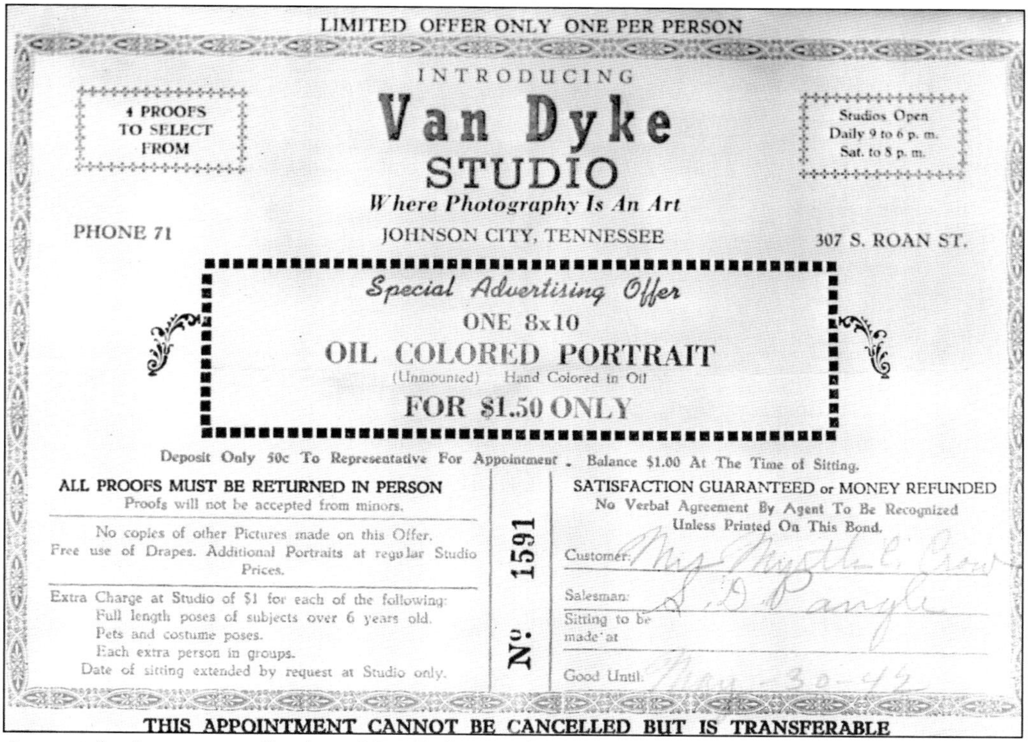

LIMITED OFFER ONLY ONE PER PERSON

INTRODUCING

4 PROOFS TO SELECT FROM

Van Dyke
STUDIO
Where Photography Is An Art

Studios Open Daily 9 to 6 p. m. Sat. to 8 p. m.

PHONE 71 JOHNSON CITY, TENNESSEE 307 S. ROAN ST.

Special Advertising Offer
ONE 8x10
OIL COLORED PORTRAIT
(Unmounted) Hand Colored in Oil
FOR $1.50 ONLY

Deposit Only 50c To Representative For Appointment . Balance $1.00 At The Time of Sitting.

ALL PROOFS MUST BE RETURNED IN PERSON
Proofs will not be accepted from minors.

No copies of other Pictures made on this Offer.
Free use of Drapes. Additional Portraits at regular Studio Prices.

Extra Charge at Studio of $1 for each of the following:
Full length poses of subjects over 6 years old.
Pets and costume poses.
Each extra person in groups.
Date of sitting extended by request at Studio only.

No. 1591

SATISFACTION GUARANTEED or MONEY REFUNDED
No Verbal Agreement By Agent To Be Recognized Unless Printed On This Bond.

Customer: Mrs Myrtle C. Crow
Salesman: S. D. Pangle
Sitting to be made at
Good Until: May 30-42

THIS APPOINTMENT CANNOT BE CANCELLED BUT IS TRANSFERABLE

A special advertising offer from Van Dyke Studio, located at 307 South Roan Street, shows their phone number as 71. One 8x10 oil-colored portrait was only $1.50. Mrs. Myrtle C. Crow purchased this certificate from S.D. Pangle on May 30, 1942. (Courtesy of Doug Thompson.)

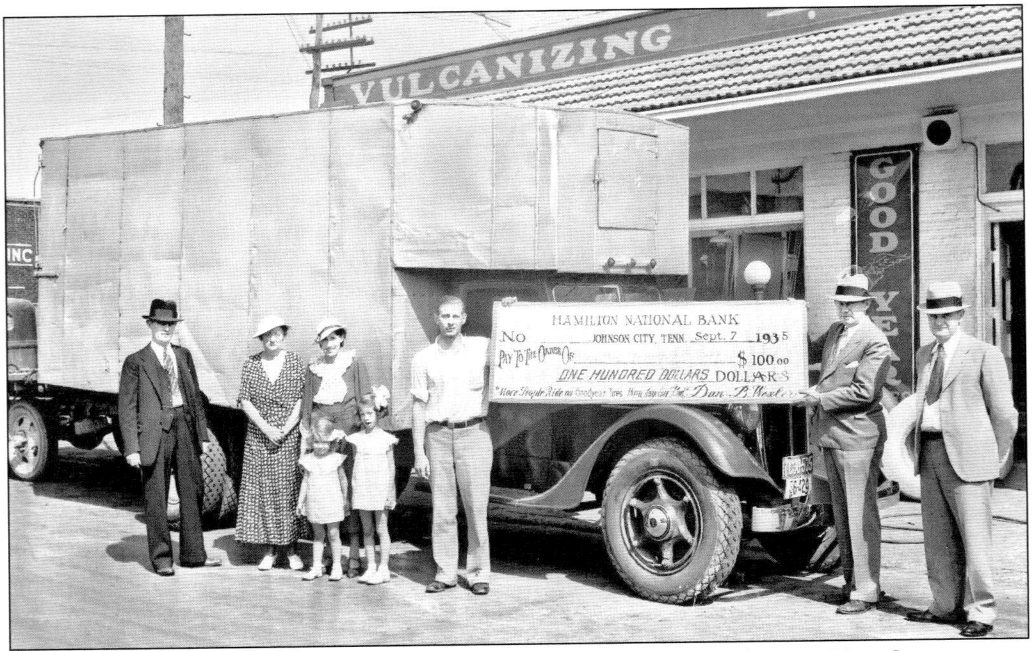

Mr. and Mrs. Herman R. Potts won $100 from the Wexler Free Service Tire Company on September 7, 1935. The "check" was issued by Hamilton National Bank and signed by Dan Wexler. The caption at the bottom of the check states that "more people ride on Goodyear Tires than any other kind." (Courtesy of Doug Thompson.)

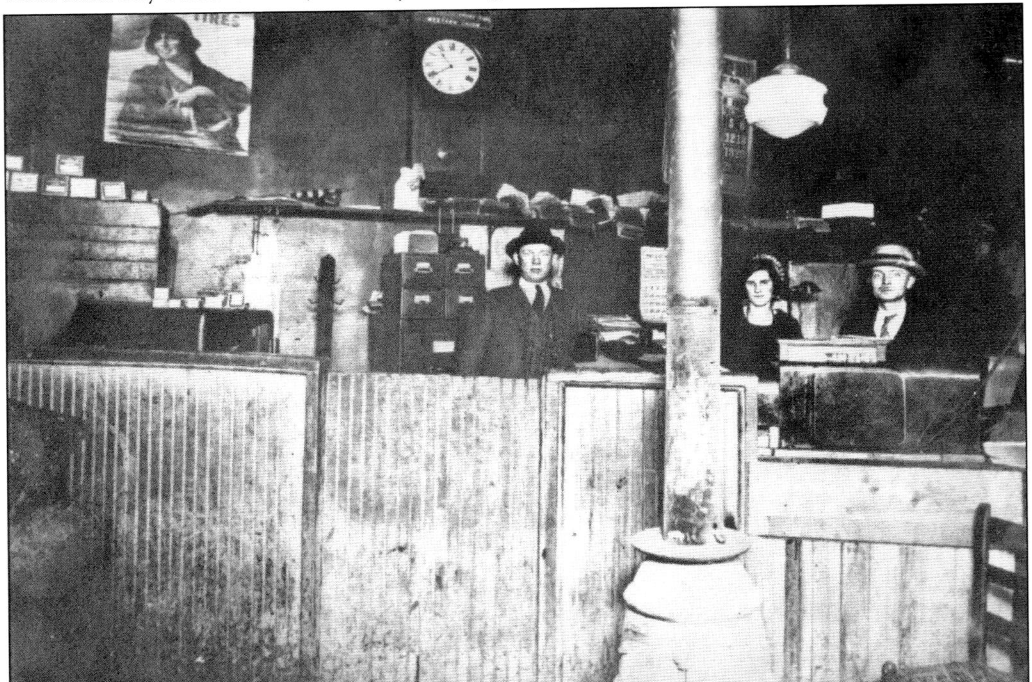

Dan B. Wexler and Robert Wiley opened Free Service Tire Company on June 25, 1919. This photograph shows, from left to right, Dan B. Wexler, Bernice Cooper, and Robert Wiley. A magnification of the calendar in the background looks like 1924. (Courtesy of Lewis Wexler Sr.)

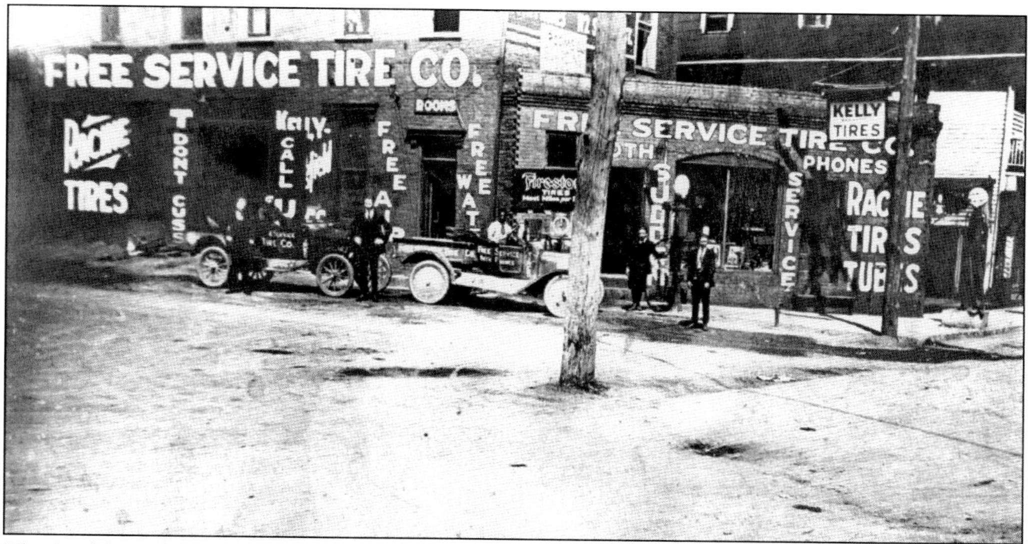

The building that housed the Free Service Tire Company in this early 1920s photo began as a railroad depot and is now part of the corporate office building at the corner of Buffalo Street and Wilson Street. The grand opening announcement for Free Service Tire Company advertised "service of the automobile public from daylight to midnight." (Courtesy of Lewis Wexler Sr.)

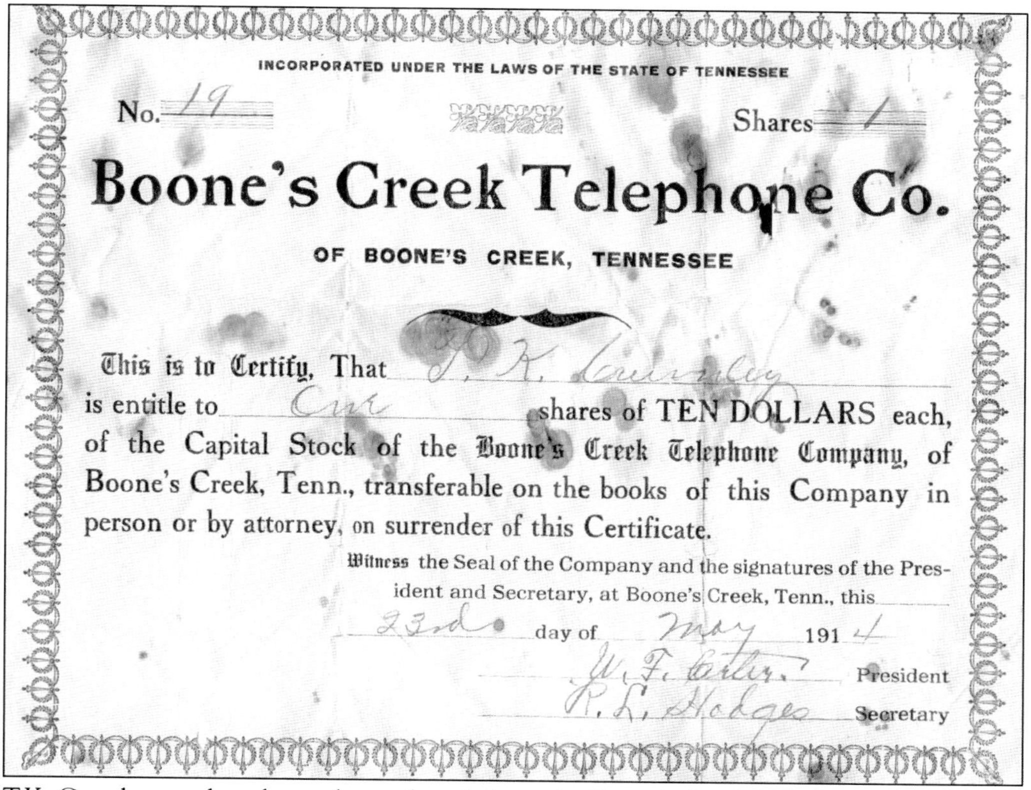

INCORPORATED UNDER THE LAWS OF THE STATE OF TENNESSEE

No. 19 Shares 1

Boone's Creek Telephone Co.

OF BOONE'S CREEK, TENNESSEE

This is to Certify, That T. K. Crumley is entitle to One shares of TEN DOLLARS each, of the Capital Stock of the Boone's Creek Telephone Company, of Boone's Creek, Tenn., transferable on the books of this Company in person or by attorney, on surrender of this Certificate.

Witness the Seal of the Company and the signatures of the President and Secretary, at Boone's Creek, Tenn., this 23rd day of May 1914

W. F. Carter President

R. L. Hodges Secretary

T.K. Crumley purchased one share of stock from the Boone's Creek Telephone Company on May 23, 1914, for $10. W.F. Carter, president, and R.L. Hodges, secretary, signed the certificate. (Courtesy of Don and Sarah Walters.)

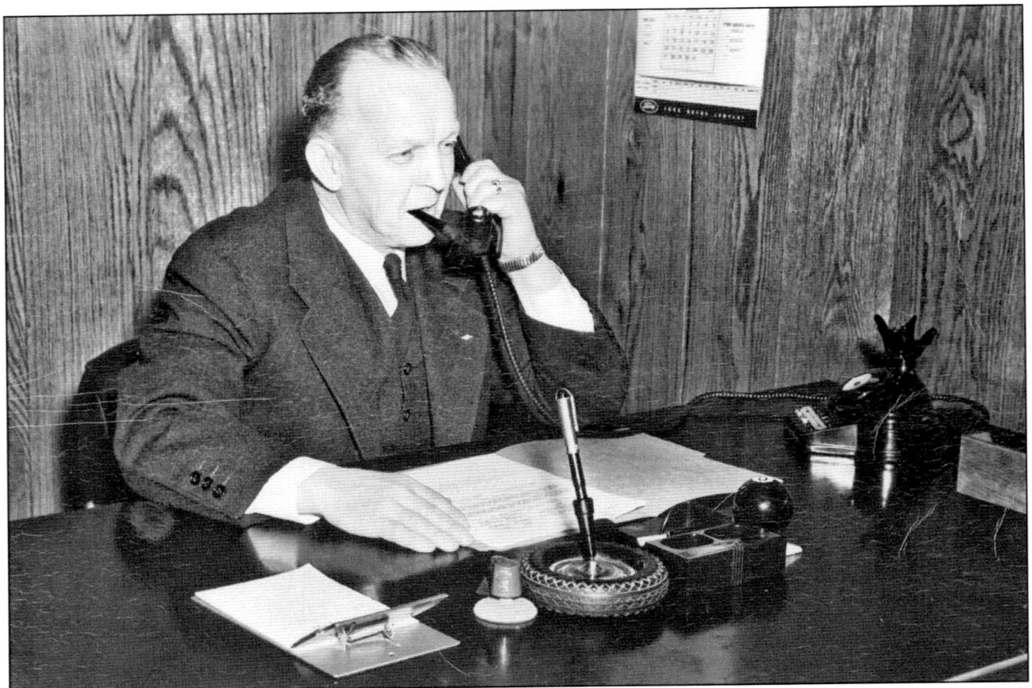

Gates W. Kidd, shown here *c.* 1947, came to the area in 1938 from Milwaukee to buy half interest in Kraft Motors of Kingsport. He met W.C. Adams, owner of Tennessee Motor Company and Royal Crown Bottlers, while he was staying at the John Sevier Hotel. Adams gave Kidd a good deal, so he purchased Tennessee Motor Company instead. (Courtesy of Bruce and Mildred Kidd.)

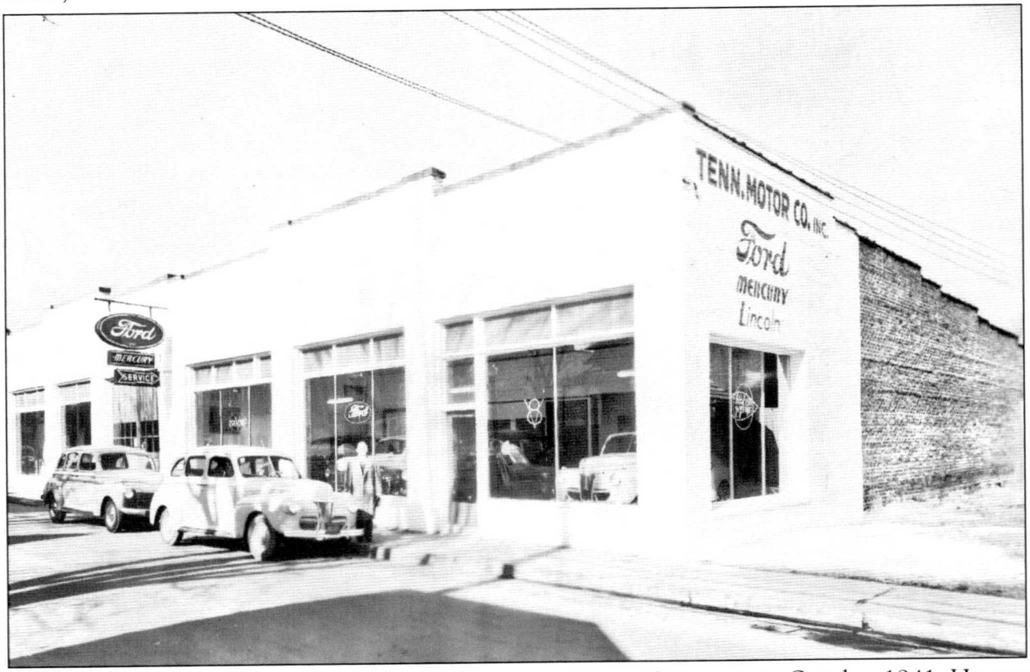

Gates W. Kidd, owner, stands outside the Tennessee Motor Company in October 1941. He was president and owner from 1938 until 1961. (Courtesy of Bruce and Mildred Kidd.)

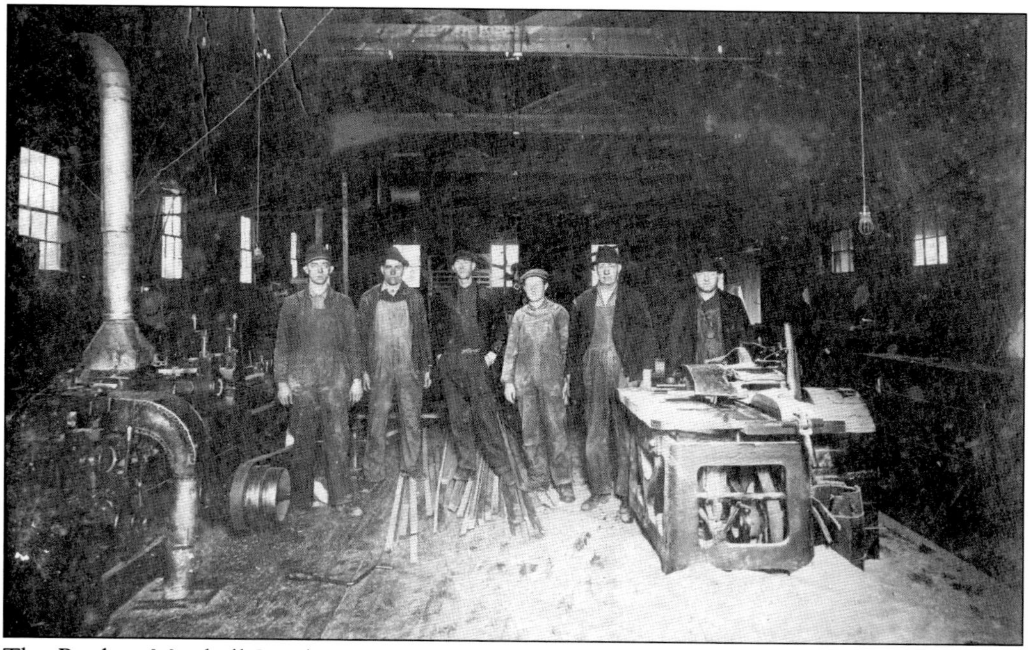

The Brading-Marshall Lumber Company began business in 1904. The company, located on Legion Street, produced a wide range of lumber and building products. Among the workers pictured here are John W. Rice, Mr. Pritchard, and Bill McClellan, *c.* 1920. (Courtesy of Earl Rice.)

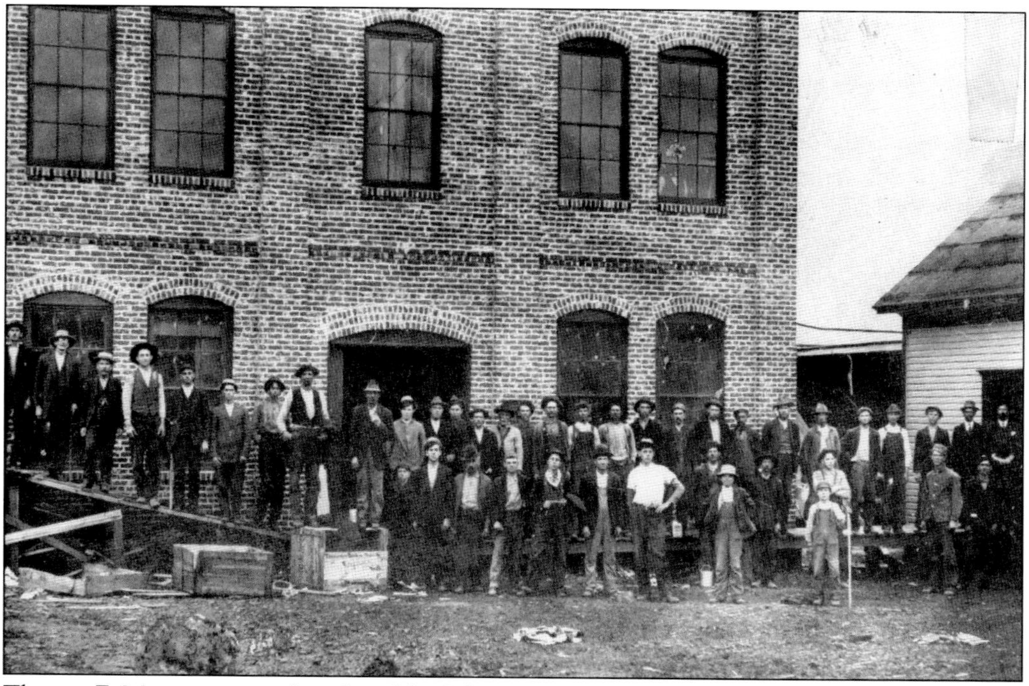

Thomas E. Matson was co-founder of the Johnson City Foundry and Machine Works, which was originally established as the Miller and Crumley Foundry and is Johnson City's oldest industry. This photograph of workers outside the foundry was probably taken in the late 1800s. (Courtesy of John G. and Etta Love.)

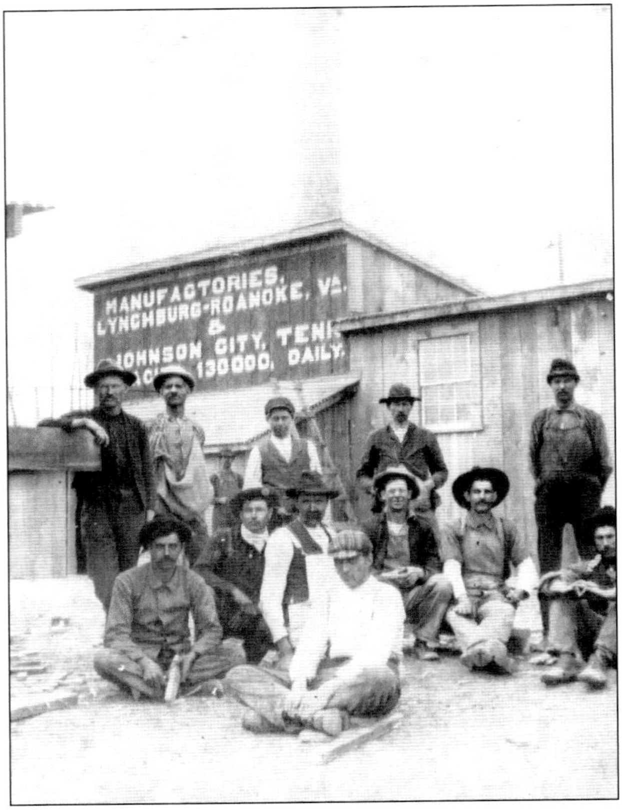

Workers from the Johnson City Foundry and Machine Works, established in 1883, stop working to pose for this picture. The foundry was the first industry to receive the Army-Navy "E" award for excellence in November 1943 when they operated at 95 percent during World War II, producing products for defense usage. (Courtesy of John G. and Etta Love.)

The Johnson City Foundry & Machine Works, Inc. built bridges, tanks, iron work, and steel plate work, among other things. Shown here is an end of the foundry building with their sign advertising, "iron or steel, draw a picture of it, we'll build it." (Courtesy of Doug Thompson.)

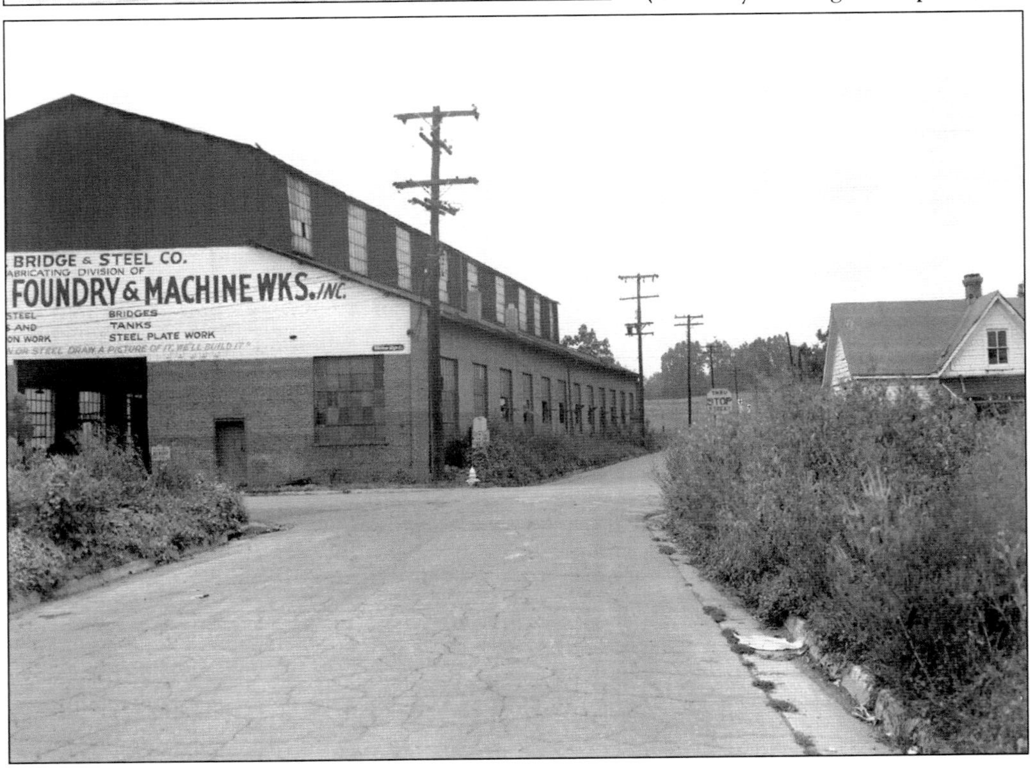

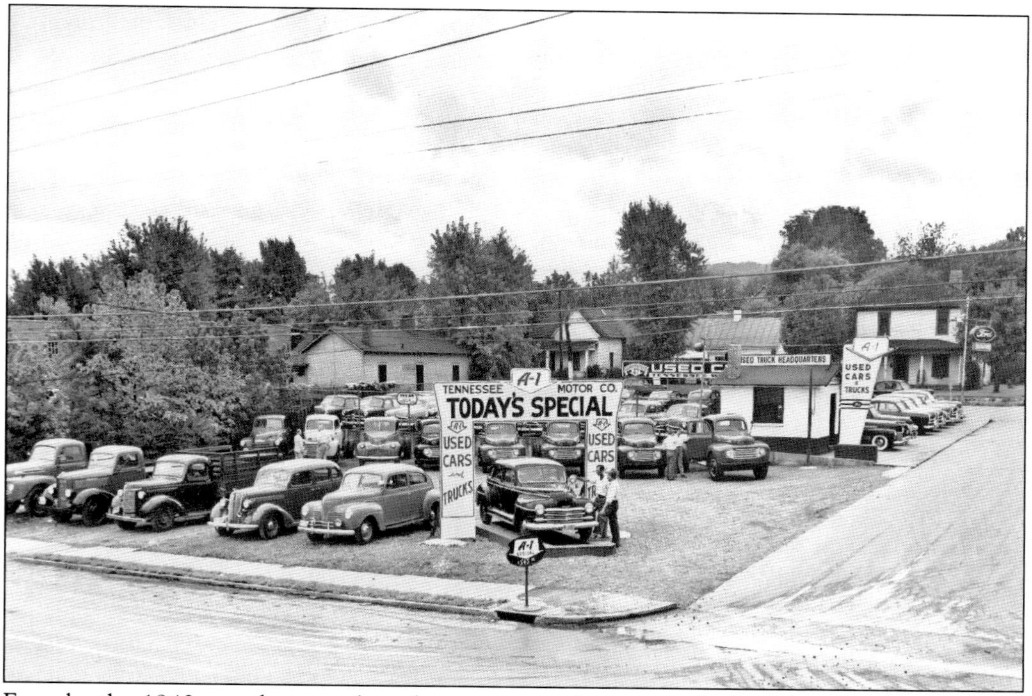

Even by the 1940s, used cars and trucks were a popular option. In this photograph, Tennessee Motor Company's A-1 special was $545. (Courtesy of Bruce and Mildred Kidd.)

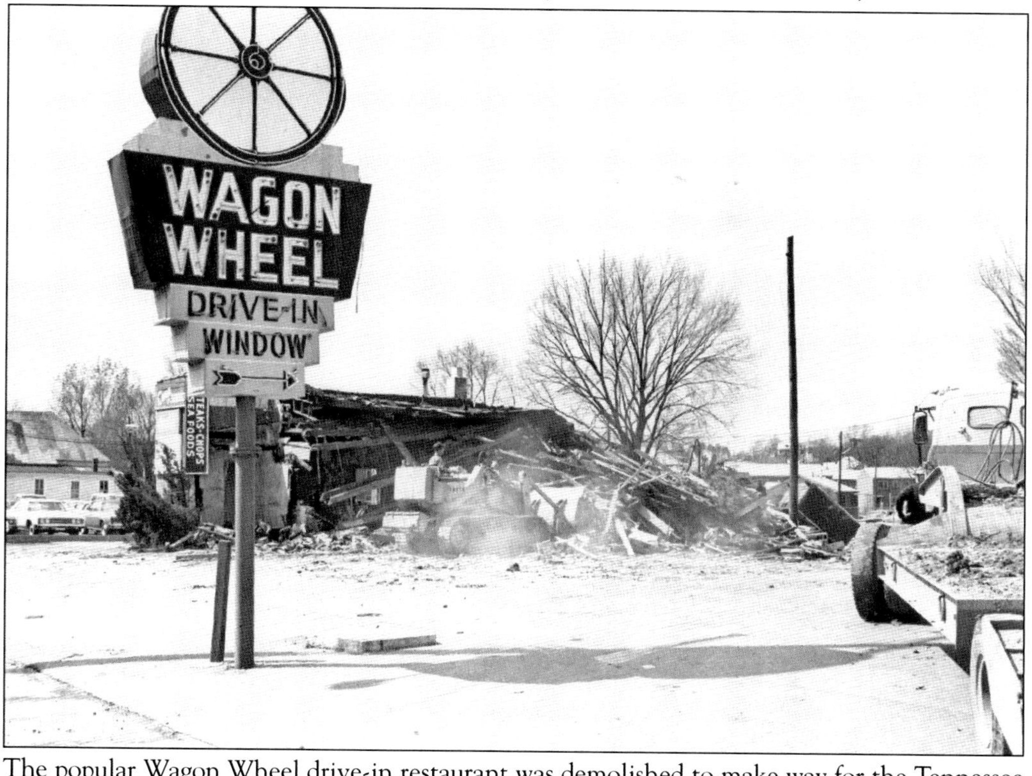

The popular Wagon Wheel drive-in restaurant was demolished to make way for the Tennessee Motor Company on Market Street. (Courtesy of Bruce and Mildred Kidd.)

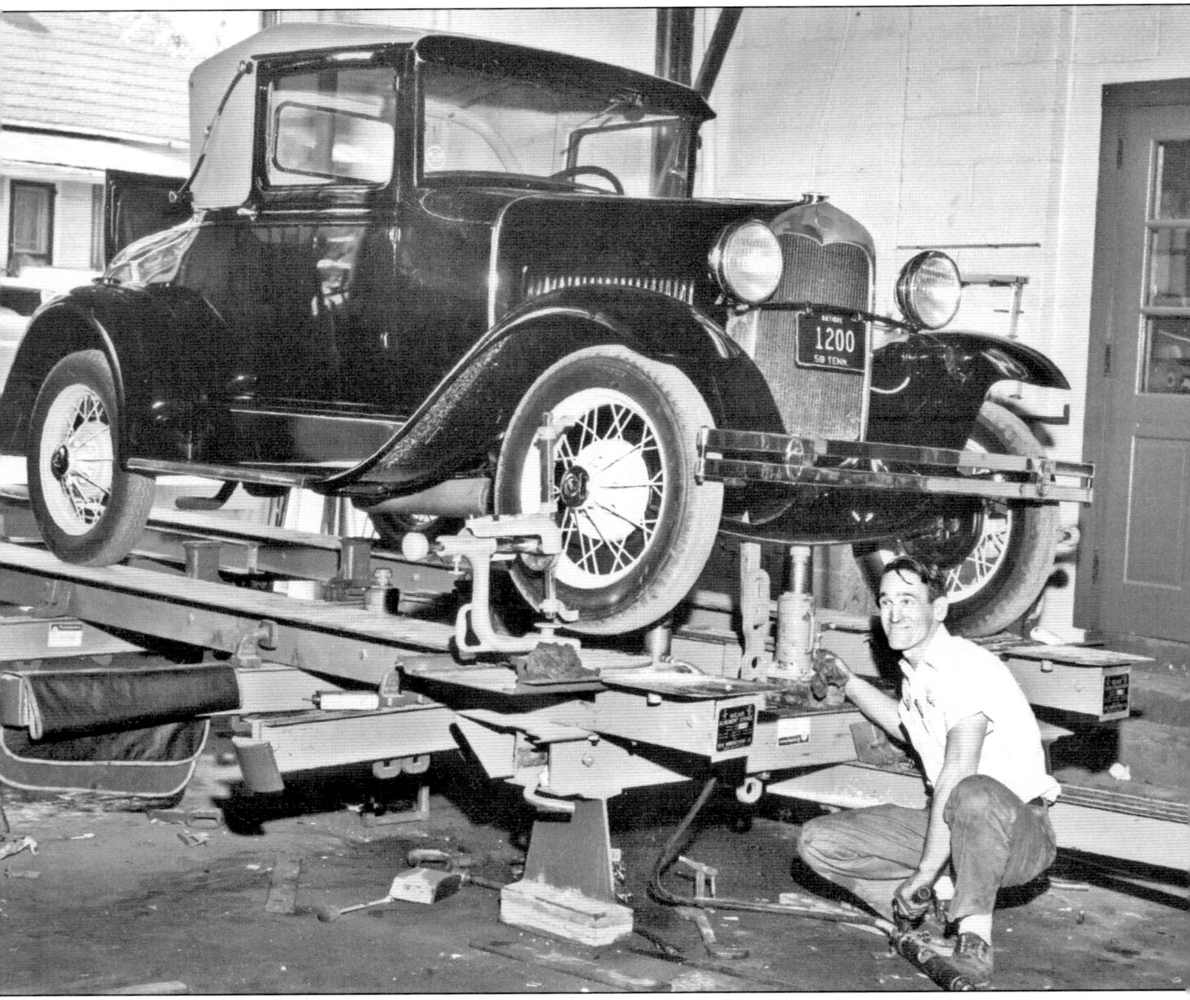

In the early days of automobiles, many people thought men who bought the "horseless carriages" should go back to the four-legged mode of transportation. Nonetheless, when Henry Ford introduced the Model T in 1908 and the moving assembly line in 1913, the future of the automobile was secure. Pictured here in 1958, an unidentified mechanic at the Tennessee Motor Company is working on a much earlier model Ford. (Courtesy of Bruce and Mildred Kidd.)

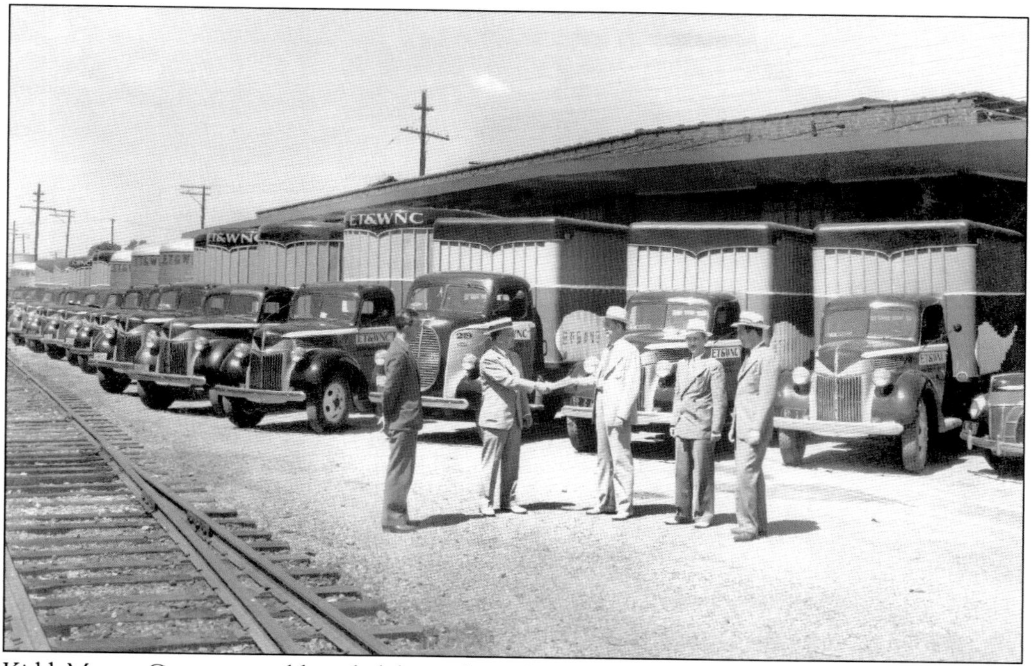

Kidd Motor Company sold and delivered trucks to the East Tennessee & Western North Carolina (ET & WNC) Transportation Company. New delivery trucks are being presented to the company in this photograph. (Courtesy of Bruce and Mildred Kidd.)

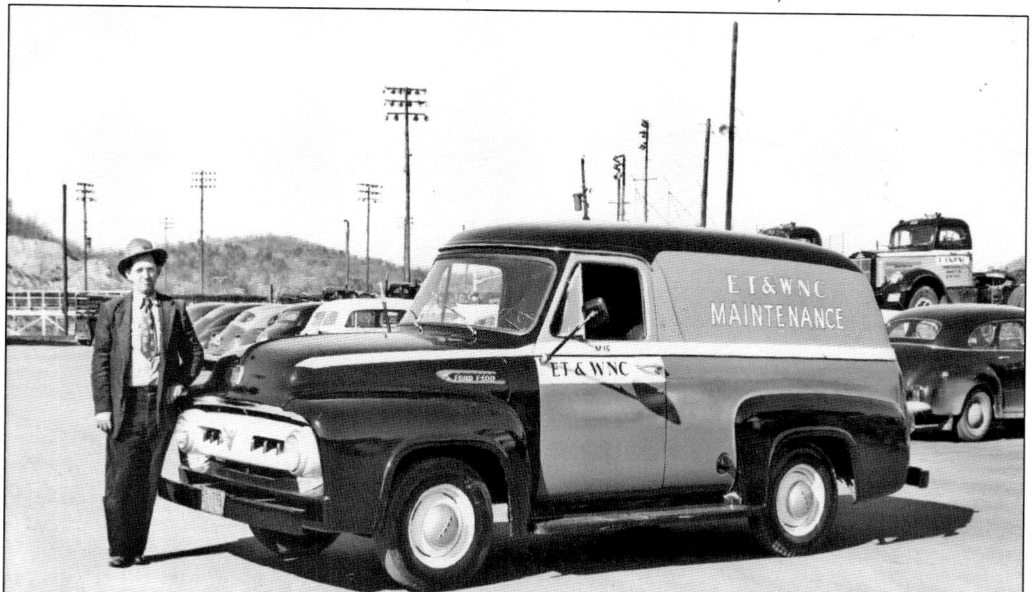

A representative from the Tennessee Motor Company is shown here delivering a new maintenance truck to the ET & WNC railroad c. 1953. The ET & WNC, the second railroad in the Washington County, was charted in May 1866. One of the main purposes was to capitalize on transporting coal, asphalt, cordwood, iron ore, and other materials through the mountains. (Courtesy of Bruce and Mildred Kidd.)

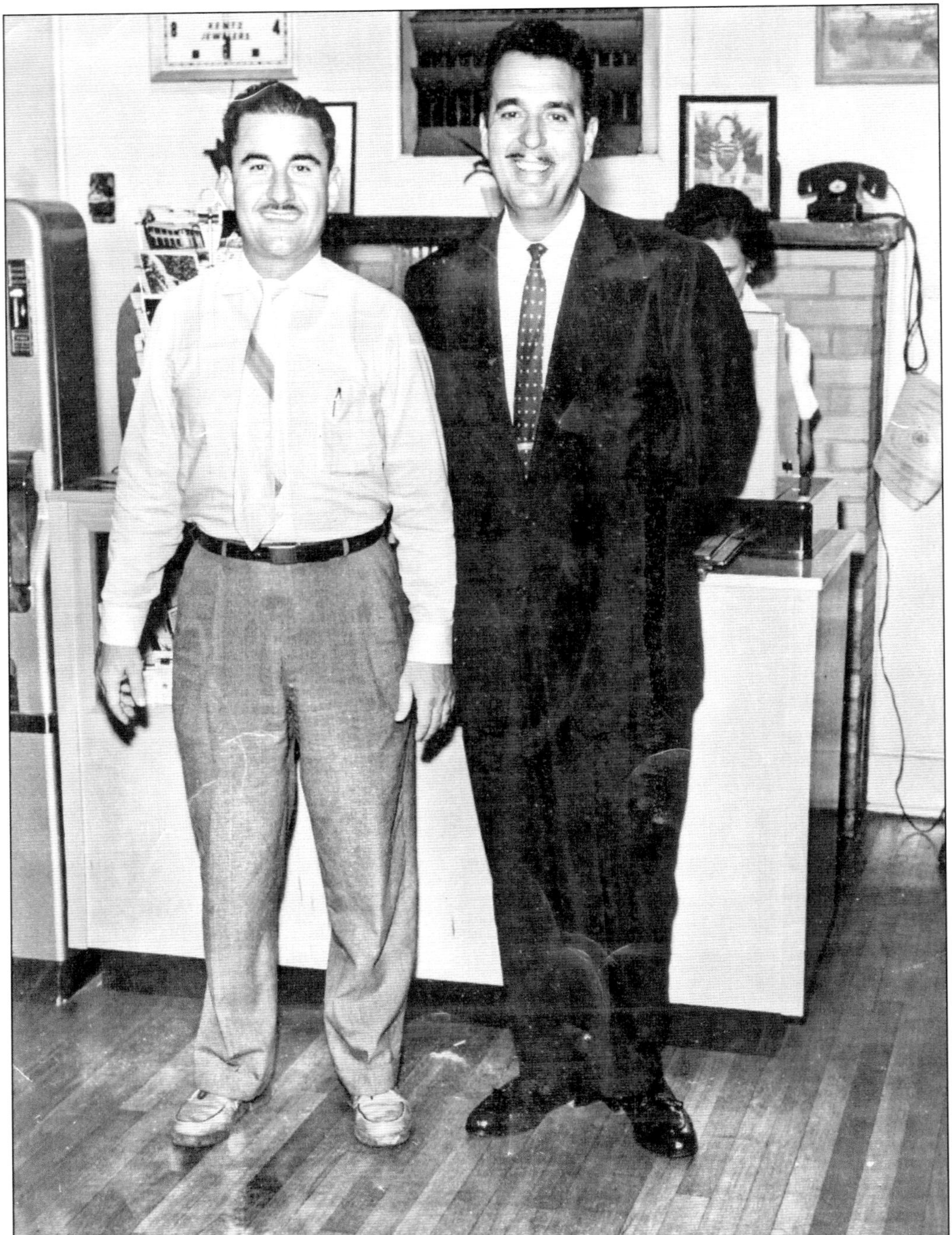

Peerless owner Jim Kalogeros (left) poses with singer Tennessee Ernie Ford in this c. 1950 photo. Over the years, the Kalogeros family and Peerless staff have hosted numerous well-known patrons, including governors, senators, movie stars, rock stars, and racecar drivers. (Courtesy of Jim Kalogeros.)

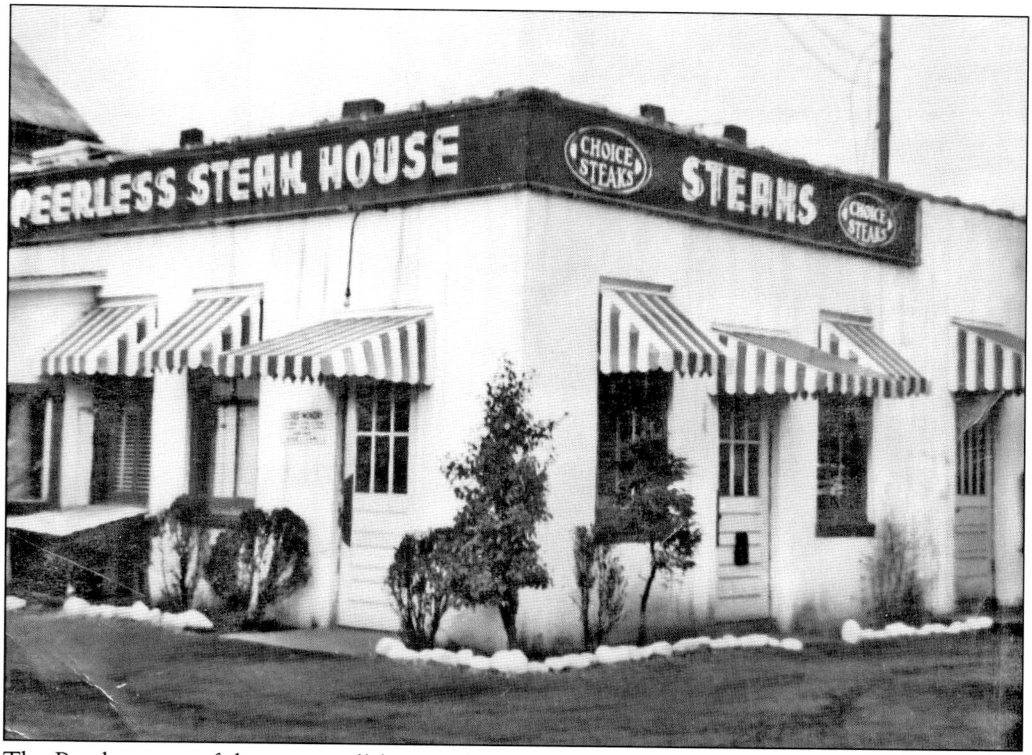

The Peerless, one of the most well-known fine-dining establishments in the Tri-Cities area, was captured in this 1938 photo. The restaurant opened as a barbeque stand at 321 West Market Street. (Courtesy of Jim Kalogeros.)

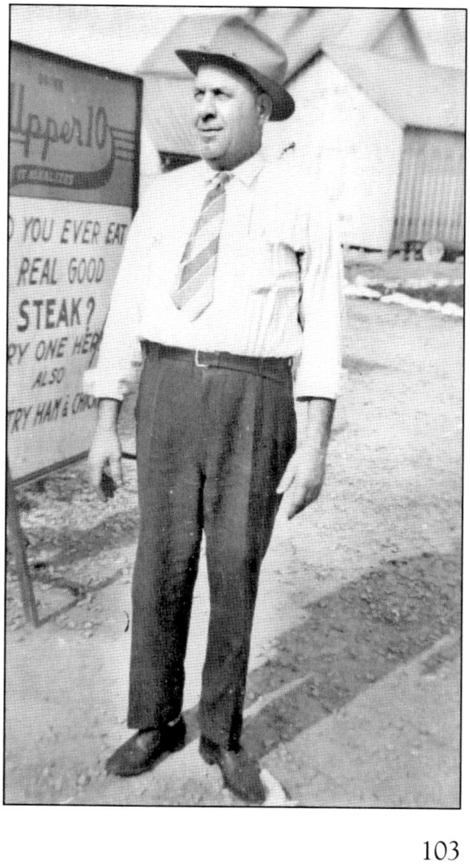

John Kalogeros changed the Peerless over to a steak restaurant in 1939, and the establishment became famous for its Grecian salad. John died in 1947 of a heart attack. His son, Jim, is now owner and continues the tradition of fine food dining. (Courtesy of Jim Kalogeros.)

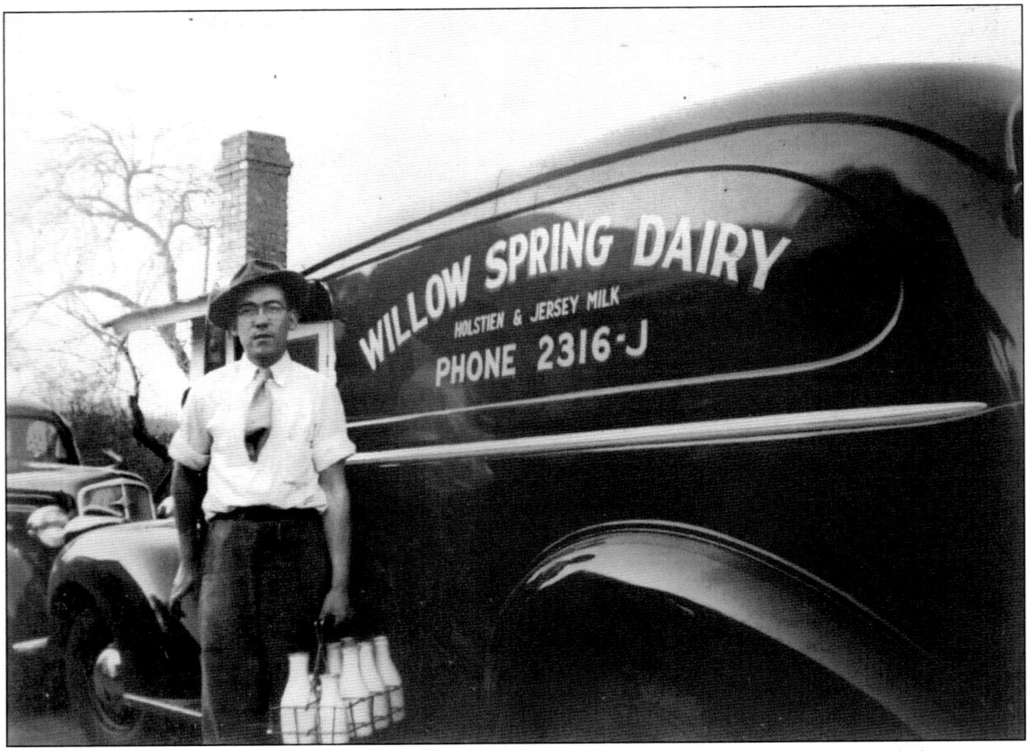

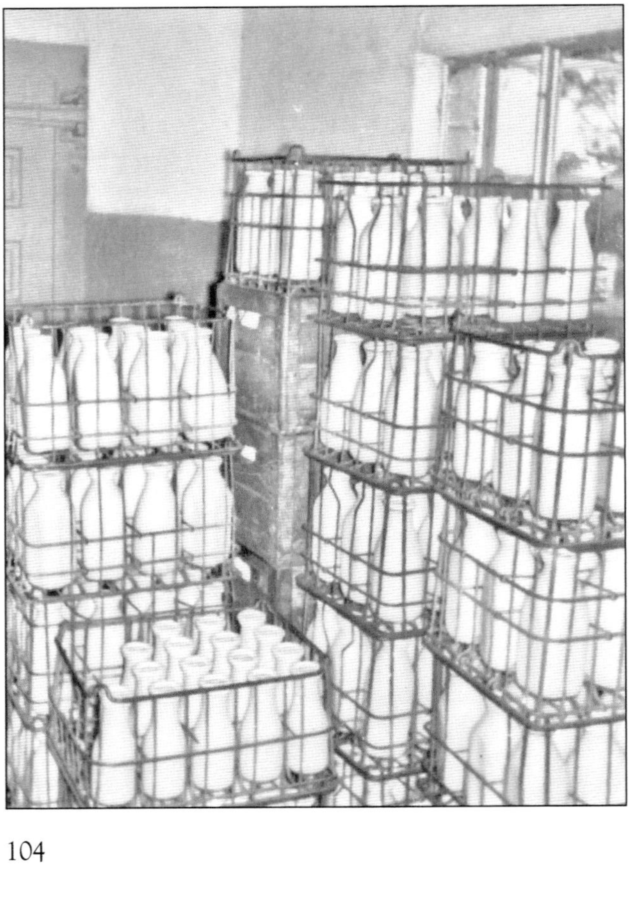

Millard Wilson started the Willow Springs Dairy in 1918 as a horse-and-buggy business. His son Robert N. Wilson took over the business around 1940 and continued delivering bottled raw milk until 1956, when a law was passed requiring pasteurization. Robert stopped home delivery c. 1965. William E. Wilson took over the business in 1977 and continued bulk processing until 1988. (Courtesy of William E. Wilson.)

Millard Wilson delivered bottles of raw milk to patrons throughout Johnson City in the early 1900s. An aerial photograph of the farm can be seen on page four. There are only a few acres remaining of the farm today, as most of it has been sold off for the use of developers. A small portion has been retained as grazing land for beef cattle. (Courtesy of William E. Wilson.)

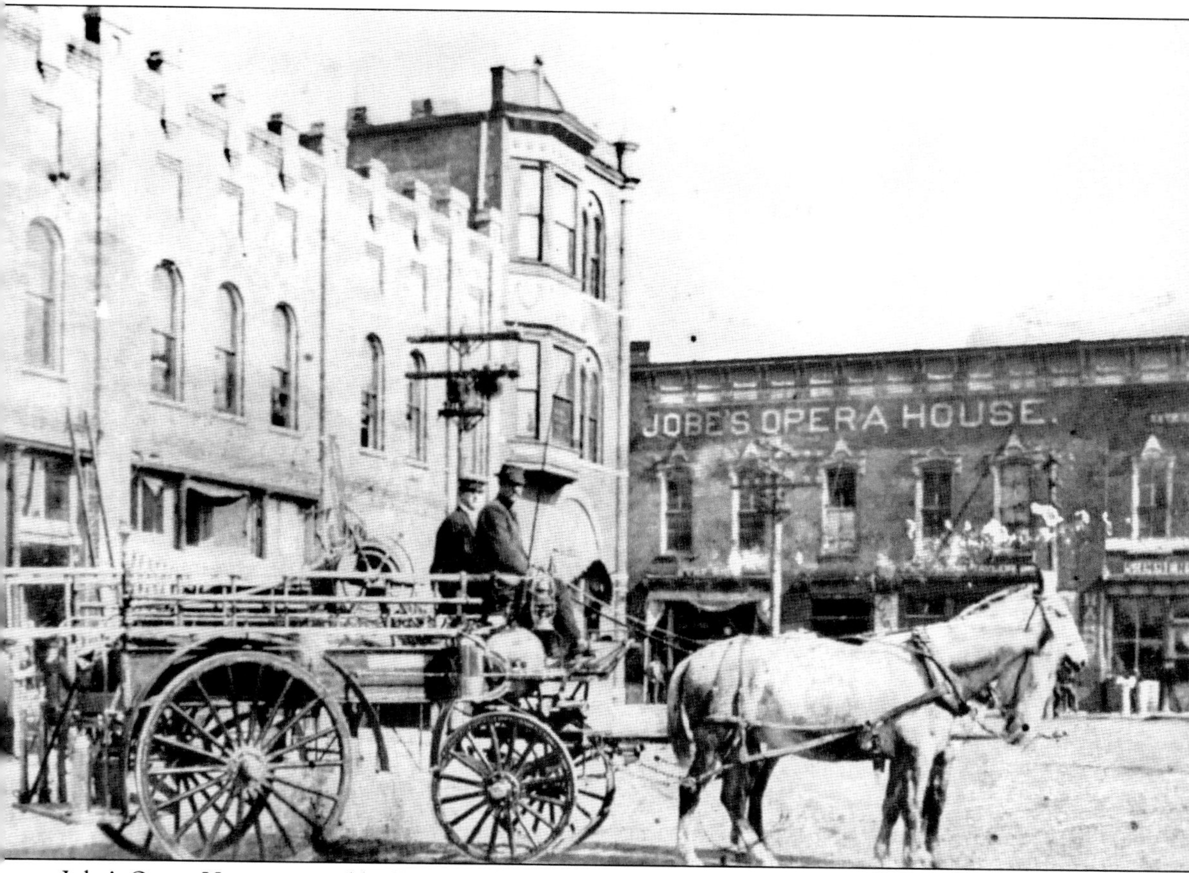

Jobe's Opera House, owned by Tipton Jobe, was a popular Johnson City site from 1884 to 1905, when it was torn down. In the foreground is an 1890 horse-drawn fire wagon, a fine example of early firefighting equipment. In addition to constructing the opera house, Jobe donated the land on the corner of Roan and Water Streets for the location of what would become Science Hill High School. He also donated land to the Georgia Railroad Company for the construction of a Johnson City depot. (Courtesy of Rocky Mount Historical Association.)

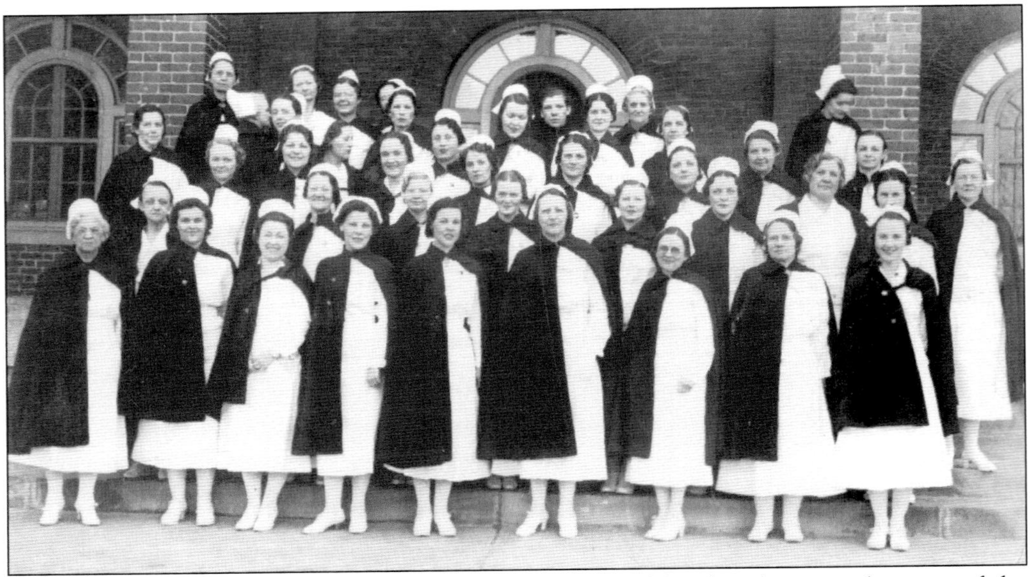

The nurses of the Veterans Administration Hospital posed for this photo on the steps of the nurses' home c. 1936. The sixth nurse from left in the front row is superintendent Marie Glauber. (Courtesy of Glady and Cindy Landreth.)

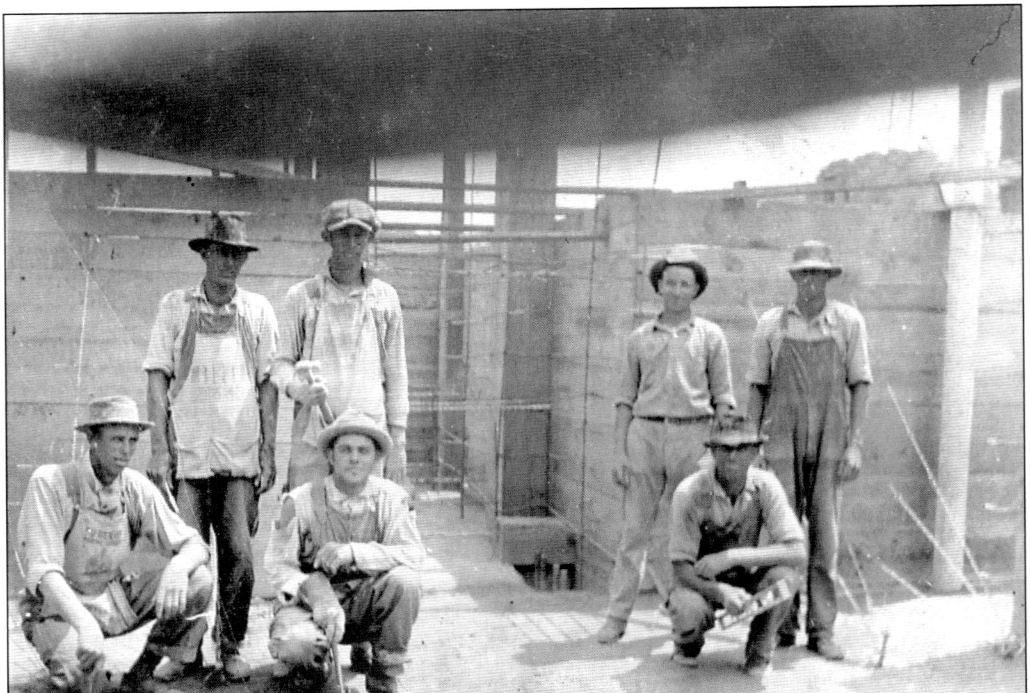

Holding hatchets, hammers, and levels, these construction workers are ready to build. One of the aprons says "Miller Brothers." The man second from the left on the front row is Ralph Eugene Scott Sr. of Route 1, Johnson City. (Courtesy of Elaine Cantrell.)

Gladys Whitt and Verna Walker were two of the many nurses who cared for "Babb," whose mother died during childbirth in 1932. The nurses raised him until he was two years old, when he was adopted. The photo was taken on the steps of the Appalachian Hospital. (Courtesy of Gladys and Cindy Landreth.)

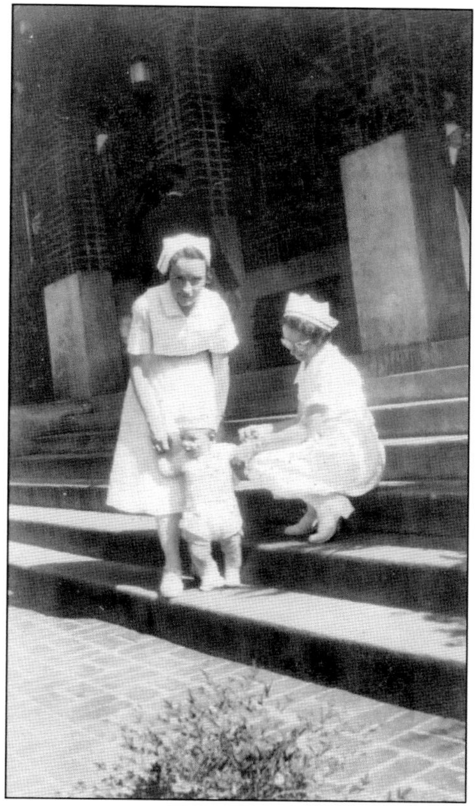

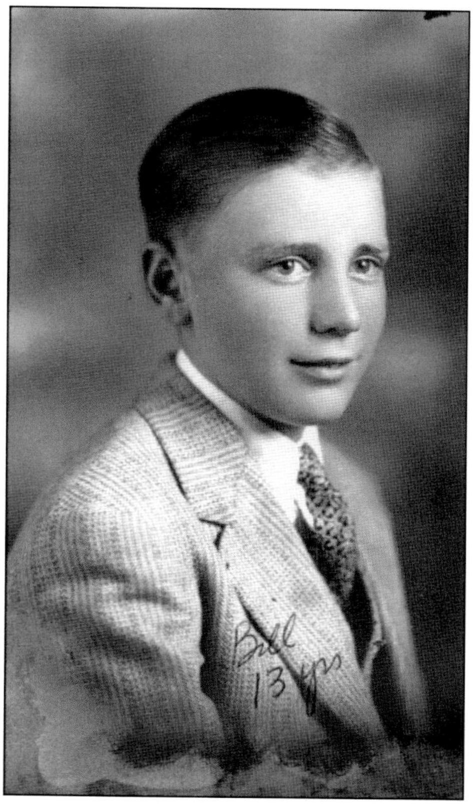

William H. Smith (June 12, 1914–June 27, 1991) graduated from Science Hill, where he played football during the undefeated 1934 season. William went to work for ET & WNC, then Summers Hardware, where he worked his way up from truck driver to vice president of sales. This photo was taken when he was 13 years old. (Courtesy of Barbara G. Smith.)

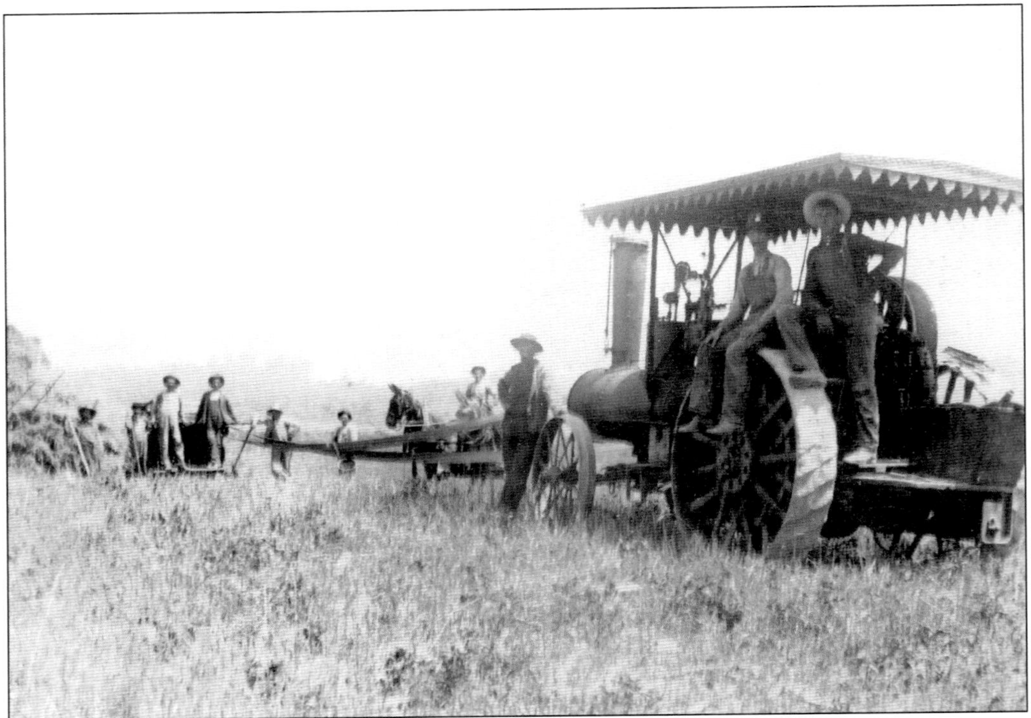

The threshing outfit of Winnam Carathers and Will Goodman was an impressive mechanism for the early 1900s, especially with Carathers's steam engine. The top photo was taken in 1909, the bottom photo in 1910 at Carathers's farm in Knob Creek. (Courtesy of George and Margaret Holley.)

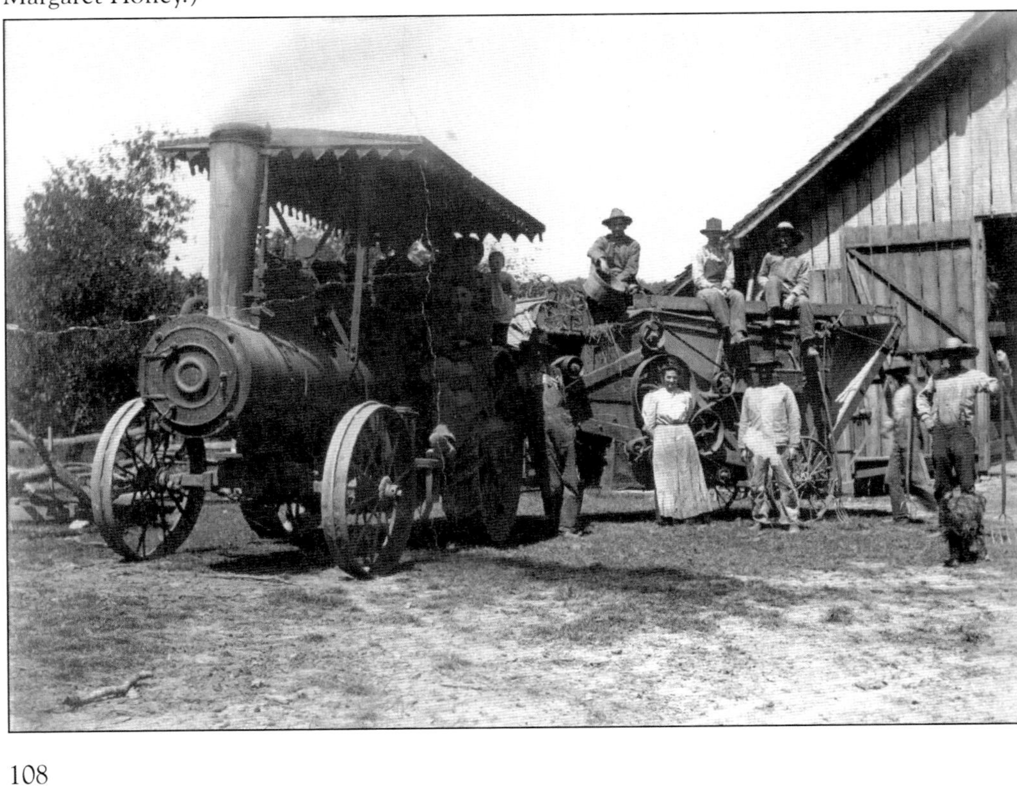

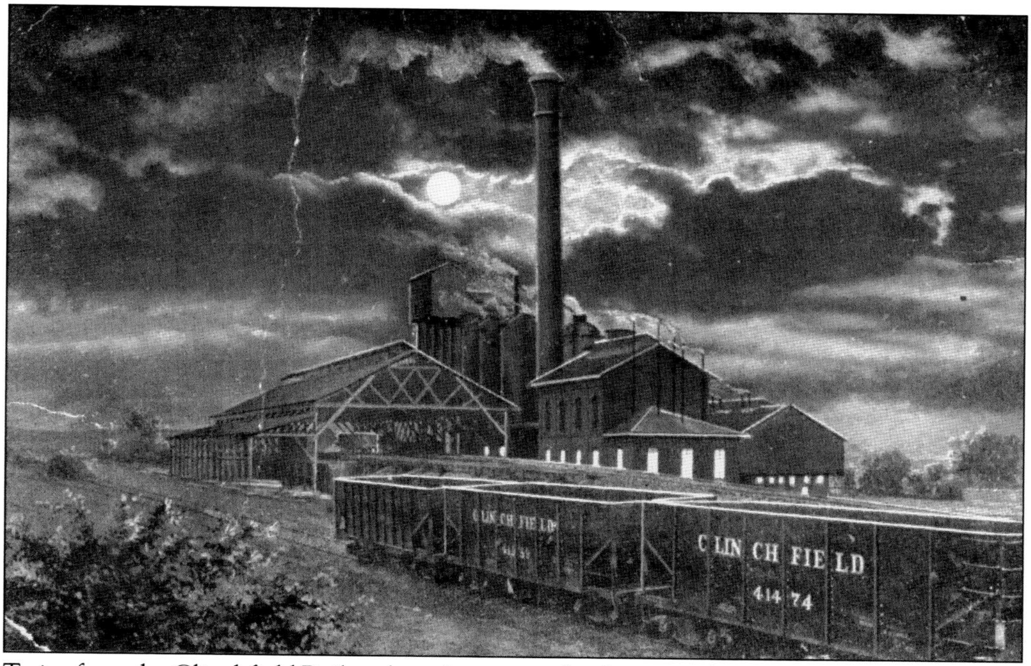

Trains from the Clinchfield Railroad can be seen in the foreground of this postcard highlighting the Cranberry Furnace at night. The railroad line to Cranberry was completed in 1882, and the Cranberry Furnace was built sometime after that in the Carnegie section of Johnson City. Workers at the furnace processed iron ore brought from Cranberry, North Carolina. The furnace closed in 1929. (Courtesy of Betty Jane Hylton.)

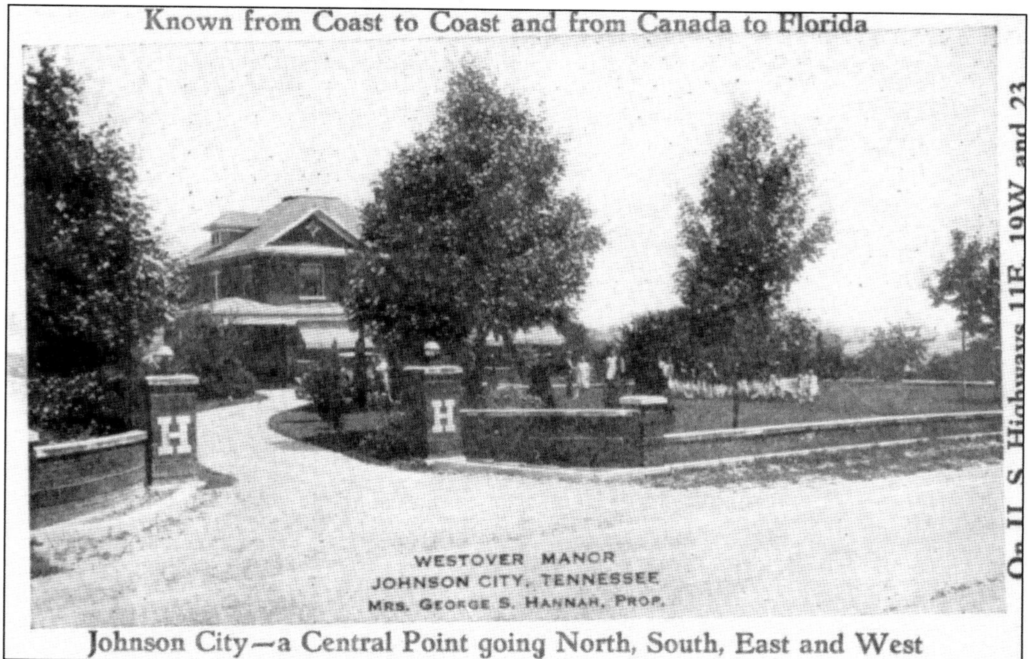

A postcard of Westover Manor boasts of Johnson City as a "central point going north, south, east and west." Mrs. George S. Hannah was the proprietor of Westover Manor. (Courtesy of Betty Jane Hylton.)

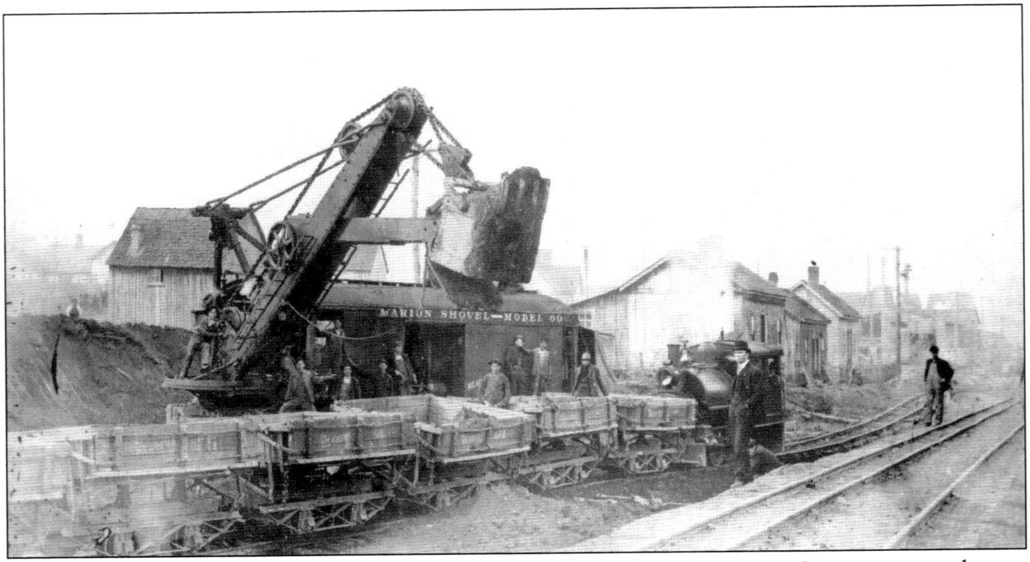

Residents ultimately rejected a proposal to change Johnson City's name to Carnegie in exchange for a $100,000 public library and a large steel mill that had been offered by Andrew Carnegie. A Carnegie community did arise, however, as John Thomas Wilder planned the development of the Carnegie area where this railroad depot was photographed, probably just before the financial depression of 1883. (Courtesy of Elaine Cantrell.)

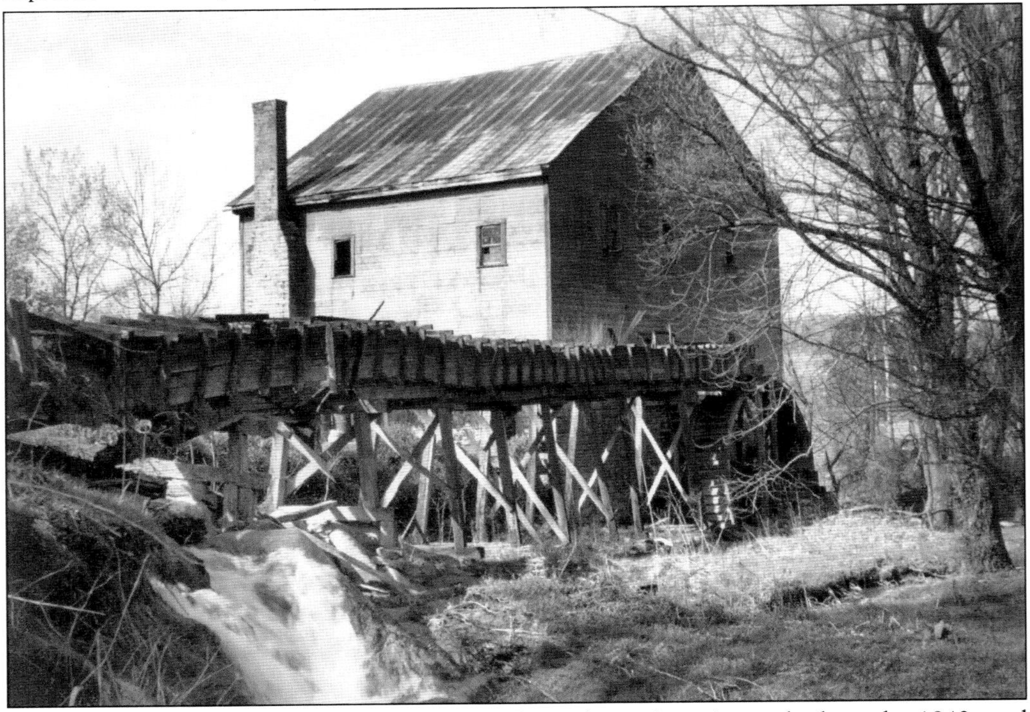

The Henry Bashor Mill, located on Denny Mill Road near Lowe's, was built in the 1840s and went into operation in 1848. Henry Bashor married Elizabeth Bowman, daughter of deacon Joseph Bowman of Knob Creek. When the mill ceased operation in 1952, the last two millers were Robert L. Denny and Niles Hodge. This photograph was taken by Frank Tannewitz in the early 1950s. (Courtesy of George and Margaret Holley.)

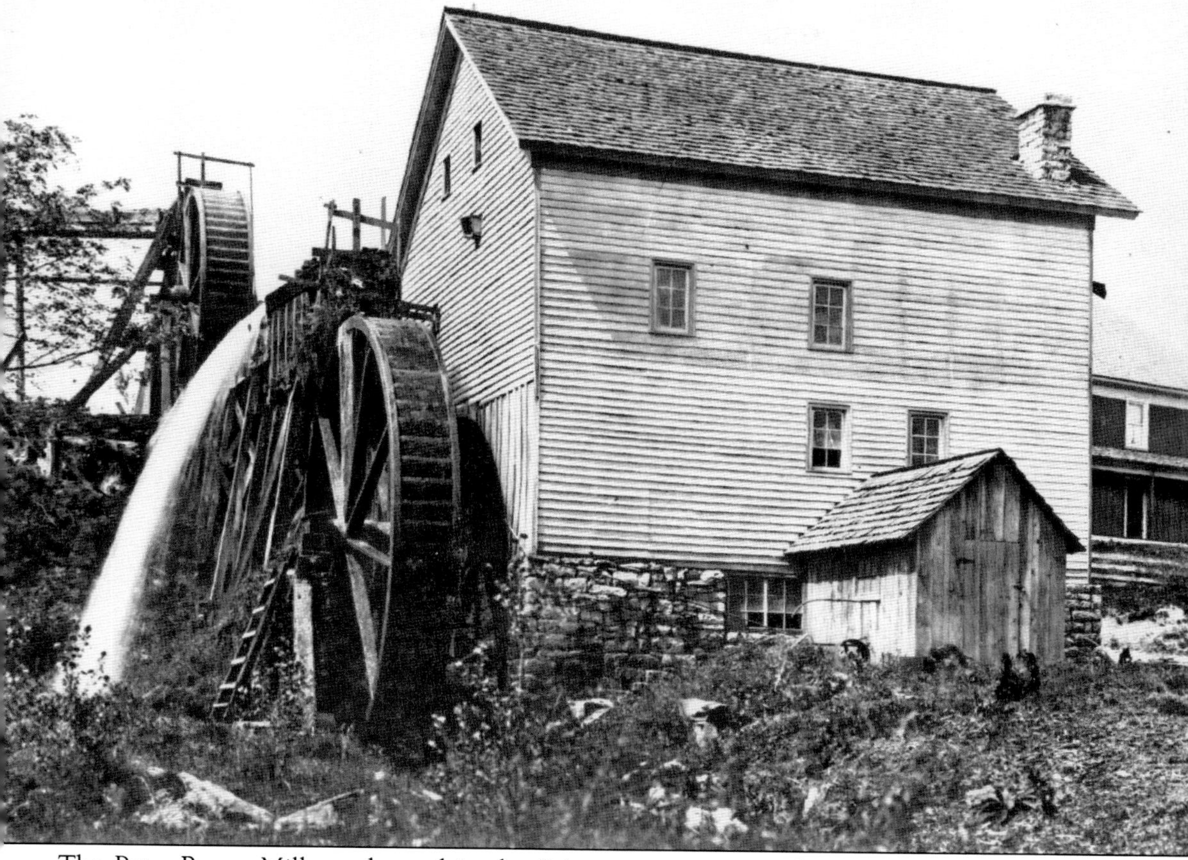

The Peter Range Mill was located in the Princeton community that is now East Oakland Avenue. The mill later served as a slaughter house for Morton Brothers Packing Company. Peter Range's home on Oakland Avenue was built in the late 1700s. (Courtesy of George and Margaret Holley.)

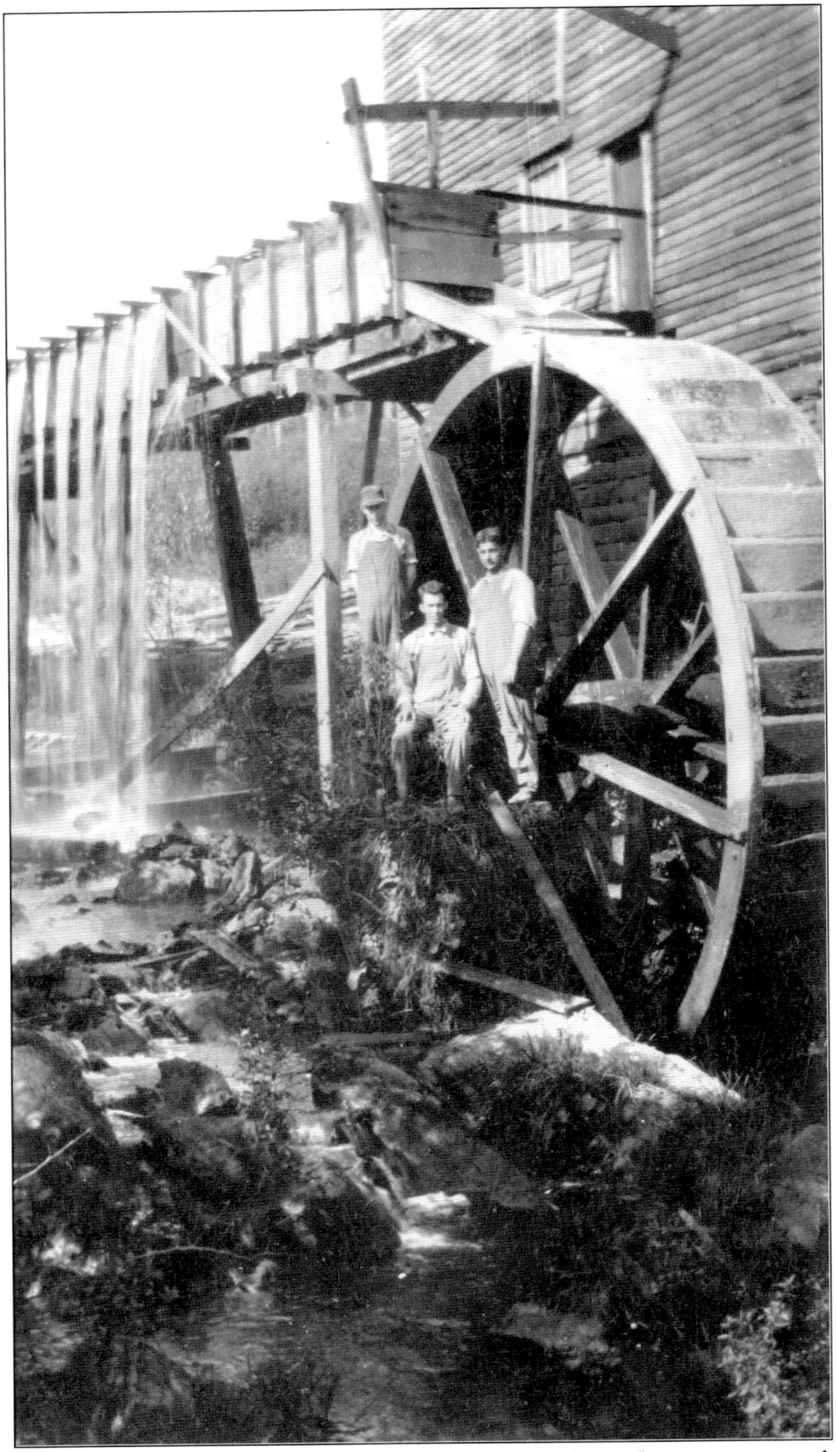

This is the wooden water wheel of the Henry Bashor Mill and overflowing water in the forebay on Knob Creek. Henry and Homer Sells owned and ran the mill for numerous years until Henry died and Homer became ill in the 1920s. Pictured here at the mill, from left to right, are unidentified, Homer Sells, and John Sherfey. (Courtesy of George and Margaret Holley.)

Eight

MILITARY

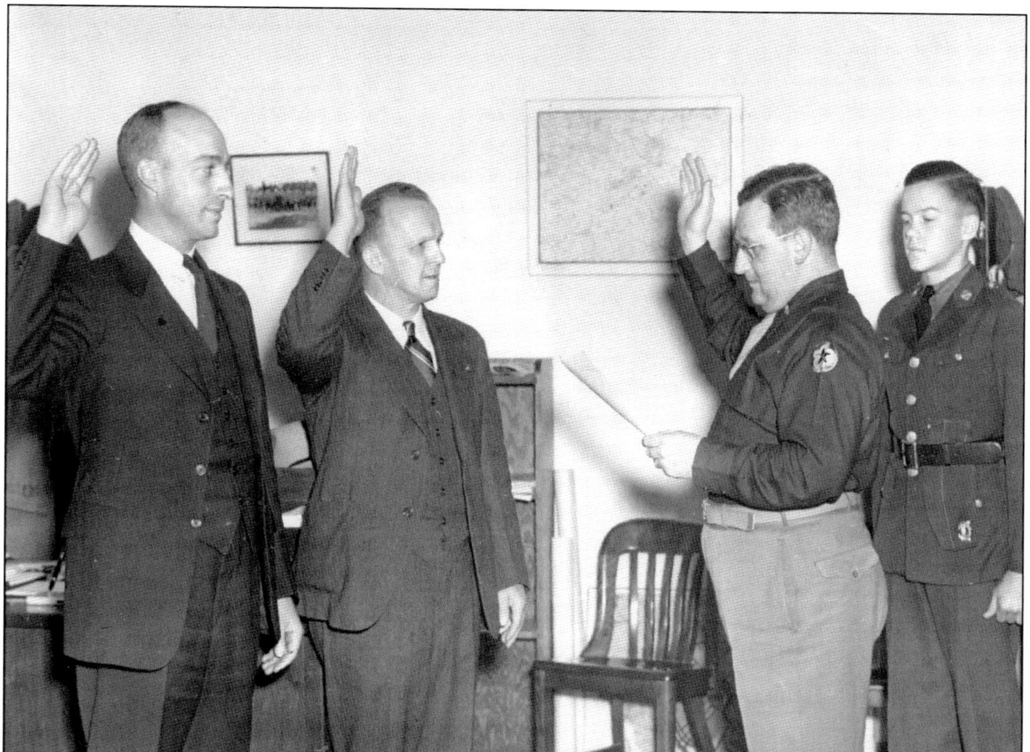

Gates Warriner Kidd, owner of Tennessee Motor Company, chose to join the military rather than be drafted. Present at his swearing in ceremony, from left to right, are William E. Washburn (also swearing in), Gates W. Kidd, an unidentified officer, and G. Bruce Kidd. (Courtesy of Bruce and Mildred Kidd and the *Kingsport Times News*.)

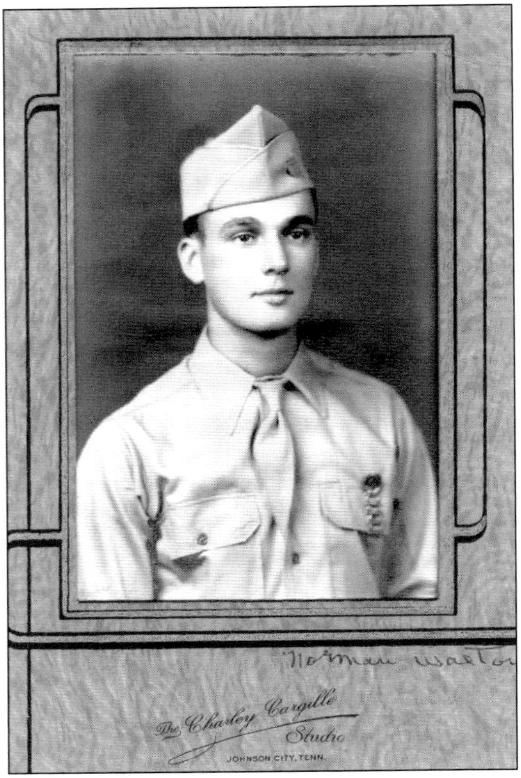

Norman K. Walters (October 8, 1925–November 9, 2003) served in World War II. He received an American Theatre Ribbon with two bronze stars, a Good Conduct Medal, and a World War II Victory Medal. Norman's parents were Dewey and Glenna Huffine Walters. (Courtesy of Elaine Cantrell.)

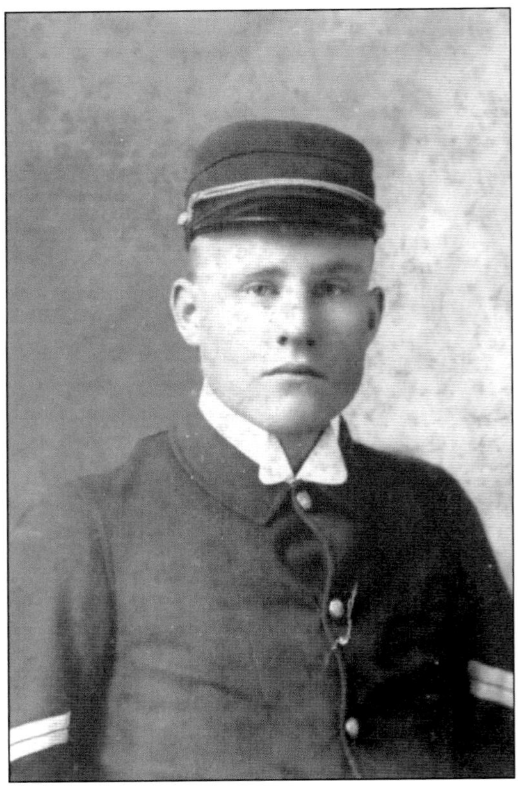

Francis Patton Bowman (October 10, 1845–September 18, 1916), of Route 1 in Johnson City in the Cherokee area, served as a soldier during the Civil War. (Courtesy of Elaine Cantrell.)

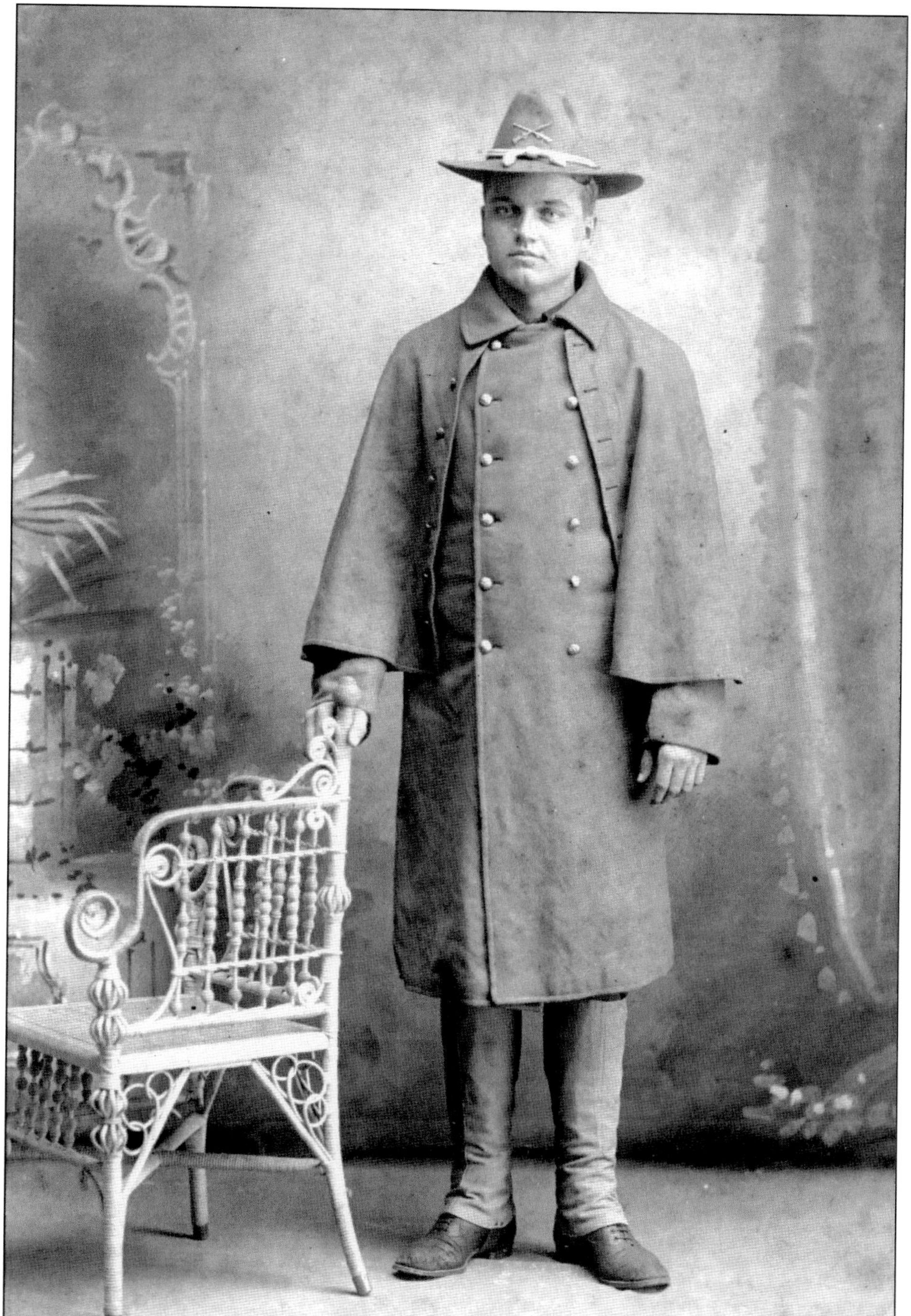

During the Civil War, Tennessee was surrounded by slave-holding states. While there were slaves in East Tennessee, most of them were domestic workers. There were also free African Americans in the area. Thus, sympathies in Johnson City went both ways. According to Ray Stahl's *Greater Johnson City: A Pictorial History*, more than 30,000 of the 45,000 men eligible served for the Union army. Here, Sam Denton poses in his Civil War uniform, which might be a Confederate uniform due to its lighter color. (Courtesy of Elaine Cantrell.)

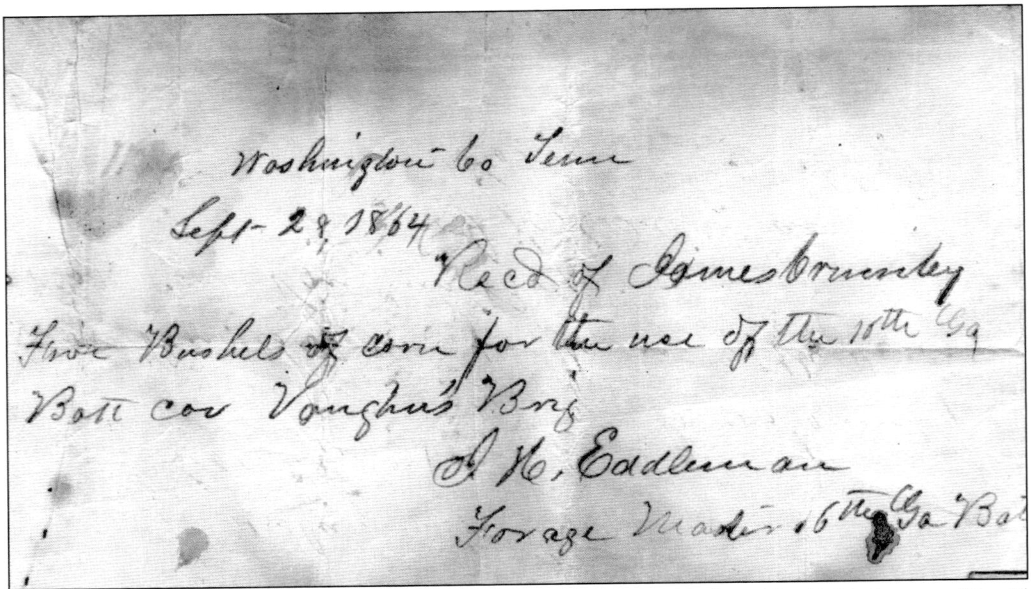

Washington Co Tenn

Sept 28 1864

Rec'd of James Crumley

Five Bushels of corn for the use of the 16th Ga

Batt cov Vaughn's Brig

J. H. Eddleman

Forage Master 16th Ga Bat

This remarkably well-preserved paper is a receipt dated September 28, 1864. It says, "Rec'd of James Crumley five bushels of corn for the use of the 16th US (?) Batt cov Vaughn's Brig." Although both Confederate and Union soldiers left these "payment vouchers," very few individuals received restitution for goods taken. (Courtesy of Don and Sarah Walters.)

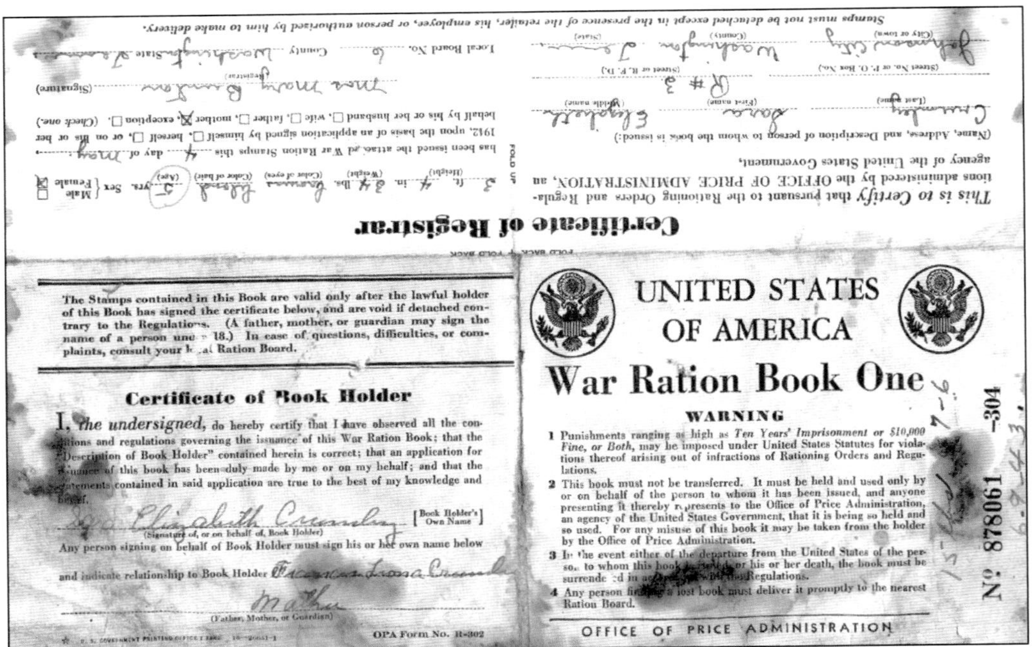

Certificate of Registrar

This is to Certify that pursuant to the Rationing Orders and Regulations administered by the OFFICE OF PRICE ADMINISTRATION, an agency of the United States Government,

The Stamps contained in this Book are valid only after the lawful holder of this Book has signed the certificate below, and are void if detached contrary to the Regulations. (A father, mother, or guardian may sign the name of a person under 18.) In case of questions, difficulties, or complaints, consult your local Ration Board.

Certificate of Book Holder

I, the undersigned, do hereby certify that I have observed all the conditions and regulations governing the issuance of this War Ration Book; that the "Description of Book Holder" contained herein is correct; that an application for issuance of this book has been duly made by me or on my behalf; and that the statements contained in said application are true to the best of my knowledge and belief.

Sara Elizabeth Crumley [Book Holder's Own Name]

(Signature of, or on behalf of, Book Holder)

Any person signing on behalf of Book Holder must sign his or her own name below and indicate relationship to Book Holder Francis Leona Crumley

Mother

(Father, Mother, or Guardian)

OPA Form No. R-302

UNITED STATES OF AMERICA

War Ration Book One

WARNING

1 Punishments ranging as high as *Ten Years' Imprisonment or $10,000 Fine, or Both,* may be imposed under United States Statutes for violations thereof arising out of infractions of Rationing Orders and Regulations.

2 This book must not be transferred. It must be held and used only by or on behalf of the person to whom it has been issued, and anyone presenting it thereby represents to the Office of Price Administration, an agency of the United States Government, that it is being so held and so used. For any misuse of this book it may be taken from the holder by the Office of Price Administration.

3 In the event either of the departure from the United States of the person to whom this book is issued, or his or her death, the book must be surrendered in accordance with the Regulations.

4 Any person finding a lost book must deliver it promptly to the nearest Ration Board.

OFFICE OF PRICE ADMINISTRATION

Nº 878061 -304

As a child, five-year-old Sarah (incorrectly spelled "Sara" on the book) Elizabeth Crumley was eligible to receive war rations. Sarah's mother, Francis Leona Crumley, was permitted to apply for and redeem the coupons on Sarah's behalf. This particular book of rations was received May 4, 1942. (Courtesy of Don and Sarah Walters.)

Nine

COMMUNITY

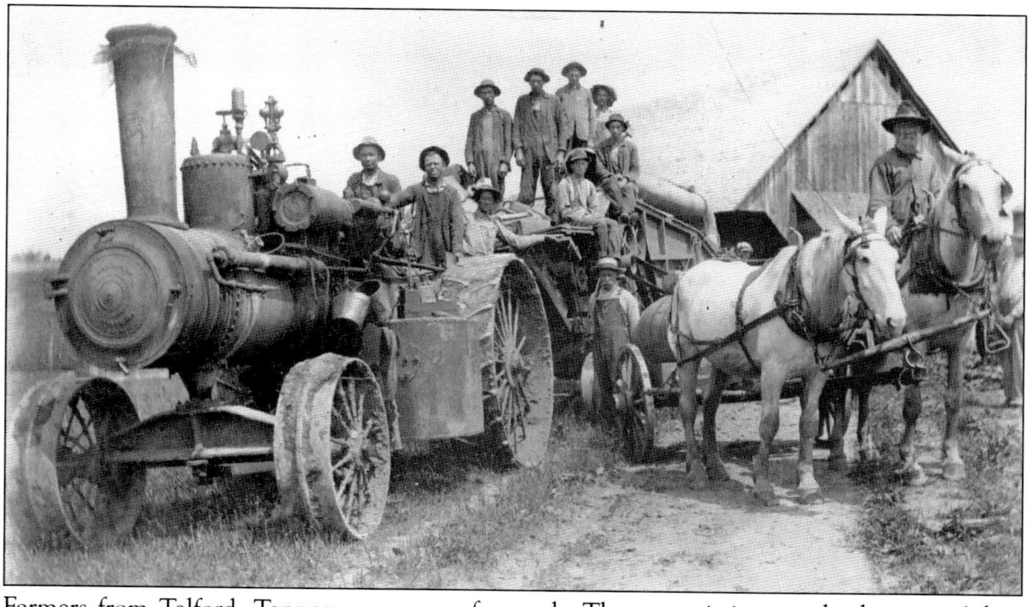

Farmers from Telford, Tennessee, prepare for work. The man sitting on the horse is Adam McCracken, who was born November 2, 1850, and died January 28, 1914. The photo was probably taken shortly before his death. Adam's sons are on the tractor, and the other men came to help during the threshing season. (Courtesy of Betty Jane Hylton.)

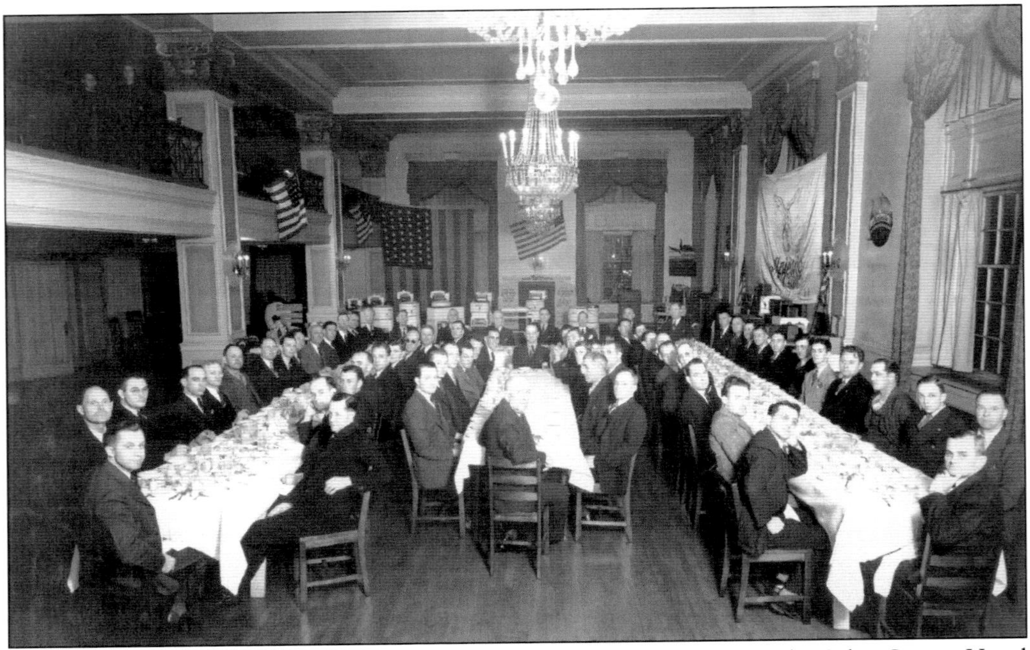

A meeting of the Majestic Radio and Meadows Washer was held at the John Sevier Hotel ballroom on Friday night, March 8, 1940. The flag in the background only holds 46 stars. An enlargement of the photo also reveals advertisements for the washers with "a more economical wash dry," "famous 'controlled' water action," and an "exclusive safe and convenient wringer." (Courtesy of Julia Wade.)

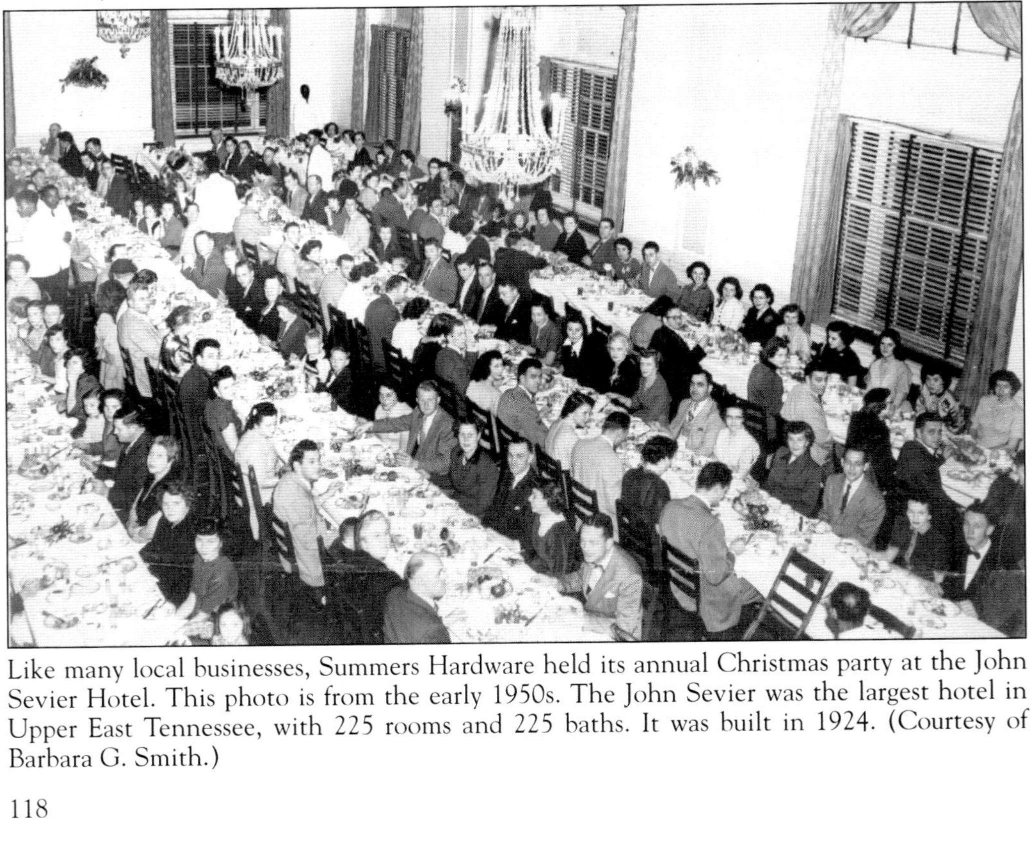

Like many local businesses, Summers Hardware held its annual Christmas party at the John Sevier Hotel. This photo is from the early 1950s. The John Sevier was the largest hotel in Upper East Tennessee, with 225 rooms and 225 baths. It was built in 1924. (Courtesy of Barbara G. Smith.)

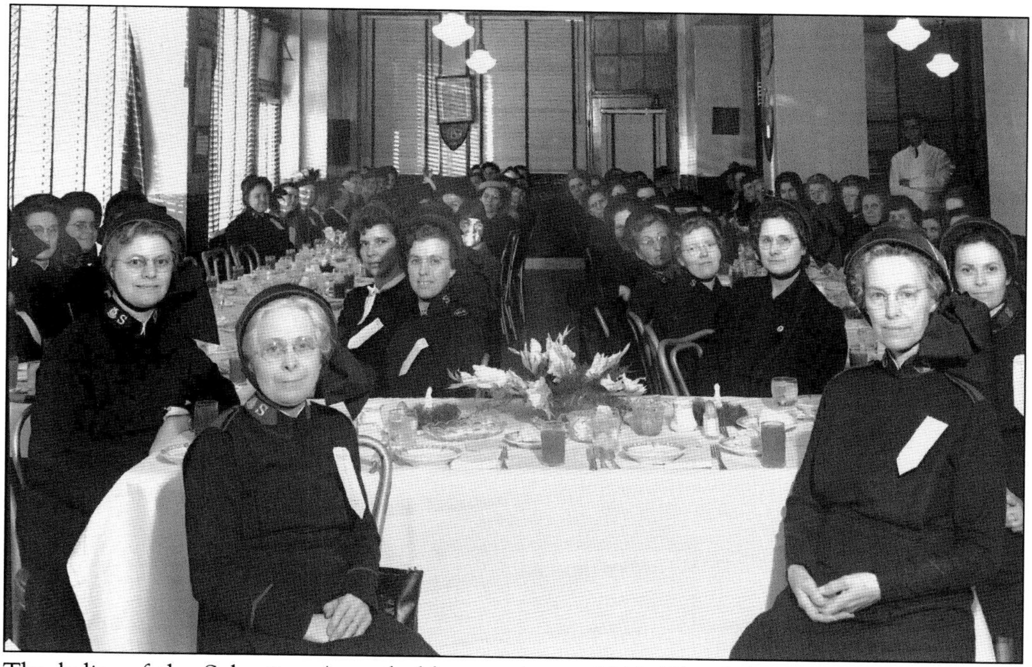

The ladies of the Salvation Army hold a meeting *c.* 1940. The Salvation Army was started in 1865 by William Booth, who wanted to minister to people not being welcomed by the established church. The group began work in Tennessee in 1890, with its mission being to lead people to Christ and to serve people in Christ with food, shelter, and clothing. (Courtesy of Doug Thompson.)

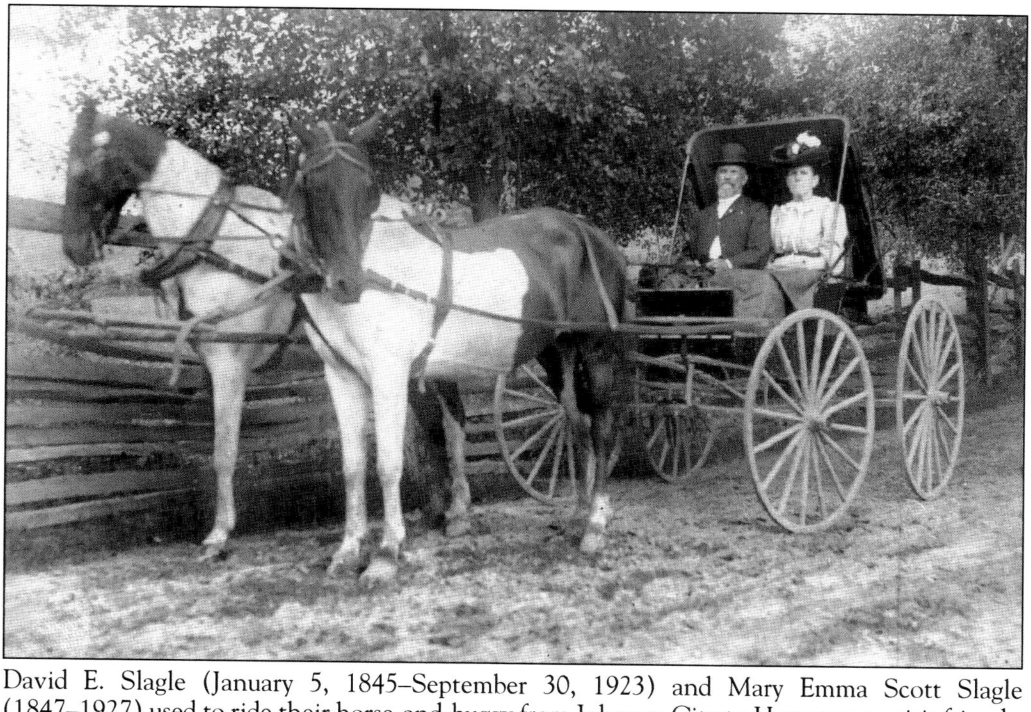

David E. Slagle (January 5, 1845–September 30, 1923) and Mary Emma Scott Slagle (1847–1927) used to ride their horse-and-buggy from Johnson City to Hampton to visit friends. (Courtesy of Elaine Cantrell.)

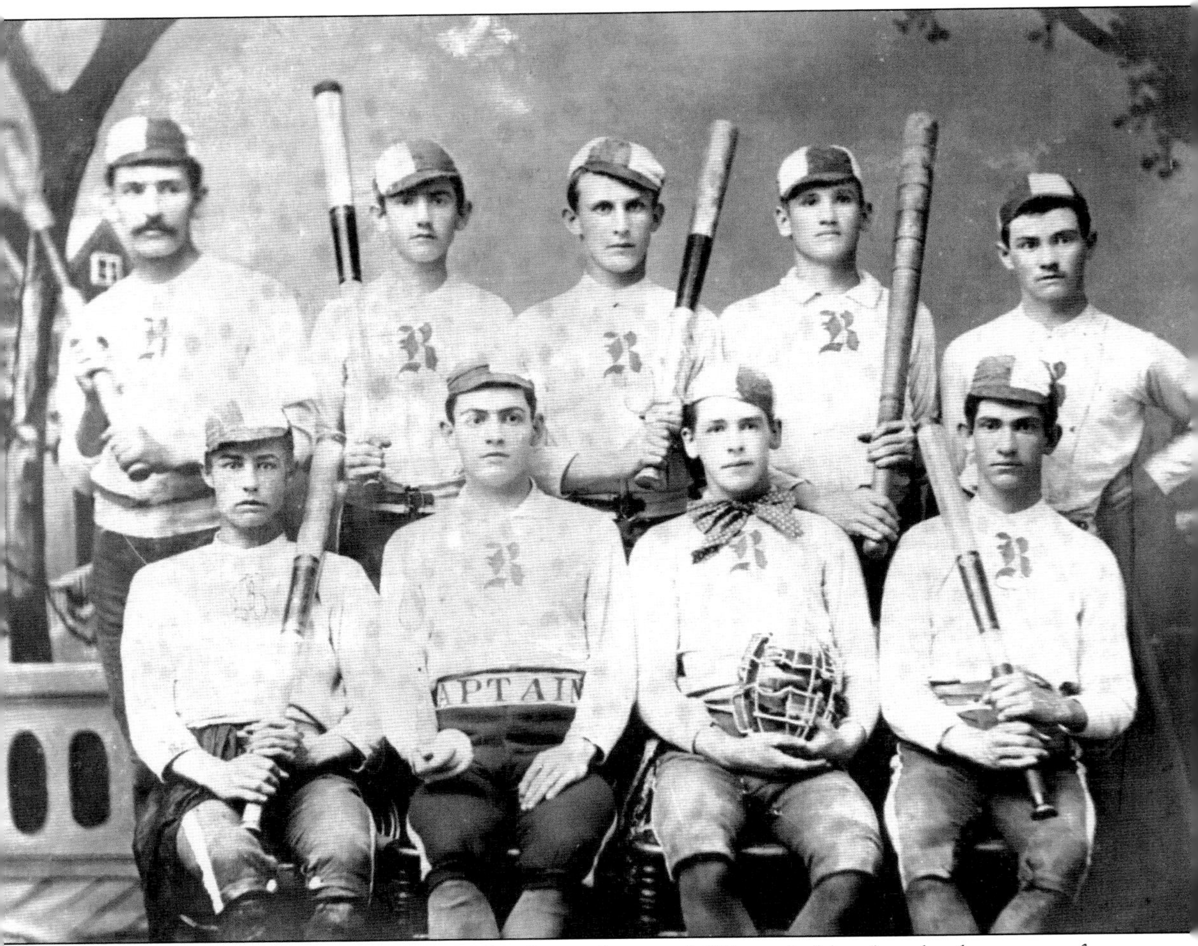

Members of the Johnson City Reds, shown here *c*. 1886, probably played other teams from Northeast Tennessee and Southwest Virginia, as baseball had begun to cross the nation as a booming sport in the late 19th century. The Reds probably consisted mostly of amateurs with a few outstanding paid players. The Reds and other local teams were the precursor of the Appalachian League, which was born in 1911, disbanded in 1914, and reformed in 1921. Johnson City's first team in the new league was called the Soldiers, after the National Soldiers' Home. (Courtesy of Doug Thompson.)

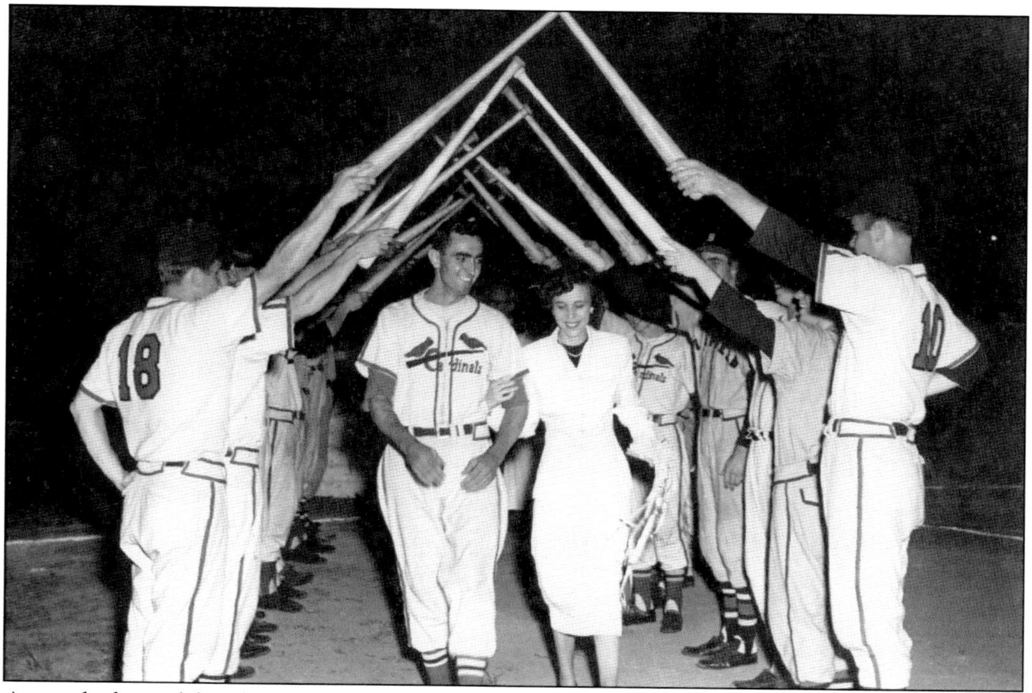

An arch formed by the Cardinal team serves as the passageway for Cardinal pitcher Gary Blaylock and Joy Watson, who were married on June 1, 1951. Joy's father, Alfus Watson, gave the bride in marriage. (Courtesy of the Johnson City Cardinals.)

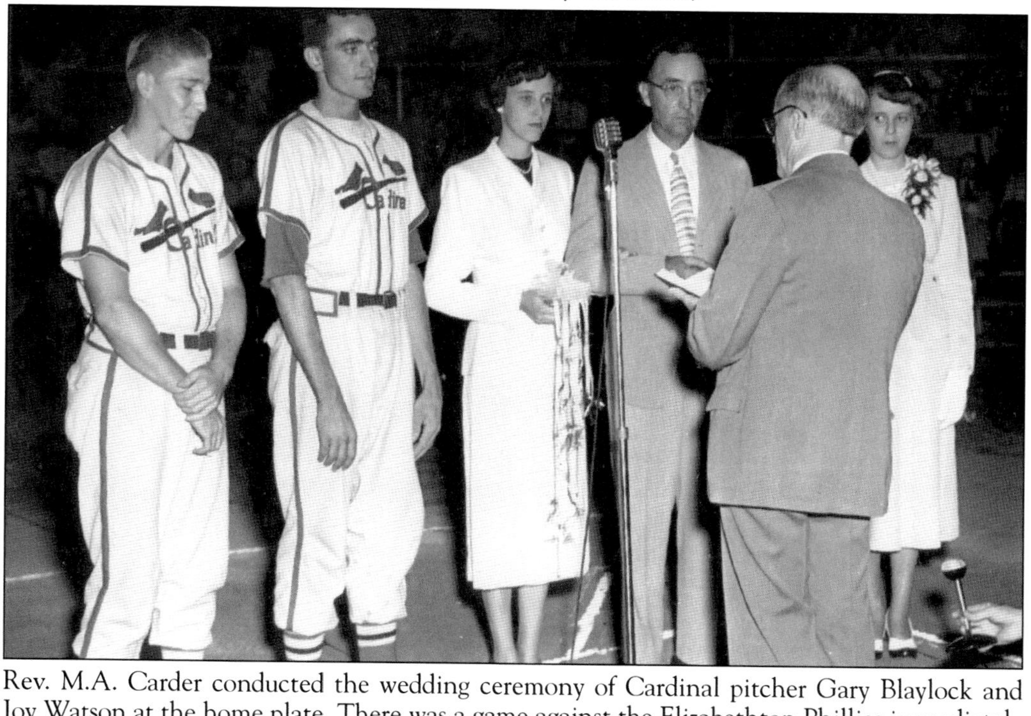

Rev. M.A. Carder conducted the wedding ceremony of Cardinal pitcher Gary Blaylock and Joy Watson at the home plate. There was a game against the Elizabethton Phillies immediately following the Friday night wedding and a reception after the game at the John Sevier Hotel. (Courtesy of the Johnson City Cardinals.)

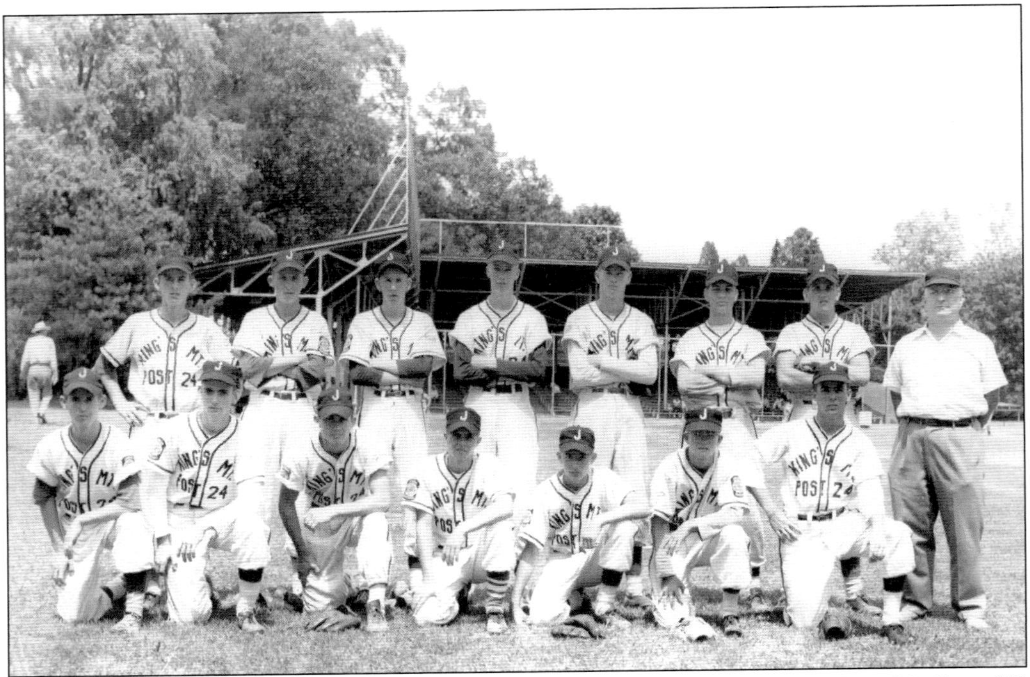

The American Legion baseball team pictured here was from King's Mountain Post 24. Gates W. Kidd, owner of the Tennessee Motor Company, sponsored baseball teams for several years after World War II. This photo was taken c. 1950. (Courtesy of Bruce and Mildred Kidd.)

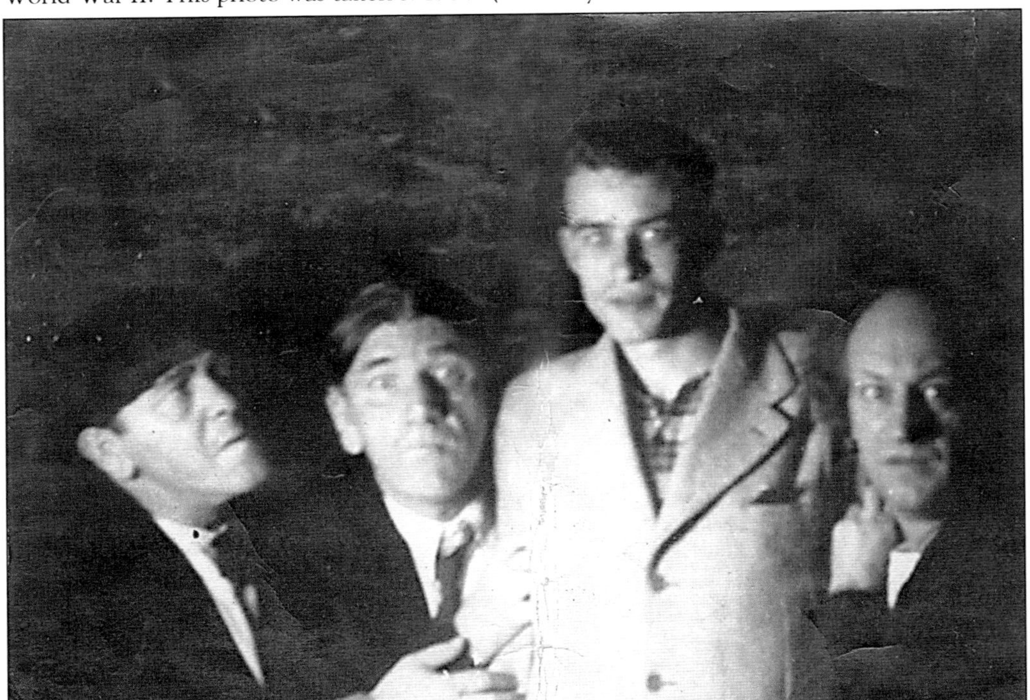

Weldon Nelson, of Boone's Creek, had this photograph taken with the Three Stooges in Johnson City in October 1947. Pictured from left to right are Moe Howard, Shemp Howard, Weldon Nelson, and Larry Fine. (Courtesy of Chuck and Nancy Mason.)

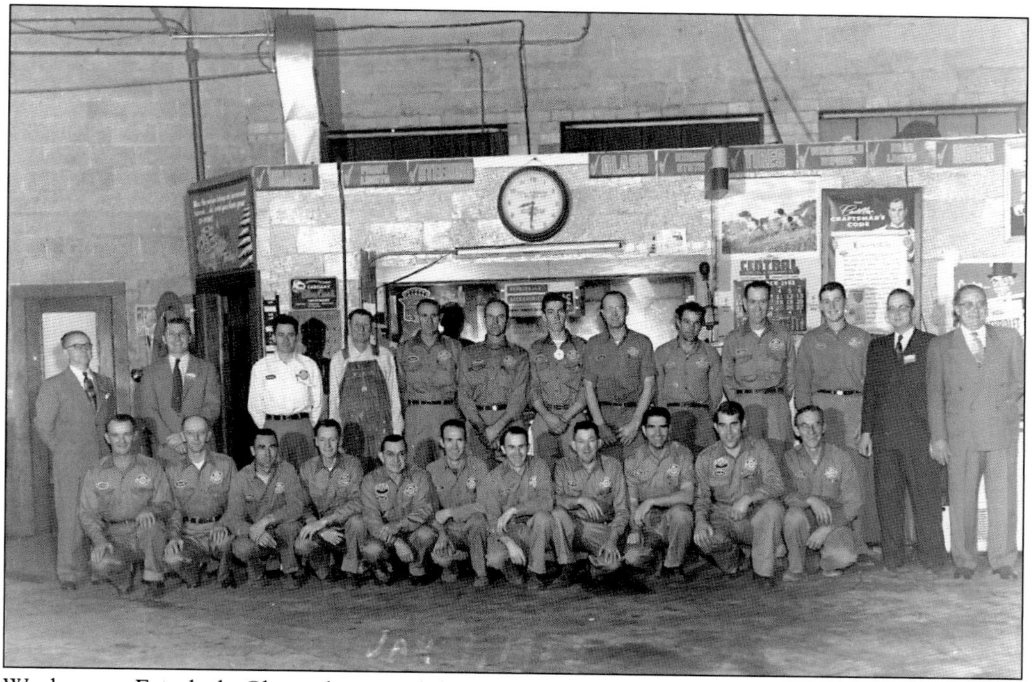

Workers at Faircloth Chevrolet posed for this photograph in December 1952. (Courtesy of Karen Wise Bennett.)

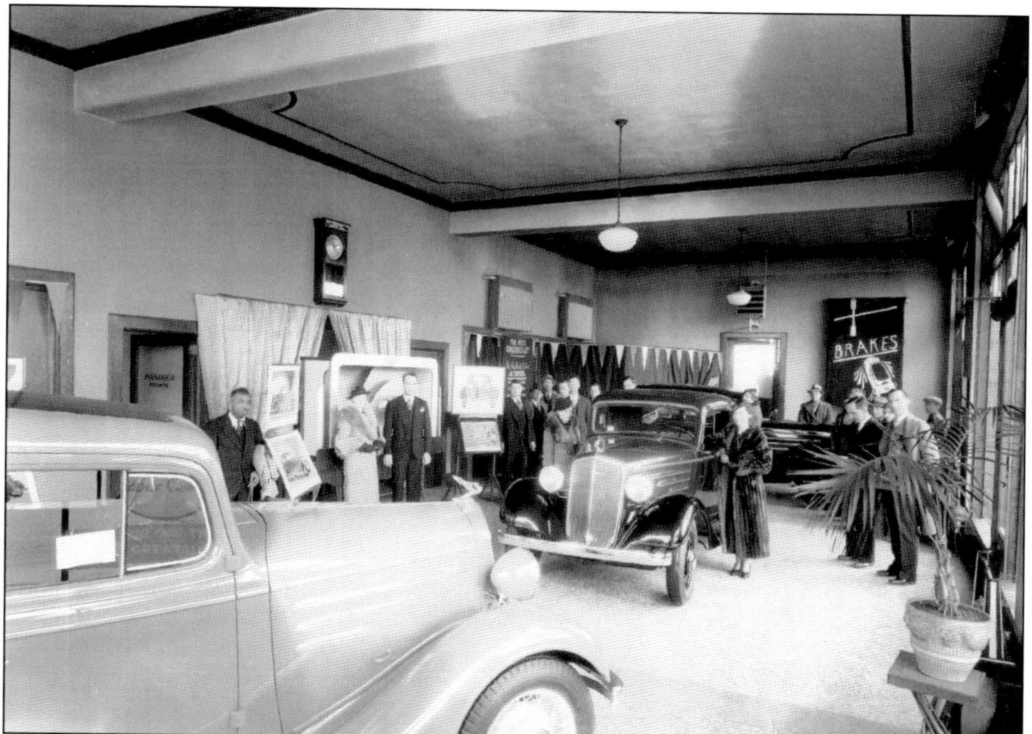

The interior of automobile retailers looks much the same today as it did in 1935, when this photograph was taken at the Faircloth Chevrolet Company in downtown Johnson City. (Courtesy of Karen Wise Bennett.)

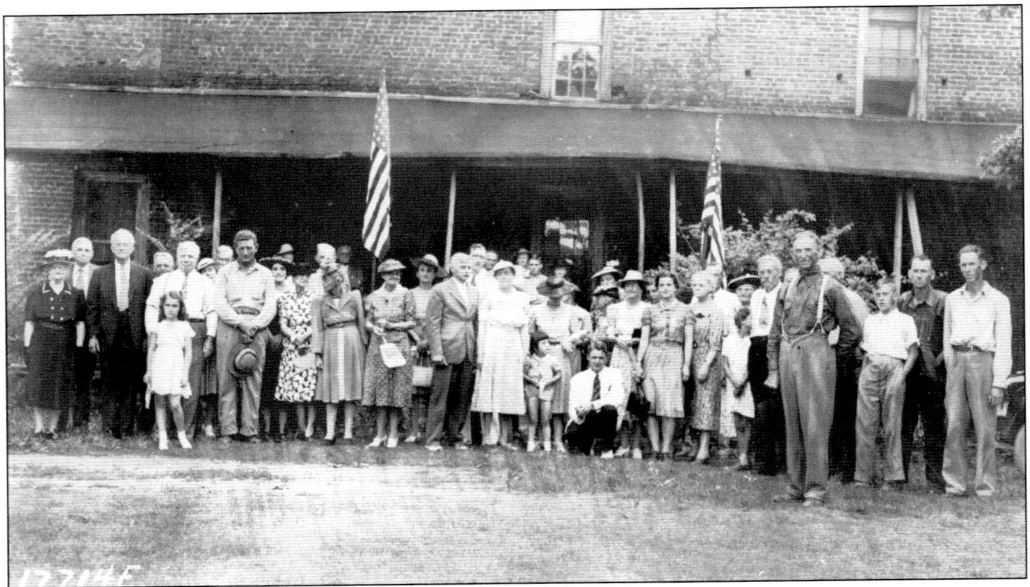

Taken at the Cobb home on the river in 1941, this photograph shows "all Cobb descendents." On the back of the photo, it also lists the home as the Nelle Brown/Read home. The photo was taken just before the home was torn down. (Courtesy of the Rocky Mount Historical Association.)

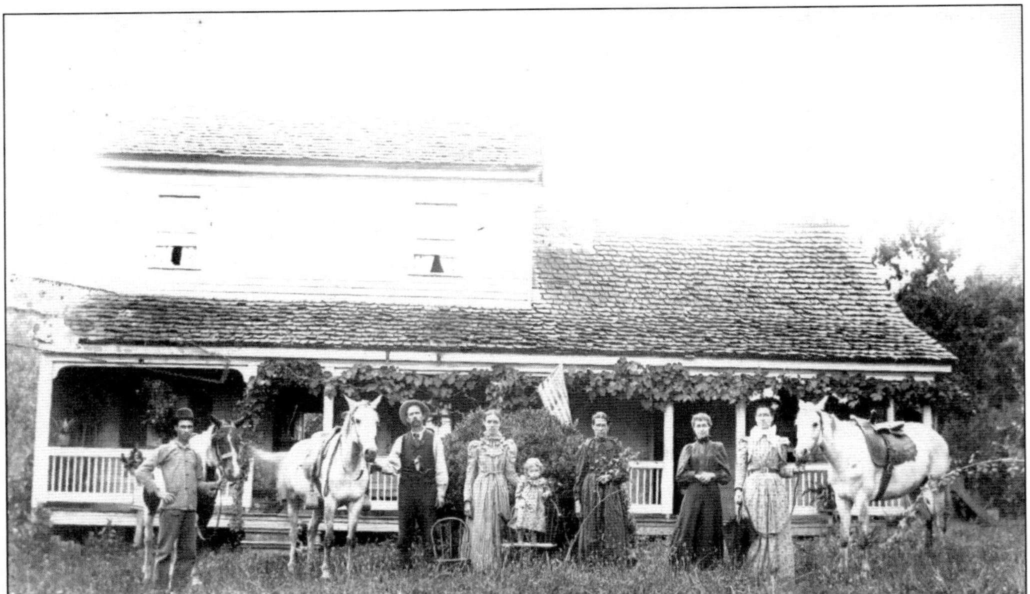

Pictured from left to right at the James Crumley homestead in 1898 are John Goodman (a neighbor); Thomas King Crumley; Thomas's wife, Mary Johnson Crumley; George, son of Thomas and Mary Johnson; Mary Elizabeth Crumley; Martha Ann Crumley; and Sarah Catherine Crumley. (Courtesy of Don and Sarah Walters.)

Gladys Whitt Landreth still remembers witnessing the hanging of Mary the elephant on September 13, 1916. Four-year-old Gladys was visiting grandfather Jonathan Hatcher in Erwin. Mary was hanged from a railroad derrick for killing one of her trainers in Kingsport on September 12. She was buried in the Clinchfield Railroad yard after circus authorities removed her tusks. (Courtesy of Gladys and Cindy Landreth.)

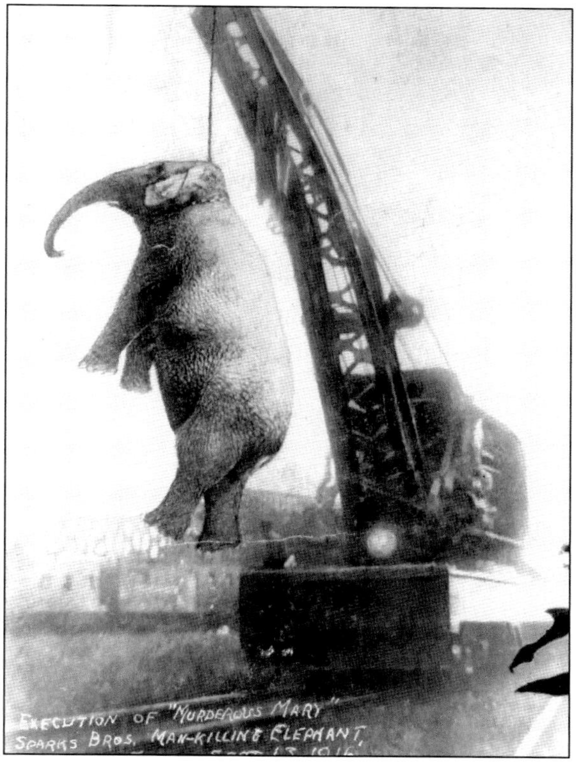

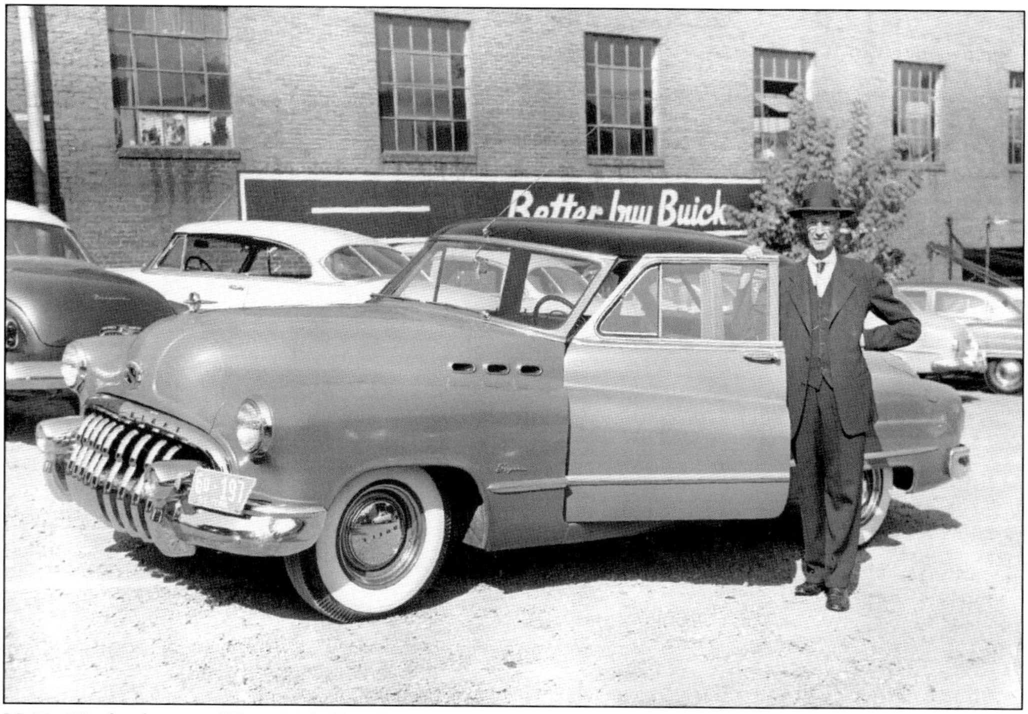

H.H. Wade shows off his 14th Buick in 1951. Wade lived at 711 West Maple Street in Johnson City with his wife, Golden, and their son, Harry. Wade was a salesman at Summers Hardware. (Courtesy of Julia Wade.)

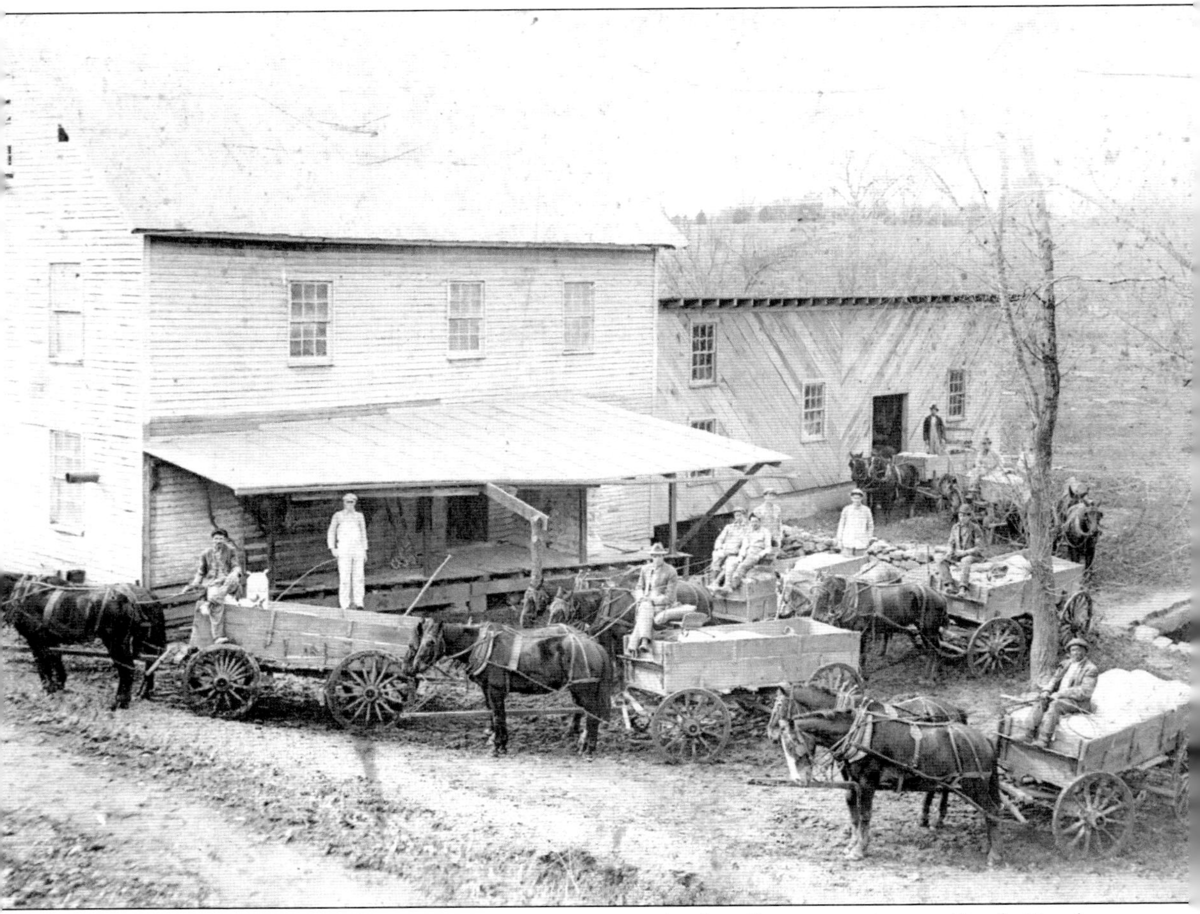

The Star Mill, shown here in 1914, was a water-wheel mill in operation on Brush Creek on the east side, or Watauga area, of Johnson City, now Woodlyn Road. Like all mills of the early 1900s, it ground flour, meal, and feed for cattle. Joseph A. Brown, sixth from the left, was the owner. The second man from the left is Frank VanHuss. (Courtesy of Grace Brown Miller and June Miller Gouge.)

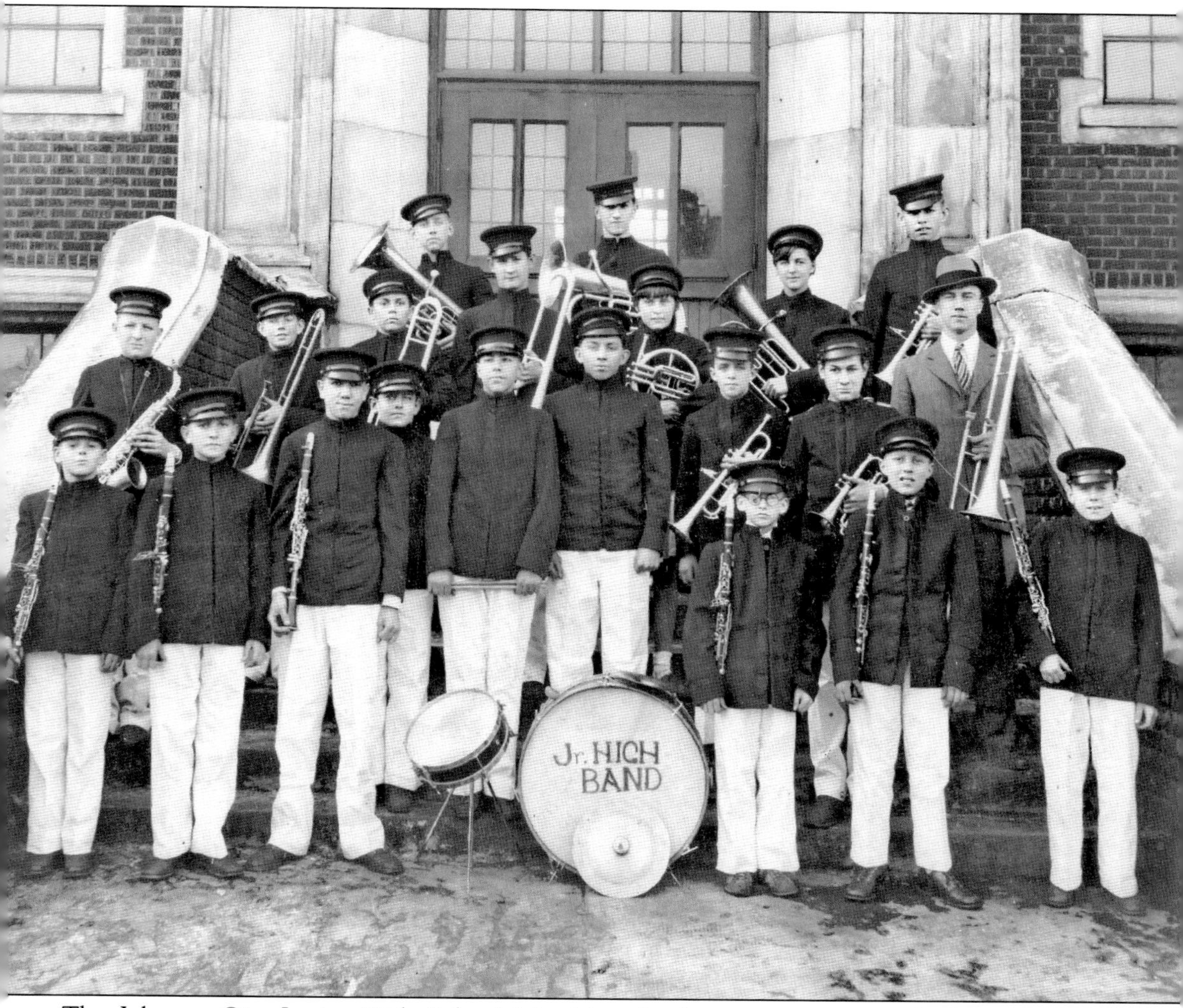

The Johnson City Junior High School Marching Band was an impressive-looking group of young people *c.* 1925. Among the members were Henry Blackwell, Coring Cox, Albert Miller, Rutledge Miller, Grace Brown, Harry Gastiger, and Eugene Loggins. The instructor was Mr. Broaduss, on the far right of the second row. (Courtesy of Grace Brown Miller and June Miller Gouge.)

About the Author

Sonya Haskins has a bachelor's degree in English from King College in Bristol, Tennessee. She has written hundreds of articles for newspapers and magazines, including *Writer's Digest*, *Guideposts for Teens*, *Decision*, *Physician's Practice Digest*, *College Bound*, *Educational Dealers*, and *Homeschooling Today*. Sonya is also the author of Images of America: *Jonesborough*. She lives near Johnson City, Tennessee, with her husband, Chris, and children, Sarah, Micah, Christopher, Daniel, and Hannah.

Bibliography

Calloway, Brenda C. *America's First Western Frontier: East Tennessee*. Johnson City, The Overmountain Press, 1989.

———. *History of Washington County, Tennesseee 1988*. Upper East Tennessee: Watauga Association of Genealogists, 1988.

Stahl, Ray. *Greater Johnson City: A Pictorial History*. Virginia Beach, Virginia: The Donning Company, 1983.

Washington County Historical Association, Inc. *History of Washington County, Tennessee*. Johnson City, Tennessee: The Overmountain Press, 2001.